Philip Larkin
SUBVERSIVE WRITER

For Sue, Ian, and my parents

Philip Larkin

SUBVERSIVE WRITER

STEPHEN COOPER

sussex
ACADEMIC
PRESS

Brighton • Portland

2 4 6 8 10 9 7 5 3 1

First published 2004 in Great Britain by
SUSSEX ACADEMIC PRESS
Box 2950
Brighton BN2 5SP

and in the United States of America by
SUSSEX ACADEMIC PRESS
920 NE 58th Ave   Suite 300
Portland, Oregon 97213-3786

British Library Cataloguing in Publication Data
A CIP catalogue record for this book is available from the British Library.

Library of Congress Cataloging-in-Publication Data
Cooper, Stephen, 1959–
  Philip Larkin : subversive writer / Stephen Cooper.
    p. cm.
  Includes bibliographical references and index.
  ISBN 1-84519-000-9 (hardcover: alk. paper)
    1. Larkin, Philip—Criticism and interpretation.   2. Sex
  roles in literature.   3. Sex in literature.
  I. Title.
    PR6023.A66Z615 2004
    821'.914—dc22
                                                    2004015674
                                                    CIP

Typeset & Designed by G&G Editorial, Brighton
Printed by The Cromwell Press, Trowbridge, Wiltshire
This book is printed on acid-free paper.

Contents

List of Illustrations

Plate Section

1   James Ballard Sutton, untitled portraits of girls, oil on canvas, private collection of Daphne Ingram, London. Photographed by S. Cooper, January 2001.

2   James Ballard Sutton, untitled portraits of girls, wash on paper, private collection of Daphne Ingram, London. Photographed by S. Cooper, January 2001.

3   James Ballard Sutton, untitled portrait of a girl, oil on canvas panel, private collection of Maeve Brennan. Photographed by S. Cooper, October 2000.

4   (a) James Ballard Sutton, untitled building scene, oil on canvas, private collection of Daphne Ingram, London. Photograph reproduced by Maeve Brennan, May 2000.

    (b) James Ballard Sutton, untitled girl on bed, charcoal on paper, private collection of Daphne Ingram, London. Photographed by S. Cooper, January 2001.

Embedded Sketches

James Sutton's drawing of himself as a drowning soldier beneath naval vessels, p. 92.

Extract from Larkin's dream-record depicting stylised racecourse diagram, p. 136.

Larkin's drawing of himself as a two-headed individual looking at paintings on opposite sides of a gallery, p. 147.

Appendix

1 Unpublished drawing from *Life With A Phairy Phantasy: A Morality in Pictures*. Drawn by Mr P. A. L. 1943. Bodleian Library.

2 University Labour Federation leaflet, *A Grave Step*, Cambridge. Enclosed in an unpublished letter from Philip Larkin to Catherine Larkin, May 24, 1941. Brynmor Jones Library.

3 W. R. A. C. recruitment coupon, *Daily Mirror*, May 30, 1953

4 W. A. A. F. recruitment poster, c. 1941. Imperial War Museum.

5 Leaflet, early 1900s.

6 Article in *Today*, weekly magazine, August 17, 1963.

List of Abbreviations

BTH, 1992	*Philip Larkin: Writer*, James Booth (Hemel Hempstead: Harvester Wheatsheaf)
BTH, 2000	*New Larkins for Old*, ed. James Booth (Basingstoke: Macmillan)
BTH, 2002	*Trouble at Willow Gables and Other Fictions*, ed. James Booth (London: Faber and Faber)
CEJL II	*The Collected Essays, Journalism and Letters of George Orwell* vol II, 'My Country Right or Left: 1940-1943', ed. Sonia Orwell and Ian Angus (London: Secker and Warburg, 1968)
CP	*Philip Larkin: Collected Poems*, ed. Anthony Thwaite (London: The Marvell Press and Faber and Faber, [1988], 1990)
John Betjeman, CP	*John Betjeman: Collected Poems*, ed. Frederick Birkenhead (London: John Murray, [1958], 2000)
LFI	*Letters from Iceland*, W. H. Auden and Louis MacNeice (London: Faber and Faber, [1937], 1985)
W. B. Yeats, SP	*W. B. Yeats: Selected Poetry*, ed. Timothy Webb (Harmondsworth: Penguin, 1991)
BJL	Brynmor Jones Library, University of Hull
u/p	Unpublished
W. A. A. F.	Women's Auxiliary Air Force
W. R. A. C.	Women's Royal Army Corps

Acknowledgements

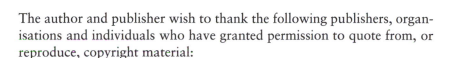

The author and publisher wish to thank the following publishers, organisations and individuals who have granted permission to quote from, or reproduce, copyright material:

Faber and Faber Ltd for excerpts from the *Collected Poems, Jill, A Girl in Winter, Trouble at Willow Gables and Other Fictions* and *Required Writing* by Philip Larkin.

The Marvell Press for excerpts from 'Lines on a Young Lady's Photograph Album', 'Wedding-Wind', 'Places, Loved Ones', 'Reasons for Attendance', 'Dry-Point', 'Next, Please', 'Going', 'Wants', 'Maiden Name', 'Born Yesterday', 'Wires', 'Church Going', 'Myxomatosis', 'Toads', 'Poetry of Departures', 'Spring', 'Deceptions', 'Absences', 'If, My Darling' and 'At Grass' from *The Less Deceived* by Philip Larkin.

The Society of Authors as the Literary Representative of the Estate of Philip Larkin for extracts from unpublished correspondence and manuscripts of Philip Larkin.

Excerpts from the *Collected Poems* by Philip Larkin. Copyright © 1988, 1989 by the Estate of Philip Larkin. Reprinted by permission of Farrar, Straus and Giroux, LLC.

Excerpts from the novel *Jill*, copyright © 1976 by Philip Larkin, reprinted with permission of The Overlook Press.

Excerpts from the novel *A Girl in Winter*, copyright © 1947, 1976 by Philip Larkin, reprinted with permission of The Overlook Press.

Acknowledgements

Excerpt from an unpublished letter, copyright © 1946 Kingsley Amis. Reprinted by Jonathan Clowes Ltd., London, on behalf of the Literary Estate of Sir Kingsley Amis.

Hazel Holt for excerpts from the unpublished correspondence of Barbara Pym to Philip Larkin.

Daphne Ingram for excerpts from the unpublished correspondence of James Sutton to Philip Larkin and for a selection of James Sutton's paintings and drawings.

The Imperial War Museum, London, for the reproduction of the poster 'Serve in the WAAF with the Men who Fly' by Jonathan Foss, *c.* 1941.

The publishers apologise for any errors or omissions in the above list and would be grateful to be notified of any corrections that should be incorporated in the next edition or reprint of this book.

I am also grateful to those scholars and writers who have shared with me their insights into Larkin's life and work and who have influenced the book in various ways. My thanks go to Richard Allen, Richard Brown, John Carey, Steve Clark, Julia Courtney, Robert Crawford, Barbara Everett, Robert Fraser, Jane de Gay, Jean Hartley, Dennis Healey, Douglas Hurd, Andrew Motion, John Osborne, Tom Paulin, Adam Piette, István Rácz, Neil Roberts, Diccon Rogers, Anthony Thwaite and Terry Whalen.

In addition, the following have provided invaluable assistance in locating unpublished material and in advising on numerous other matters: Sally Brown (British Library), Helen Roberts (Brynmor Jones Library, University of Hull), Brian Dyson (formerly of BJL), Julie Maylon (formerly of BJL), Sue Hodson (Huntington Library, San Marino, California), Chris Petter (McPherson Library, University of Victoria, Canada) and Judith Priestman (Bodleian Library, Oxford). Thanks also to Liz Mallett and Jo Parker (both of the Open University Library, Milton Keynes) for their help with the electronic research.

Special thanks are also due to James Booth, for sending me the transcripts for *Trouble at Willow Gables and Other Fictions* in advance of that book's publication, and Janice Rossen, for her sustaining interest during the research and for her help in tracing archival papers. I am especially grateful to the late Maeve Brennan for sharing her personal recollections of the writer, for her kind hospitality during my trips to Hull, and for her strenuous efforts in tracing James Sutton's paintings. In this respect I am also indebted to Daphne Ingram and Madge Sutton for generously granting me unrestricted access to Sutton's studio and for allowing me to photograph a wide selection of drawings and paintings, some of which are reproduced in this book.

Above all, I am deeply grateful for Stephen Regan's enthusiastic and painstaking supervision of the PhD thesis that formed the basis of this study and for his continuing friendship and guidance. My joint supervisor, Andrew Swarbrick, has also provided many suggestions, offering meticulous advice on the typescript and giving generously of his time in many a Sunday evening discussion. In the latter stages of the original research period Katie Gramich's scholarly expertise was also most welcome.

I would like to thank Jeremy Crowe of the Society of Authors for his sound counsel on copyright matters. Anthony Grahame and Tim Andrews of Sussex Academic Press also deserve gratitude for their judicious editing of the typescript.

Finally, I would like to thank my family for their unwavering support throughout the six years I have dedicated to Larkin scholarship. Sincere thanks are extended to my parents, Margaret and Ivan Cooper and to my mother-in-law, Elizabeth Leslie, for their nourishing interest and helpful support. For their enduring patience and understanding I am eternally grateful to my wife, Sue, who read countless drafts whilst pursuing a challenging City career, and my son, Ian, a scholar of Tonbridge School, who offered his own shrewd critical observations. Without their belief and encouragement this book would never have been written.

STEPHEN COOPER
TONBRIDGE
JULY 2004

'To me I seem very much an outsider, yet I suppose 99% of people would say I'm very establishment & conventional. Funny, isn't it?'

Philip Larkin, letter to Norman Iles, July 4, 1972
(*Selected Letters*, 460)

Introduction

Since the publication of the *Selected Letters* (Thwaite, 1992), Philip
Larkin's reputation has been tarnished by those critics who have chosen
to allow the sexist, racist and reactionary tendencies expressed in the
correspondence to influence our perception of the poet's work. However,
a review of the structural aesthetic of the entire range of Larkin's writing
now available – including the 'juvenilia' and other neglected archival
material – suggests that a very different view of Larkin's national and
sexual politics exists. The interplay of signs and motifs in the early work
orchestrates a subversion of conventional attitudes towards class, gender,
authority and sexual relations; close analysis of the later works reveals
that they share many of the concerns first articulated in the novellas.

The political attitudes in Larkin's poetry have been fiercely contested
throughout the 1990s. The ostensibly vile sentiments of some of the
published letters provoked Lisa Jardine into a merciless caricaturing of
the poet as 'a casual, habitual racist, and an easy misogynist' (Regan,
1997, 6). Her indignation at jibes such as 'all women are stupid beings'
and remarks about 'niggers and wogs' (cited in Regan, 1997, 4) endorsed
Germaine Greer's assessment of the *Collected Poems* (1988) as 'anti-intel-
lectual, racist, sexist, and rotten with class-consciousness' (Greer, 1988,
27). For Tom Paulin, too, the letters' hateful views revealed 'the sewer
under the national monument Larkin became' and he called for a more
extensive publication of the letters that would 'place, analyse and under-
stand – socially and psychologically – Larkin's racism, misogyny and
quasi-fascist views' (Paulin, 1992, 15). However, by drawing extensively
on hitherto unpublished letters by both Larkin and his friend, James
Sutton, this book presents evidence which counters the notion that
Larkin's 'quasi-fascist views' are expressed – at least with an unironic
intention – in his poems, plays and novels. Using material from the letters
– both the liberal-minded and the politically incorrect – an enhanced

understanding of the texts is presented here. The overriding concern, throughout Larkin's literary career, was to unsettle many of those very same reactionary attitudes that he expresses in some of the published letters. Moreover, other letters, which have until now remained unpublished, reveal a distinct detachment from such attitudes in their plea for alternative constructs of masculinity, femininity and social and political organisation.

Larkin's detractors habitually ignore the extent to which offensive attitudes are invoked in the texts for the express purpose of being parodied and pilloried. Not surprisingly, critics sympathetic to Larkin's work have already taken issue with the way that Jardine, Paulin and Greer have approached the poems. With regard to orthodox gender politics, for instance, Steve Clark detects in Larkin's poems an 'opting out of the coercive force of contemporary sexual ideology' (Regan, 1997, 127). Taking a similar line on Larkin's social attitudes, Stephen Regan detects 'a dissident political voice' in the early poems (BTH, 2000, 125). Similarly, Terry Whalen's study of the depiction of traditional identities finds Larkin to be 'subverting the role requirements of both the chivalric and the Bourgeois Male' in the 'major' poems (BTH, 2000, 119). There now exists a pressing need to register the *full* extent of Larkin's thematic and stylistic interests from the 1940s until the late 1970s. As well as the unfinished novels and the Coleman novellas – recently published in *Trouble at Willow Gables and Other Fictions* (BTH, 2002) – there is a neglected archive of poetry and verse drama, dream-records and autobiographical sketches whose structural principles corroborate a strong subversive impulse in Larkin's 'major' poems. Collections in the Brynmor Jones Library, the British Library, the Bodleian Library and the McPherson Library help to uncover the full range of Larkin's interests, which are undocumented in most critical studies.

A major advantage of appraising the extended Larkin canon is that it allows us to appreciate the way in which texts as diverse as *Trouble at Willow Gables* (1943), 'At Grass' (1950) and 'MCMXIV' (1960) interrelate in their gestures away from establishment ideals. 'Deceptions' (1950), *A New World Symphony* (1953) and *A Girl in Winter* (1947) share the same radical concerns about women who are entrapped by the bonds and gestures of patriarchal society. 'Conscript' (1941), *No For An Answer* (1949) and *Night in the Plague* (1946) all confront the imperialistic creed of jingoistic heroism through a subtle invocation of common tropes and symbols. To recognise, in the augmented oeuvre, the persistent chafing at convention – with regard to gender, class and capitalism – is to understand that Larkin's 'major' poems are only one element of a literary voice which speaks through genres as various as girls' school fiction, poetic prose, dramatised debate and verse drama, all of which illustrate lighter and darker shades of the same subversive imagination. Unlike previous accounts of Larkin's poems, which allude only scantily to the early writings, often questioning their aesthetic worth and discarding them as marginal experiments, this book adopts an entirely different approach, submitting them to close analysis as works of art in their own right. By appraising these texts in a systematic fashion, through the application of critical methods such as structuralism, historicism and feminism, their centrality, in terms of rectifying Larkin's literary reputation, and in terms of the insights they offer about his 'mature' poems, will be emphasised throughout.

Chapter 1 appraises the Coleman writings – 'What Are We Writing For?' (1943), *Trouble at Willow Gables, Michaelmas Term at St Bride's* (1943) – and *Jill* (1946). **Chapter 2** considers *A Girl in Winter*, the unfinished novels, *No For An Answer* and *A New World Symphony*, together with the debates *Round the Point* (1950) and *Round Another Point* (1951). **Chapter 3** presents an analysis of Larkin's 1940s poetry, as well as a study of the unpublished play, *Night in the Plague*. Finally, in **Chapter 4**, the insights gained in previous chapters will assist in tracing the subversive aspects of the 'major' poems and in locating the cultural and historical contexts from which Larkin's most widely read work emerges.

Substantiating the various strands of the above argument will require excursions into Larkin's adaptation of other writers' work. In the case of W. B. Yeats, Edward Thomas, W. H. Auden and John Betjeman, Larkin's borrowings are predictable, but the affinities with James Joyce and Virginia Woolf are more surprising and innovative. It is often assumed that early and late Larkin were two different writers. James Booth, for instance, refers to the 'neat mid-century division between a pre-1950 novelist and a post-1950 poet' (BTH, 2002, xli) and Stan Smith has conducted 'a statistical breakdown of how [Larkin's] vocabulary differs between the two periods' (Smith, 2000, 260). This study, however, argues strongly for the *continuities* in Larkin's writing – at both a formal and a thematic level – which allow us to retrace his early commitment to prose to the end of his literary career. Larkin's grasp of the world and his unease with certain aspects of it did not, essentially, change during some forty years of writing: as such, his master-images recur frequently, adapted only to meet the needs of new experiences and circumstances that his work encountered. A brief example of this stability of interest can be seen in the enduring application of Woolfian signification which pervades not only *The North Ship, Jill* and *A Girl in Winter*, but also 'Absences' (1950) and 'Wants' (1950) several years later. It is even visible in the later poems 'Friday Night in the Royal Station Hotel' (1966) and 'To the Sea' (1969).

These poems' interest in the symbolic power of waves and the allure of self-shedding recalls scenes and characters in *To the Lighthouse* (1927) and *The Waves* (1931). The impact that the latter novel had on Larkin's writing is underestimated, though its style and concerns bind together texts that might otherwise be separate. Larkin's high regard for the book can be seen in a letter to Sutton:

> 'The Waves' is bloody fine, in my opinion: I shall probably keep rereading it till I know it well. There are many books that are worthless, but 'the Waves' [sic] is not one of them. I remember being crazy about it at school, and writing 'Trio' under *its expansive influence*. (my emphasis, u/p letter, 29.x.43)

In the Coleman writings this 'expansive influence' is spelled out in terms that are crystal clear:

> The late Mrs Woolf in *The Waves* likened the sound [of the sea] to falling logs; that is good, but even more exact would be the collapsing of buildings. When I was very young I would lie and imagine that the sound of the sea was the sound of ancient cities falling. (BTH, 2002, 235)

This is taken from Brunette Coleman's autobiography, *Ante Meridian* (1943). It is notable, not merely for its direct reference to *The Waves* and the characteristic Woolfian sea imagery, but also for its sense of natural forces triumphing over human structures: 'collapsing . . . buildings' and 'ancient cities falling'. We can detect a similar sentiment thirty years later as 'Show Saturday' (1973, CP, 199–201) records the waves of communal feeling that '[break] ancestrally each year' in order to beat back the 'Sale-bills and swindling' of worldly enterprise. A line from 'The School in August' (*c.* 1943, CP, 271) aptly expresses the interconnectedness of Larkin's oeuvre: 'And seniors grow tomorrow / From the juniors today'.

Larkin's early writing is not a false start on a career that never materialised, but part of the dynamic whole of an output in which every aspect illumines, and is illumined by, every other. In a later episode of *Ante Meridian*, Brunette and her father confront the elements together on a lonely cliff-top:

> We two stood up on the cliff-top, in the howling wind, seeing the little village almost as a stage where a scene of destruction was being enacted. My father was no doubt quoting texts, but the gale tore away his words before they reached me. (BTH, 2002, 237)

These lines contain echoes which reverberate throughout Larkin's writing. The natural threat that the 'little village' faces recalls the 'Villages [that] were cut off' by wintry conditions in *A Girl in Winter* (11). Equally, the passage is imbued with Larkin's enduring obsession with the limitations of language and human codes when faced with larger elemental forces. 'The gale tore away [Mr Coleman's] words' echoes the 'wind [that] . . . took away [the speaker's] words' in 'I put my mouth' (1943–4) and anticipates the 'untalkative' natural realm in 'Here' (1961) or the 'blue air' of 'High Windows' (1967) which, 'Rather than words', communicates 'Nothing, and is nowhere, and is endless' (CP, 276, 137, 165).

Two further passages from Coleman's autobiography confirm its centrality in the structure of Larkin's aesthetic landscape. The first describes, in a farcical way, the return to shore of a lifeboat crew who have successfully completed their mission: the leader 'staggered ashore, wet through, his hair tumbling over his eyes, a picture of *exhausted heroism*' (my emphasis, BTH, 2002, 238). The italicised phrase refers to the sailor's physical state but it also alludes to a construct of masculine behaviour which places unreasonable expectations on speakers in several of the later poems. The clichéd masculine ideal of being 'Stubbly with goodness' springs to mind, as does the desire to get 'The fame and the girl and the money' in 'Toads' (CP, 85, 90). These characters feel the pressure to re-enact heroic, 'masculine' routines but the poems' effort is the same as *Ante Meridian*. All three texts invite the reader to take a critical look at the 'exhausted' stereotypes of gendered identity.

The second passage returns to the idea of acting a part:

> I have furnished many rooms and houses in my time, but somehow,
> it is like designing sets for a play – one can never subscribe to the illu-
> sion in front of the curtain when the play is acted. (BTH, 2002, 239)

Like 'Toads' and 'Poetry of Departures' (CP, 89, 85) these lines highlight the illusion of satisfaction that we create for ourselves, but they have tap-roots, too, in the deeper sub-soil of Larkin's psychological make-up. The most consummate actor in the passage is the speaker 'herself'. Brunette Coleman is a character played by Philip Larkin whose attempts 'To be that girl' (CP, 279) represent an opting out of the 'printed directions' and 'tabled fertility rites' ('Wants', CP, 42) of conventional gender roles in the early 1940s. At the same time, the adoption of the female perspective provided Larkin with an insider view of the alternative structures of a female world.

1

Jill and the Coleman Novellas

"Feminising" the Male and Empowering Femininity

Trouble at Willow Gables

Any new appraisal of Larkin's writing must take into account the stylistic and thematic influences of his youthful experiments in prose: *Trouble at Willow Gables*, and its incomplete sequel, *Michaelmas Term at St Bride's*. Analysis of the novellas' structural principles demonstrates how their motifs overlap with, and anticipate, the poetry's persistent concern with rebellious and conformist attitudes. First, it will be helpful to review the major critical responses towards this latest addition to the Larkin canon.

Commenting on the novellas as early as 1993, Andrew Motion claimed that 'they allow us to see some aspects of Larkin's mind that he normally kept hidden, and others that he didn't know existed' (Motion, 1993, 89), hinting that the texts might repay closer inspection. Motion focuses primarily on the texts' mild eroticism and finds, 'at the heart of [*Trouble at Willow Gables*] . . . voyeurism, sado-masochism, and a pleasure in taking advantage of those who . . . cannot easily defend themselves' (Motion, 1993, 92). The laureate's observation that the novellas 'allowed [Larkin] to create a private imaginative world when the real world was threatening to overwhelm him' (Motion, 1993, 96) anticipates more recent enquiries into the psychological and cultural motivations for Larkin's Brunette phase. In 1995 Andrew Swarbrick identified, in the Coleman works, 'the construction of personae which evolves into John Kemp's "Jill" and, finally, [into] a poetic technique' (Swarbrick, 1995, 31). For John Carey, too, Brunette Coleman allows Larkin to express different facets of his personality, most notably his 'feminine' and 'masculine' elements. Like Motion, Carey suggests that the stories 'are clearly written to produce male sexual arousal, and . . . seem to have been partly for the entertainment of Larkin's male friends' – the 'male and female elements or voices [in Larkin's work] here co-operate in an unusual way – the imagined female self subordinates itself to and gratifies the male' (BTH, 2000, 55). However, in a review of Booth's edition of the fiction, Carey scotches the idea that the stories are pornographic: rather, they are 'a celebration of innocence' and demonstrate 'Larkin's envious delight in [the schoolgirls'] youth and naïveté' (Carey, 2002, 38).

Mark Rowe is another critic to attach importance to the novellas' air of innocence. For Rowe, Larkin's homosexual leanings in the early 1940s left him 'stricken with guilt, self-loathing and remorse'; 'Sexual relations *between* women were the one kind of sexual relationship which was not sullied' (BTH, 2000, 87). Rowe complicates his psychological interpretation of the Coleman texts by claiming that they also represent a desire to punish women for the indifference they showed Larkin in real life. Moreover, the idea of assuming a female consciousness granted Larkin access to women in a way that was denied to him as a man (BTH, 2000, 86–8). In the introduction to *Trouble at Willow Gables and Other Fictions*, Booth pursues a similar line, claiming that the works express the same concerns as 'I see a girl dragged by the wrists' (CP, 278–9) in which the male protagonist wants 'To be that girl'. For Booth, Larkin's 'self-feminisation' (BTH, 2002, xi) offered refuge from conventional male destinies: in 1943 Larkin would have felt alienated from traditional manly roles on account of his rejection from military service. These attempts to explain the texts in terms of Larkin's psychological profile can be extremely illuminating, though the Coleman novellas provide much more than therapy for their author. As well as assuaging Larkin's emotional turmoil, the stories offer, within the confines of their own closed cosmos, a thoughtful probing of conventional opinion on matters such as authority, gender and moral judgement.

In *A World of Women* (1999), Rosemary Auchmuty explains how writers of girls' school fiction utilise the genre to unsettle orthodox notions of sexual politics: 'In this world girls [are] relatively free to negotiate an identity and relationships outside patriarchal constraints' (Auchmuty, 1999, 3). What is particularly attractive to authors of girls' school fiction is the way that power and influence – traditionally the preserve of men – can be wielded by girls and women: 'hence the head-mistress becomes, in a sense, a surrogate male figure governing her surrogate community, the school' (Auchmuty, 1999, 110). Perhaps the chief advantage, though, for writers intent on subverting dominant patterns of thought, is the way that the stories *appear* to uphold the very values that they seek to question:

The popular support enjoyed by girls' school stories in this period was in large part due to a perception that they promoted traditional family values and appropriate gender roles. But in their depictions of parenting, as of marriage, these apparently conservative novels often challenged cultural norms in ways which encouraged their young readers to think beyond the usual stereotypes. (Auchmuty, 1999, 78)

In Coleman's essay on literary practice, 'What Are We Writing For?', Larkin explores almost exactly the same attributes of girls' school fiction as those noted by Auchmuty. Through the texts of his subversive pseudonym, Brunette Coleman, Larkin seeks to empower women, to grant them their own 'Copernican universe, controlled by the Headmistress' (BTH, 2002, 268). Coleman refers to the working out of her characters' destinies in terms that suggest alternative, 'feminine' principles of social organisation: in Brunette's stories 'Vast webs of friendships, hatreds, loyalties . . . reconciliations, and adorations must arise' (BTH, 2002, 270). Male characters are ejected from Coleman's fictional domain: 'they are so *tabu* that I hardly dare mention the matter. We must construct a closed, single-sexed world, which Mr Orwell would doubtless call a womb-replica' (BTH, 2002, 269). However, in drawing a comparison between Coleman's sentiments and Auchmuty's claims about girls' school story writers, we must tread cautiously. 'What Are We Writing For?' was written by a man, and the result is partly a parody of the political concerns of the girls' school writers Dorita Fairlie Bruce, Elinor Brent-Dyer and Elsie Oxenham. Nevertheless, Larkin / Coleman's reference to these authors as 'my sister-writers', together with the strong desire to 'construct a closed, single-sexed world . . . a womb-replica' (BTH, 2002, 270, 269), alerts us to Larkin's empathy with the female perspective.

Auchmuty claims that the girls' school story enables an author to subvert cultural norms from within an apparently settled and traditional framework. Such a scheme chimes perfectly with Coleman's blueprint for a leading character whose specific function is to revolt against the institution to which she belongs so that alternative values are imposed:

As [the principal character] reaches the middle school her nature breaks out fiercely into rebellion, and she really sets out to set at defiance all the rules of the school, until she sinks rapidly to the position of the worst girl in the school . . . Public opinion is against her, and she has to stand alone against her enemies with no weapons at all, suffering in consequence many gross humiliations until her steadfast resolution wins the rest of the school over to her side, and she emerges, with some suitable climax, triumphant over all. (BTH, 2002, 271–2)

Coleman's fascination with the free-booting rebel is critical because characters in many of Larkin's later texts display a similar interest in unorthodox lifestyles. Just as 'Toads' and 'Poetry of Departures' (CP, 89, 85) invite the reader to 'work through' arguments both for and against conformity, so Coleman in 'What Are We Writing For?' asks that we 'grade the behaviour of [her] characters' against 'conventional modes of good and evil' (BTH, 2002, 268). The following appraisals will show that it is the conventional categories, as well as the characters' behaviour, that are 'grad[ed]' or evaluated by the novellas' aesthetic structures.

The Prologue to *Trouble at Willow Gables* opens in an almost cinematic way, as the reader is swept through the countryside with the movement of the postman's bicycle. This journeying motif stresses the existence of a world beyond the classrooms and dormitories of Willow Gables within which the plot will unfold. Anticipating how mail forges comforting connections at the end of 'Aubade' (CP, 209), the postman's letters bring part of the wider community into the school in the form of liberal attitudes which run counter to the institution's codes. There is, moreover, a striking contrast between the freedom of the postman's movements up to the point where he arrives at the school, and the sense of curtailment shown thereafter. Whilst still some way off from Willow Gables he 'bowl[s] along at his own pace, swooping from patches of shadow to patches of sunlight' (BTH, 2002, 6), yet on drawing near casual observations conspire to create a prevailing mood of suppression, concealment and redundancy. Near the school 'The trees are very tall and shut out the light' (BTH, 2002, 7) signalling that any news the postman bears from outside is going to be unwelcome beyond the gates. The obligatory notice '"Keep Off the Grass"' (BTH, 2002, 7) signifies the institution's reverence for traditional values which may be diminishing outside its domain. The fact that the drive 'has to be continually weeded and raked' (BTH, 2002, 7) implies that without artificial nurturing, the 'moss' of an alternative world-view may take hold, thereby choking the neatly-tended enclave of respectability. Throughout the passage Larkin superimposes, upon ordinary description, a network of signification such that the narrative is double-voiced: the 'disused fountain' (BTH, 2002, 7) symbolises further the redundant nature of certain values that Willow Gables represents.

The final paragraph firmly places this isolated school in a socio-historical context. Originally designed as an opulent 'eighteenth-century country house' (BTH, 2002, 7) it has since been 'altered . . . extensively in order to make it into a school' (BTH, 2002, 7). Thus, Willow Gables purports to be something that is less than authentic, and the final sentence suggests a façade which barely disguises snobbery and class-consciousness: 'Only the Palladian front remained in entirety, to confront the curious parent or shrinking new-girl, and to speak of more gracious and hierarchical days' (BTH, 2002, 7).

The Prologue's suggestion that the school's official values may not warrant close inspection is illustrated in numerous ways throughout the novella. The plot structure repeatedly overturns conventional depictions of authority and morality. In an early scene, the Headmistress, Miss Holden, chastises Marie Moore for re-pocketing a confiscated five pound note that her aunt had sent her: '"Do you think, then, that you are a better judge of what is fair and what is unfair in this school than I am?"' (BTH, 2002, 34). As the story unfolds it transpires that Marie is, indeed, the better judge, though at this stage it is clear that the 'theft' is merely an appropriation of what is rightfully hers. On more than one occasion, Marie justifies her retrieval of the note on ethical grounds which run counter to the school's, but which are no less consistent. '"After all, it *is* mine"' (BTH, 2002, 15) she protests, and her honourable reaction, on learning that juniors are permitted to receive no more than two pounds, is to send the money back to her aunt. The solace that Marie finds in Shylock's words – '"The villainy that you teach me I will execute, and it shall go hard but I will better the instruction"' (BTH, 2002, 16) – confirms the novella's sympathy for those who are persecuted for shunning the codes of a dominant order. Like Shylock, Marie maintains 'a strong determination not to compromise in any way with this unjustified assault from authority' (BTH, 2002, 41) but 'Such was the power of collective opinion that she almost began to believe herself guilty' (BTH, 2002, 56). These sentiments anticipate the manner in which later speakers feel 'Bound . . . to act / As if what [they] settled for / Mashed [them]' ('Places, Loved Ones', CP, 99). These lines were written long after Larkin's Coleman phase had passed, yet they convey, just as clearly, his irritation with the way that alternative values are demonised by all-powerful cultural norms.

If there are thematic links between the novella and the later poems, stylistic similarities can also be found. At the start of Chapter One Larkin employs a metonymic technique to emphasise the nature of establishment orthodoxy that the Headmistress represents. In a way that is characteristic of many of the later poems, Larkin catalogues signifiers of a traditional way of life, so that individual items become emblematic of an entire culture of power and conformity. The 'thick carpet' on the floor and the 'calf-bound' books, the 'discreet pictures hung high up' and the 'red plush curtains' (BTH, 2002, 8–9) connote a settled enclave of money and privilege. The sense of a traditional past with a strict social hierarchy, involving a servant class, is suggested by the 'disused bell-pull', and the placing of the Head's desk 'at right-angles to the door' (BTH, 2002, 9) implies a certain inflexibility of character. Moreover, the fact that 'Neither in public nor private did she smoke or drink' (BTH, 2002, 9) consolidates our impression of the Head's unswerving commitment to duty and responsibility to office.

In another, seemingly casual, description we see the alternative to such a life of regulation and order. Though the girls were forced to wear the regulation school clothing, 'The effect, curiously enough, was not one of uniformity: so many . . . different hair-styles, contrasts in age, build and height, that an observer would have been dazzled by variety rather than dispirited by any impression of mass-production' (BTH, 2002, 10). Wearing uniforms suggests outward complicity, but the irrepressibility of human nature is such that it rejects artificially imposed restraints. Accordingly, 'Girls pushed different ways: some wanted to go to one class-room, some to another: some clambered upstairs, some struggled down' (BTH, 2002, 10). This is more than a casual description in that it suggests defiance in the face of categorisation. The dangers of judging by appearances is a theme which is endemic to the whole story: misunderstandings and confusions arise as people are measured according to institutional rules and expectations which are inadequate to account for individual behaviour in a multitude of contexts. Appropriately, the passage closes with the 'Prefects' (themselves representative of authority and conformity) who 'tried *vainly* to introduce some order into the squabble' (my emphasis, BTH, 2002, 10).

Larkin's character mimicry is another technique that is traceable to the Coleman prose. Through the focalisation of Margaret Tattenham, the narrative renders her anti-establishment perspective all the more vivid: after being caught communicating with a bookmaker 'Margaret clenched her teeth in anger as she drew the door shut behind her. That fool Waley, after she'd specially told him to address his letter in long-hand!' (BTH, 2002, 11). Through the use of an indirect free style, the reader is encouraged to see the world through Margaret's eyes. Larkin's early use of this fictional mode forms the basis of the construction of voices and personae in *The Less Deceived* (1955), a volume which is heavily reliant on a range of novelistic ploys. In the passage quoted above, by aligning the reader with Margaret's viewpoint, the narrative encourages an empathy with a marginalised character. Margaret's reference to Willow Gables as 'a God-forsaken hole' (BTH, 2002, 11), and her partiality for scatalogical invective ('Christ! said Margaret bitterly to herself' (BTH, 2002, 11)) show her detachment from the genteel veneer of the established school culture. This ability to create a distinct voice for characters is utilised in poems such as 'Toads' and 'Poetry of Departures' (CP, 89, 85). These poems achieve their effects by inviting the reader to assimilate various positions in a stylised 'dialogue' and, significantly, the method of communication in 'What Are We Writing For?' is strikingly similar to this. Larkin constructs a 'discussion' in which Brunette argues each point on girls' school fiction with her 'secretary', Jacinth (BTH, 2002. 255). Larkin used the dialectical method again in the *Round the Point* debates (1950–1) which also collide judgements and values. Though conspicuous in the poetry, this is a process which has its roots in Larkin's early commitment to the methodology of prose.

As well as these obvious examples of a dialogic method the novella's entire aesthetic structure debates the attractions of escaping quotidian norms. Margaret isn't the only pupil who feels the need to spice up school life with illicit practices. Marie is overwhelmed by her novelist aunt's gift of five pounds and her enthusiastic opening of the letter suggests how correspondence can assuage depressing reality. The letter's contents transport Marie to another world, far away from school life, and the money represents 'a preposterous procession of what £5 could buy: tennis racquets, evening frocks, wristlet-watches, slave-bangles, bicycles, underwear of finest silk' (BTH, 2002, 12). Larkin's own vicarious living through the letters that he wrote and received is well documented: 'Lookahere, you, write, write & keep on writing. I'm the trapped miner you're feeding through a tube, see?' he told Sutton in 1940 (Thwaite, 1992, 5), and the sustaining power of correspondence can be seen throughout his work. John Kemp feeds his imagination in the letters he composes for his fictitious sister and mail alleviates suffering 'like doctors' in 'Aubade' (1977, CP, 209). Similarly, in 1953 the speaker of 'At thirty-one, when some are rich' bemoans 'The eyelessness of days without a letter' (CP, 69). As elsewhere in the ouevre, in the novella correspondence provides an escape from a world of tedium and imperfection.

What constitutes the novella's most searching discussion, though, is its analysis of conventional perceptions of right and wrong. Like Margaret, Marie has also broken school rules. Unlike Margaret, however, Marie has done so unwittingly, not realising that possession of the money is officially forbidden. Regrettably, her genuine innocence counts for little against what is, in terms of official policy, a 'crime'. It is ironic that she stands accused by Hilary, who, despite her trusted position, is genuinely guilty of illicit practice. In many of his poems Larkin recasts circumscribed notions of what constitutes moral worth, though it is here, in the schoolgirl world of the Coleman prose, that he hones this tactic. The use of free indirect speech at the end of the chapter provides insight into a vindictive mind made more dangerous through its approval by the dominant culture: 'Then she turned on her heel, and marched away in the direction of the

Headmistress's study. What a business it was, she reflected, keeping oneself amused' (BTH, 2002, 13). At this juncture it is a school prefect who is 'amused' by imposing strictures and rules, though in 'At Grass' innocents are recruited by a more powerful adult world in the name of spectacle and entertainment.

Elsewhere, too, the novella refashions conventional perceptions. In a descriptive passage which echoes that of Miss Holden's study, Larkin draws our attention to Hilary's room. 'The carpet was soft, the furniture well-sprung' though the 'silken cushions' and the 'heavily chiaroscuro'd' picture alleviate what would otherwise be the room's 'chaste nudity' (BTH, 2002, 16). The passage contains more than a hint of erotic potential which would have appealed to Larkin's male cronies. However, just as Larkin 'transfigure[s] the clichés of urban folklore and advertising in poems such as "Essential Beauty" or "Sunny Prestatyn"' (BTH, 2002, xvii), so he adapts the standard tropes of girls' school fiction to shatter the respectable image of privilege and power. The passage undermines the school's social hierarchy in its suggestion that Hilary's respectable taste in furnishings and books is complemented by 'a whole bottom shelf' which contains 'other, less innocent, productions, often with heavy binding concealing their original continental paper covers' (BTH, 2002, 16). By re-invoking the description of Miss Holden's study, yet at the same time distorting it – through the addition of sensual suggestion – the passage invites us to re-evaluate the moral standing of traditional sources of prestige and authority.

Despite her failings, Hilary remains, for most of the story, an official agent of authority whose exploitation of younger girls anticipates officialdom's abuse of innocence in later poems. *No For an Answer*, 'Conscript' and 'MCMXIV ' are also concerned with how the naïve and the vulnerable fall prey to a persuasive authority culture. Hilary's clandestine tutoring of Mary allows her to combine her predatory sexuality with an apparent regard for the '"good cause"' (BTH, 2002, 20) of the junior's education. Whilst discussing the arrangements for Mary's extra lessons, Hilary reveals how she exploits her position. She treats signs of friendship from younger girls as a means of 'utilising . . . cheap labour to the fullest extent' (BTH, 2002, 18) and her 'biscuit tin, half-full of cigarette ends' (BTH, 2002, 21) shows a flouting of the rules that she is supposed to uphold. It is also ironic that whereas the official 'wrong-doers', Mary and Margaret, are intent on furthering the school's career on the cricket pitch, 'Hilary was not interested in cricket' (BTH, 2002, 17).

The sporting metaphor is carried through the story and characters are judged against it. A healthy regard for outdoor pursuits – which remove girls, literally, from the confines of the school – comes to be associated with subversion and virtue, whereas those who dislike sport have outwardly responsible positions yet, secretly, are steeped in vice. Hilary is all too conscious of the fine line she treads between doing her prefect's duty and fulfilling a sexual fantasy. Unable to suppress her image of Mary as a '"tawny young lioness"' (BTH, 2002, 18), she copies the phrase 'into her diary and then furiously scratche[s it] out, aware how much such a sentiment would surprise its object, and disgust, normally, its author' (BTH, 2002, 18). Hilary's official role within the school hierarchy vies with her licentious nature which seeks to exploit those within her care. Larkin's later poems also explore how institutions that are traditionally respected exploit misguided subjects who meekly follow.

Whilst Hilary's subversive behaviour goes unnoticed, Marie's one indiscretion brings down the full weight of authority upon her shoulders. When she is accused of stealing the money for a second time the entire school conspires against her. Denied the chance to put her side of the case, she is viciously flogged, despite the lack of evidence to justify such treatment. Furthermore, the strict observance of power relations that the school upholds pits sister against sister in a cruel and unfeeling manner: Philippa 'had to take the official view-point [towards Marie]' (BTH, 2002, 48) and has little compassion for her sister, claiming that '"One's got to have some sort of authority in a school"' (BTH, 2002, 47). Subsequently, Marie's protestations of innocence are useless in the face of a dominant culture that presents a united front:

> Marie was not put into the punishment room immediately, and by the time the Fourth Form came up to bed the news had imperceptibly spread around the Lower School that she had broken into the gym box and stolen the note again. On the whole, public opinion, being as usual insufficiently informed and easily swayed, tended to side with the view-point already expressed by Philippa Moore. Few girls took the view of Margaret, that a gymnasium would be more of a hindrance than a help: to most of them a gymnasium resembled a Nirvana (of a rather active kind) that they had not expected to attain in their school lives. (BTH, 2002, 52–3)

The narrative voice of this passage evokes sympathy for one who is at the mercy of the fickle whim of gossip. The word 'imperceptibly' suggests how the party line is embraced in an axiomatic way, so that Marie's guilt goes unchallenged by the wider community. In addition, the wry observation that public opinion is generally 'insufficiently informed' aligns the reader with the narrator in the suspicion that Marie is being judged unfairly. By focalising the narrative through Marie's eyes, Larkin encourages the reader to identify with Marie's plight in a manner which fore-shadows the empathy felt for the rape victim in 'Deceptions' (CP, 32):

> Marie could not but notice the coolness that was displayed towards her as her form-mates got into bed, or hung about, chatting . . . It annoyed her, all the more so because she had expected to be an object of sympathy, and to be consoled for the real injustice she had suffered instead of snubbed for the imaginary crimes she had committed. (BTH, 2002, 53)

The novella's plainest challenge to moral justice, as it is traditionally conceived, is directed against the dominant authority, or culture. The 'crime' of taking the note is 'imaginary' and the 'real injustice' is how the dominant culture misconstrues the facts. As the story unfolds, conventional notions of right and wrong are reversed, so that those who are convicted by officialdom are morally superior to those who make the charges. There is an instance of this in Chapter Seven when Marie's innocence exacerbates her punishment, rather than mitigates against it. The Headmistress is furious that Marie will not produce the note, but as she is not the thief she is powerless to stem Miss Holden's wrath. As Marie herself wryly reflects: 'It occurred to her that if only she had the note, everything would be much smoother. Crime, once again, would have paid' (BTH, 2002, 58). Like the girl in 'Deceptions' (CP, 32), Marie is over-powered by the values of the dominant culture and, like her later counterpart too, her plight urges us to reassess fixed and inflexible conventional moral categories.

Once Marie is restricted to solitary confinement, Myfanwy, Marie's loyal friend, plays the detective and discovers the truth about the stolen money. It might be worth mentioning, at this point, the influence of Bruce Montgomery's writing on the novella. Larkin shared the same staircase with Montgomery at St John's College, Oxford, and greatly admired the popularity that Montgomery's crime writing enjoyed. Thus, if the mildly pornographic elements of *Trouble at Willow Gables* were part of an on-going 'entertainment' between Larkin and Kingsley Amis, the aping of the detective style owed something to Larkin's friendship with Montgomery, and this debt to detective fiction can be seen in the novella's middle section.

Throughout this section Myfanwy's dialogue and free indirect speech repeatedly bear the imprint of the detective genre. Phrases like 'This would seem to fix the time of the robbery', 'a valuable deduction', '"some clues to be picked up"' (BTH, 2002, 55) and 'the clue of the crowbar' (BTH, 2002, 66) confirm Myfanwy's status as a formidable sleuth. Significantly, her task of finding the real culprit is paralleled by a marked detachment from official school culture. Myfanwy's preoccupation with clearing her friend's name 'distressed her so much that . . . she was quite unable to describe the principal features of the Orinoco basin, though the previous day she had had them at her finger-ends' (BTH, 2002, 61). This signals a transference of allegiance from the official school values to an alternative scheme which shies away from formal learning. Such signification chimes with the sentiments in an unpublished letter from Amis to Larkin: 'I have been getting on with quite a bit of serious reading since coming home; outside the syllabus, of course' (u/p letter, 4.vii.46). This revolt from what later poems term 'printed directions' ('Wants', CP, 42) or 'written skies' ('Like the train's beat', CP, 288) grants Myfanwy a broader vision than the restrictive focus of the classroom. Accordingly, Marie was set 'some particularly nasty sentence-parsing' (BTH, 2002, 61) whilst in solitary confinement, though when she swims Myfanwy escapes the stultifying nature of rote-learning:

> In the water, Myfanwy was in her element. Though shy of hockey, timid at netball, incompetent at cricket, as soon as her limbs felt the sharp coldness of water she became another being. She had never learned to swim: it seemed to come naturally. She had only used text-books to correct a few minor faults in her technique, and to learn new methods which increased her speed. (BTH, 2002, 64)

Myfanwy's natural aptitude for swimming and her disregard for the 'text-books' signify her unease with the school's orthodox methods of instruction. The novella employs the same pattern of signification as Larkin's later volumes which revere water and airy spaciousness over human codes and systems. Thus, the freedom that Myfanwy finds in swimming acts as a powerful symbolic gesture. Her coursing 'through the water like a slim brown salmon' (BTH, 2002, 64) imbues her with a natural grace, or 'a devout drench' as a later poem puts it ('Water', CP, 93), and this serves as an antidote to the oppressions of the official school hierarchy.

The novella anticipates the concerns of later poems in other ways. Larkin attempts to present an unfocused persona which transcends characterisation and sets individual activity in the wider context of an indifferent universe. After Hilary discovers that Margaret is the real culprit, there follows a passage which denies the characters responsibility for their actions. An early section of Chapter Ten shows a persistent use of passive constructions. A succession of past participles minimises the impact of human significance and implies an inevitability of action despite reasoned human input: 'Time passed . . . The machinery of yet another school day was set in motion. Water began to boil, fires were lit, bacon cut up, sausages sprinkled with flour, shoes of all shapes and sizes were cleaned and polished, floors and steps scrubbed, and the brass plate on the front door, as well as innumerable doorknobs, were brightly rubbed' (BTH, 2002, 91). Later, 'Tea steamed and was sipped: bacon cut and eaten, the rinds curling on the edges of innumerable plates: toast was buttered and bit' (BTH, 2002, 92). The impression created, that human design is of scant relevance, is one that Woolf evoked in 'Time Passes' in *To the Lighthouse*. In Section II of Woolf's novel the absence of human activity throws into relief the arbitrariness of design beneath the surface of seemingly regulated life. The early Larkin passage has none of the power or seriousness of purpose of *To the Lighthouse*, but Larkin's preoccupation with a non-human realm 'cleared of me' ('Absences', CP, 49) may be indebted to Woolf's detached portrayal of elemental indifference. *A Girl in Winter*, 'Here', 'MCMXIV' and 'High Windows' (CP, 136, 127, 165) all include this impartial dimension: Larkin was developing this mode, together with a much wider range of styles and voices, during his Coleman period.

The failings of human insight are demonstrated by the headmistress's reaction to Margaret's honest account of events in the denouement. Miss Holden dismisses her pupil's allegation as an '"unthinking slanderous [assertion]"' which will do her '"more harm than good"' and brands her a '"Revolting creature"' (BTH, 2002, 97). Margaret justifies her actions in a manner that probes the moral underpinnings of Miss Holden's accusations against her. She admits to having taken the money and remarks: '"I don't think it's a very heinous crime, anyway: it belongs to Marie Moore, she said I could have it, and I meant to put it back"' (BTH, 2002, 96). Moreover, in her stalwart determination to indict Hilary, 'Margaret plunged on, like the hard keel of a ship breaking up an ice-floe' when she describes the prefect's true nature (BTH, 2002, 97). This line conveys, in the same seafaring imagery that is used in *A Girl in Winter* and *The North Ship*, Margaret's ability to cut through the frozen rigidities of conventional opinion, a theme that these later texts also address.

Repeatedly, the novella rewrites official versions of right and wrong. In 'What Are We Writing For?' Larkin's ideal principal characters 'set at defiance all the rules of the school' yet emerge 'triumphant over all' (BTH, 2002, 271, 272). An episode towards the end of *Willow Gables* throws the school rules and their moral basis into disarray. When Miss Holden sends her senior girls to Mallerton, in an attempt to track down Marie, they treat the escapade as a jolly, rather than as an opportunity to prove their loyalty. Ursula cynically informs her peers how they will merely go through the motions of finding the runaway:

> we shall proceed to the police-station, make a similar enquiry there which will be met with a similar answer, and after that we shall walk back to school across the fields, delighting in this fresh summer day, and report to Janet what we have discovered, which is sweet fanny adams. (BTH, 2002, 101)

These lines depict the slightly errant schoolgirls who figure as stock literary types in the works of Dorita Fairlie Bruce and Elsie Oxenham. At the same time, however, the scene suggests a disinterested adherence to conventional routines which is a major thematic concern of the later poems. The girls seem to do their duty but, like Arnold who is 'out for his own ends' ('Self's the Man', CP, 117), the girls disguise their selfishness with an outward display of 'proper' conduct. So, though the seniors have the full trust of the school, it is Margaret, the 'guilty' one, who tries to rescue Myfanwy from the river. Margaret chides the others for dithering but 'without waiting to complete her sentence, she leapt up onto the parapet, steadied herself, and dived at the water. In the moment of descent, she thought bitterly: Damn it, I've done it again. I could have scooted then, if I'd only thought. What an imbecile I am - and I can't swim, either' (BTH, 2002, 117). Just as it is the convict, Magwitch, who acts virtuously in *Great Expectations* (Dickens, 1860), Margaret the reprobate risks her life in a gesture which shames the official moral guardians. The episode's appeal for Larkin is the way it allows him to expose the hypocrisies of customary behaviour. In the light of the school's shattered moral universe, Miss Holden's address to new girls is laden with irony: '"I want to impress upon you that the rules are made for your protection and for the improvement of school life"' (BTH, 2002, 111). Plainly, it is Margaret's breach of school rules – by escaping from the punishment room – that enables her to try to save Myfanwy from drowning. Thus, Larkin's adaptation of the school story genre, as well as answering a sexual and psychological need (see Rowe in BTH, 2000 and BTH, 2002), provided him with an early vehicle for questioning moral codes that are officially sponsored. The episode's message can be aptly expressed in the words of 'Vers de Société': in following the 'routines [of] / / Playing at goodness' the prefects fall short of 'what should be'(CP, 181).

The novella also foreshadows the concerns of the later poems in its treatment of animals. Their vulnerable innocence can be seen in 'Midwinter Waking', 'Myxomatosis' and 'First Sight', while 'Take One Home for the Kiddies' (CP, 87, 100, 112, 130) confronts the abuse of animals by their human masters. Margaret's affinity with Toby the horse is an early manifestation of Larkin's sympathy for animals that have been recruited into the human world:

> Toby was a little shy of most humans, having learnt by experience that they approached only when there was some mowing or rolling to do, or when they wished to ingratiate themselves with him by gurgling at him in a ridiculous fashion, the while clawing his mane or causing him acute pain by thumping him heartily, saying "Good old Toby, boy!" He made, however, an exception in the case of Margaret, for she rarely came up to him without a piece of sugar and talked to him in an ordinary voice, and had once complained to the groundsman that his harness was badly-fitting, as indeed it was. (BTH, 2002, 104)

The horse has an affinity with Margaret as both are treated unsympathetically by their superiors. By according these abused and marginalised characters the vital function of helping to save Myfanwy, Larkin implies that they have a wealth of moral integrity despite their humble status. As in 'The little lives of earth and form' (1977, CP, 207) an animal-human 'kinship lingers'; Margaret's bond with unshackled nature is stressed on more than one occasion. In Chapter Ten, for instance, 'Margaret was savage' (BTH, 2002, 116), and when she escapes with Toby 'they started to gallop across the next field, the wind blowing her short tunic precisely against her body, and her flying hair making her look like some exquisite nymph riding the horse of the dawn over the Pan-guarded slopes of Arcady' (BTH, 2002, 105). The pastoral idyll with which horse and rider are associated imbues them with the freedom to counter the school's man-made constrictions, so that their flight becomes a plea for nature rather than nurture. The excerpt's most interesting detail, in terms of Larkin's thematic continuities, is the way that Toby is described as 'peacefully *cropping* the outfield' (my emphasis, BTH, 2002, 103). The phrase anticipates 'At Grass' (CP, 29–30) in which 'one [horse] crops grass' but that poem, too, is echoed by the 'badly-fitting' harness (BTH, 2002, 104) which constrains Toby as forcefully as the groom's 'bridles' in the final stanza. An interval of seven years separates the two texts yet both express, through a similar set of images and motifs, Larkin's revulsion at how innocents are coerced by flawed human regimes.

Larkin constructs for Toby a 'voice' such that his suffering and confusion are acutely felt. When prompted by a dig in the ribs he is 'a little surprised, but imagining that it must be all right if Margaret said so, broke into a smart canter' (BTH, 2002, 104). Later, when his rider drives him into the river, the narrative again focalises his point of view:

Toby, who was really a gentle horse, became quite frightened, and sped across the river once more, clambering with difficulty up the opposite bank in an effort to appease the suddenly-ferocious friend whom he had allowed to mount him. (BTH, 2002, 105)

Toby is abused in the name of a human scheme which he cannot understand. Ponies endure 'Bewildering requirements' in 'Show Saturday' (1973) and in 'Winter' (1943–4) 'each horse . . . / Long since defeated / Lowers its head' (CP, 200, 286). What makes Toby's predicament most distressing is his 'effort to appease' the mistress who causes him pain. His desire to please is reminiscent of the way that Boxer's innocent trust in authority leads to his premature death in *Animal Farm* (Orwell, 1945).

Toby suffers a physical assault, though an earlier episode shows how another suppliant is coaxed into accepting the dominant ideology by more subtle means. When Miss Holden discovers that Marie has re-appropriated her five pounds, she decides that the money should be allotted to the gymnasium fund:

Miss Holden publicly inserted the note into the wooden cashbox attached to the wall next to the plaque commemorating the Great War of 1914–18. No mention was made of the element of compulsion in the gift, and Marie experienced the wholly delightful feeling of having the approval of the whole school bestowed upon her. (BTH, 2002, 37)

Just as Toby endured Margaret's harsh treatment in order to win her approval, so Marie is persuaded to accept her loss in exchange for the 'delightful feeling of having the approval of the whole school'. In both cases, authority internalises in the subject its own values, such that 'the element of compulsion' passes unnoticed. In the words of 'The Importance of Elsewhere' (1955), Marie's cultural deference to her own 'customs and establishments' makes it 'more serious' for her 'to refuse' (CP, 104). It is significant that the gymnasium cashbox is situated 'next to the plaque commemorating the Great War'. The implication is that acceptance of the war's ideals is secured by the same means as donations for the gymnasium fund: in both cases the dominant culture uses public praise to underline 'proper' behaviour. Larkin's sympathy for those who are manipulated by a dominant order's socialisation process resurfaces seventeen years later in 'MCMXIV ' (CP, 127).

A further aspect of Larkin's concern with oppression is the marginalisation of women on account of their low social and professional status. This is a major theme of *A Girl in Winter*, *A New World Symphony*, 'Wedding-Wind' and 'The Whitsun Weddings' (CP, 11, 114), though, once again, the girls' school story provides Larkin with the perfect vehicle from which to launch his proto-feminist campaign. As Auchmuty has shown, one of the chief attractions of the girls' school story is the way it assigns responsible positions to women. *Trouble at Willow Gables* accords with this dictum to the letter, disregarding patriarchal realism's designated roles for women and girls. Thus, the depiction of Hilary as 'a big girl, with a strongly-moulded body' (BTH, 2002, 13) cuts across stereotypes of female meekness. Similarly, Miss Holden keeps order by 'peer[ing] severely down the tables from behind her *Times*' (BTH, 2002, 31). In her role as Head she has acquired all the gestures and idiosyncrasies of the typical (male) manager. Her girls, too, continually flout roles that are conventionally designated 'feminine'. Their preferred sport is cricket and Margaret is an enthusiast of 'touch-rugger' (BTH, 2002, 36). In addition, Myfanwy solves the mystery of the missing note by consulting 'a text book on Mechanics' (BTH, 2002, 61), thereby side-stepping orthodox notions of appropriate reading for girls. Later in the story Marie's escape is inspired by the cross-dressing in *As You Like It*. '"People might take me for a boy"' (BTH, 2002, 78) she tells Pat as she pulls on the trousers that, to her father, are '"sinful and fast"' (BTH, 2002, 79). Repeatedly, the novella puts women in situations that overturn patriarchal conceptions of feminine conduct; 'An old labourer . . . muttered up at [the seniors] disapprovingly' (BTH, 2002, 101) when he sees them smoking. Interestingly, in the light of Larkin's own rejection from military service in 1942, he describes the senior girls – whose real-life counterparts would have been sidelined from the war – as 'three trained Commandos' (BTH, 2002, 109), and after expelling Hilary, Miss Holden suggests '"a fresh start in some other sphere of life: perhaps the A. T. S. . . . "' (BTH, 2002, 124).

At the same time as encroaching on traditional manly behaviour, however, Larkin's female characters rigidly adhere to a code of mutual support that implies sisterly solidarity in the face of hardship. Thus, even as they plan Mary's 'illegal' tutorials, Philippa thinks of the junior's welfare: '"Don't let her stay later than eleven, because she must get plenty of sleep. I don't think losing an hour every other night does any harm, do you?"' (BTH, 2002, 21). In the same way, Margaret recognises that she cannot benefit from the new gym '"but still, others will enjoy it"' (BTH, 2002, 39). Ultimately, though, women's liberation from a life of subservience can best be achieved by personal wealth (see Auchmuty, 1999, 20). Marie, for one, fully appreciates '"How nice it is to have a rich aunt"' (BTH, 2002, 12) and Margaret observes, with great perspicuity, that '"It's not brains you need to get [to Oxford], it's money"' (BTH, 2002, 39). Significantly, Margaret's own attitude towards money contrasts starkly with a later character who 'let[s] [money] lie . . . wastefully' ('Money', CP, 198). Her honourable intention of sharing her winnings with Marie anticipates 'Show Saturday' (CP, 199–201) in that human relations transcend financial interest: in that poem 'Sale-bills and swindling' are overshadowed by a 'Regenerate union' of understanding.

However, though it is possible to discern a coherent set of patterns and motifs in the novellas, any artistic integrity the work aspires to is compromised by its concessions to adolescent titillation. Philippa's belt fetish is one example of this; another is the manner in which Margaret rides away from the school: 'she noted for future reference that bare-backed riding without knickers was a pleasurable occupation' (BTH, 2002, 105). In addition, Margaret's penchant for swearing would undoubtedly have amused Larkin's student chums: 'Margaret . . . plunged into the realms of scatology, of which she seemed to be mistress' (BTH, 2002, 110), and later we learn she was 'beginning to enjoy her farrago of obscenity' (BTH, 2002, 110). Nevertheless, such a manner of speaking would have been more common amongst men than women in the early 1940s and so Larkin's all-female world allows its characters to invade territory – linguistic and otherwise – that would customarily have been inhabited by men (see Auchmuty, 1999, 39). In 'High Windows' and 'This Be The Verse' (CP, 165, 180) Larkin utilises demotic terminology as a negationist gesture of detachment from settled structures. To claim that this was the intention in *Trouble at Willow Gables* would be to over-read Larkin's juvenilia. Nevertheless, when we consider Margaret's alienation from conventional attitudes, her expletives might provide what Stephen Burt calls 'subcultural indicators' of alternative values (Burt, 1996, 18). The use of coarse colloquial diction, then, might constitute another way in which the novella foreshadows what was to follow in Larkin's later writing.

Ultimately, whether or not we accept a serious intention behind *Trouble at Willow Gables*, it shows, quite clearly, important literary influences on the young Larkin. Something of the debt to Woolf has already been mentioned, though borrowings are not restricted to stylistic presentation. When they are alone together, Hilary and Marie settle down to their cosy tutorial: the 'reading-lamp shed a cone of light on the open page' whilst 'out in the night, darkness stretched' (BTH, 2002, 85). Cones, wedges and triangles figure prominently in Woolf's work as signifiers of essential selfhood which confirm inner worth in the face of a hostile environment. Thus, Mrs Ramsay sees herself as 'a wedge-shaped core of darkness' (*To the Lighthouse*, 60) in her retreat from the pressures of surface reality. Larkin's similar imagery evokes Hilary's need to lead, simultaneously, the life of orthodox prefect and secretive lesbian. Moreover, Hilary's reflection on 'the apt coherence of time, place and desire' (BTH, 2002, 85) conveys that sense of epiphany which is so often expressed in Woolf's novels.

The novella is also shot through with echoes of Edward Thomas. After Marie escapes from the punishment room, she faces a difficult trek across rough terrain. In this environment 'trees stood as close together as palings of a fence' (BTH, 2002, 99) and the land 'far from being grassy, was uneven and covered in a knee-deep growth of brambles, nettles, spear-grass, dry bracken and other impediments' (BTH, 2002, 99). As Motion has shown, physical and mental landscapes conflate in Thomas's poems, so that veering off the well-trodden path imposes penalties that go beyond the geographical (see Motion, 1980). So, after experiencing discomfort in the woods, Marie is desperate 'to get back to the comfortable sanctuary of Willow Gables . . . Bread and water in the punishment room was prefer-able to this wilderness of spiders, slugs, nettles, and - possibly - predatory ploughmen' (BTH, 2002, 100). By leaving the straight course Marie yearns for freedom, yet she discovers, finally, that such freedoms are illu-sory and that familiar paths are more amenable than uncharted ones. Larkin revisits these sentiments in 'Here', 'High Windows' and 'Poetry of Departures' (CP, 136, 165, 85) though they first appear in the juvenilia, albeit embedded in a form and a genre different to those poems, but avail-able, nevertheless, to be re-invoked at a later date. One of Larkin's reasons for not developing his novel writing was the difficulty he had in finding a suitable background for the characters (Thwaite, 2001, 49). Thus, to compare the novella with the later poems is to understand how Larkin sifted out, from the extraneous detail of prose, 'a single emotional spear-point' (Larkin, 1983, 95) which could be intensified by poetic scrutiny.

Michaelmas Term at St Bride's

The story follows on from that of *Trouble at Willow Gables*. Mary Burch, who was molested by Hilary at school, begins her student existence in the knowledge that she must share rooms with her old adversary. As the story unfolds Hilary and Mary become intimate friends and Hilary instils in the younger girl an outlook that will ensure her survival at the college. In particular, Hilary protects Mary against Mary de Putron, a swaggering hearty who uses her wealth and arrogance to tyrannise staff and students alike. A sub-plot involves the Moore sisters of the previous novella – here re-named Woolf – and traces Marie's efforts to cure Philippa of her obses-sion with belts. The story is incomplete, though other significant episodes include the preparations for a socialite's party and a pub crawl in which Larkin's own friends make an appearance.

Because the work is unfinished we can be less sure of Larkin's overall intention, and the incorporation of real-life figures – such as Diana Gollancz and Bruce Montgomery – into the plot confuses the piece still further. Even so, several of its scenes are worthy of serious consideration, in that they show a similar disruption of settled perspectives to those of *Trouble at Willow Gables*. As in that novella, the main areas of contestation are matters of cultural and sexual identity and the extent to which customary modes of understanding can be illusory or misleading.

At an early stage we are reminded that Mary is a thoroughly respectable middle-class girl who has been brought up in the appropriate manner:

> In the vacations she had helped her mother in their house in Yorkshire, read books from the local Boots', and gone walks and pony rides: for a fortnight she had had a girl friend from school to stay with her, and she knew that this friend – Marie Woolf – would even now be waiting for her at St Bride's, along with several other of her old school-chums. Everything was as it should be, and her only anxiety was whether her china had survived the long journey . . . (BTH, 2002, 132)

The 'local Boots'' and the pony rides are indicative of a cultural hinterland of privilege and good breeding in which 'Everything was as it should be'. The china's brittle nature symbolises the fragility of Mary's conformist background when confronted with the alternative lifestyles of her new environment. Moreover, the foreboding nature of college life is evoked through the Grimm-like description of the portress, who was 'an aged woman dressed all in black and flourishing a bunch of rusty keys' (BTH, 2002, 133). Her dialogue contains the same sense of goodness being lured by bad that permeates Larkin's *Phairy Phantasy* cartoons (1943), which are contemporaneous with *Michaelmas Term* and which draw on Larkin's own oscillation between clean living and debauchery whilst a student at Oxford. One of the most graphic illustrations depicts Larkin's 'good angel' pouring strong drink down the washbasin whilst Larkin looks on in a state of dejection (see Appendix, p. 184, u/p drawings). The portress warns Mary of future temptation in similar terms:

> "Afore the leaves 'ave fallen, afore the Christmastide of their first term, they're asmoking at cigarettes."
> "Yes, but— "
> "Awearing of short skirts!"
> "But— "
> "'Avin' fellers to tea!"
> "Look, if— "
> "Goin' to dances!"

"My— "

"And in their second term," ended the crone, sinking her voice to a tone of blood-curdling finality, "*the mischief's done*. So my advice to you my dear is, go, while the goin's good! Go, while you can still hold up your head in innercence!" (BTH, 2002, 133)

Mary has ambivalent feelings towards her new room-mate and former persecutor. On the one hand, she is attracted to Hilary's glamour, experiencing a 'transient curiosity' (BTH, 2002, 134) in her array of cosmetics; on the other, she is repelled by the presence of her old 'tutor'. Recognising the 'calf-bound book that caused all her previous premonitary feelings to return' she is seized with 'A sudden terror [that] well[ed] up from some hiding-place deep-set in her nature' (BTH, 2002, 136). This last quotation provides an early clue that, as in 'Dockery and Son', 'Innate assumptions' can be misguided (CP, 153), though what is most significant is that the two girls will be sharing rooms. This implies not so much a bifurcation of the ideals that they represented in *Trouble at Willow Gables* but, instead, the symbiotic relationship between rebellious and conformist attitudes that is explored in 'Toads' and 'Poetry of Departures' (CP, 85, 89).

In the same way as its predecessor, the narrative voice of *Michaelmas Term at St Bride's* slides easily from one character's perspective to another. Though character development is still minimal, each girl is presented as a means of ventriloquising certain attitudes. Thus, on hearing about the room-sharing Marie informs Mary of its advantages in tones which suggest a decentred view of formal education:

"She'll probably influence you a good deal – teach you things you didn't know before, you know, and give you new ways of looking at things. After all, that's what Oxford is really for – they say that half one's education comes unofficially, from the people one meets". (BTH, 2002, 143)

The suggestion is that by tempering her conventional bourgeois upbringing with a sprinkling of radicalism, Mary will attain something of a fully rounded personality. Indeed, since her expulsion from Willow Gables, Hilary's career is testimony to the fact that falling foul of officialdom has its compensations. She tells Mary:

"As soon as I left school, I went to a divine school near Paris for a year. That was marvellous. I learnt more there than I learnt in six years at Willow Gables – and my French was perfect. Then I lived a bit in Switzerland, and finally my mother took me round the world. My mother's a big-game huntress. We stopped in Africa for some time, and she caught a little lioness for me". (BTH, 2002, 148)

This passage, like so many in *Trouble at Willow Gables* and the unfinished novels, inverts standard preconceptions as to what constitutes success. Though she has been educated along unorthodox lines, Hilary '"learnt"' more during her foreign travels than she did in school, where knowledge is conventionally acquired. However, Hilary's education has not been confined to glamorous extra-curricular pursuits; her experience has resulted in her '"perfect"' French. Compared to such a life, Mary's orthodox schooling seems woefully uninspired and even she must confess to having done '"nothing much . . . Just ordinary things"' (BTH, 2002, 149). Indeed, Hilary's mocking reference to Mary's medal for '"Leadership and Character"' (BTH, 2002, 149) further undercuts any claim to superiority the life of conformity may bring. In a passage that is reminiscent of *Jill* – in which Kemp's social awkwardness is contrasted with Warner's social ease – Mary 'looked in agony at her bed, and her pyjamas on top of it. Ah, if only she were in both of them!' (BTH, 2002, 150). That Hilary was already in bed, looking at 'her continental pages' (BTH, 2002, 151) suggests that her school expulsion and subsequent avante-garde education have given her a confidence which will be invaluable in the turbulent undergraduate world.

There are other occasions, too, when the story invites us to reassess glib judgements. Hilary's close proximity makes Mary's instinctive reaction a 'detestation of the alarming onset of her Oxford life' (BTH, 2002, 151) though in tracing her re-evaluation of events the narrative disturbs the notion of settled moral absolutes. Consequently 'things were never so bad, nor so good, as they appeared at first sight' (BTH, 2002, 138) and Hilary, far from being villainous, 'was by no means as bad as she might have been' (BTH, 2002, 152). Mary finds that 'Hilary's attitude was invariably urbane and gentle, and entirely free from predatory tendencies', and the two girls 'settled down to live on fairly amicable terms' (BTH, 2002, 152). Thus, the novella highlights the folly of erecting, too hastily, clichéd constructions of 'good' and 'bad' characters. The best example, though, of false categorisation, comes in Chapter Two when the new girls contemplate their peers:

> The four strolled out together, glancing defensively at the other freshers, trying to size up the swotters, the brilliant slackers, the social types, the *ingénues*, the sophisticated, the afraid, and seeing instead nothing but a harlequinade of faces, spectacled and unspectacled, of hair-styles, fair and dark, of figures, and of all shapes and colours of jumpers and skirts. (BTH, 2002, 140)

In spite of their efforts to pick out 'social types', Mary and her chums see 'nothing but a harlequinade of faces' and their desire to measure and label is thwarted by the 'shapes and colours' that elude firm identities.

Two further scenes demonstrate how the rigid observance of prescribed roles can hinder, rather than assist. The first occurs when Mary is late for class. Hilary tells her not to '"get into a stew over missing a lecture"' as they are '"a very poor form of entertainment"' (BTH, 2002, 153). However, Mary feels compelled to attend, even if it means taking a bicycle that does not belong to her. In the pursuit of her academic duty Mary is unaware that her 'borrowing' constitutes something more serious. The bicycle's owner, Mary de Putron, enlightens her in terms that are crystal clear: '"There's another name for that sort of thing, and I'm not afraid to tell you it if you don't know what it is – stealing!"' (BTH, 2002, 155). The scene is a comic one: Mary is not really a thief and de Putron's offensive stance is unwarranted. The episode's purpose, though, is to show that events can be construed in different ways depending on the point of view. Larkin's enduring interest in the fracturing of customary perceptions is evident in much of the later work, though we see it first in Brunette's farcical romances.

After the bicycle incident Mary concludes that de Putron is '"rude and offensive"' (BTH, 2002, 156), though her arrogance and wealth have earned her a status that is almost regal: 'The servants were deferential to her, and received hard words and hard cash: the dons were respectful, and received condescending invitations to tea' (BTH, 2002, 155). Rather than being ostracised for her bullying swagger, de Putron is rewarded with social status and the narrator points out how Mary is 'educated' into an alternative value system where being '"rude and offensive"' brings its own success: '[Mary] felt in the position of a newly-arrived courtier who learns that the testy old gentleman in the washrooms whom he elbowed away from the roller towel was the sovereign himself' (BTH, 2002, 157–8).

At the hockey trial, Mary's fortunes on the pitch are expressed in terms which suggest far more than sporting endeavour. The scene's interest resides in the fact that Mary is made to play as right back when her usual position is left winger. Of crucial significance is the fact that she adopts a role that is unfamiliar to her. The narrative expresses her anxiety:

> Vague memories of text-books haunted her, that she had read on becoming Captain of Willow Gables, but before she had time to think of them, an attack swiftly developed, and the colours forwards rushed the ball into the goalmouth. (BTH, 2002, 165)

These lines contain a metaphoric import akin to those which describe Myfanwy's swimming prowess in *Trouble at Willow Gables*. As in the earlier novella, knowledge contained in 'text-books' is unable to assist with the pressures of real life, where adaptability far outweighs 'printed directions' (CP, 42).

The structural principles of *Trouble at Willow Gables* are repeated elsewhere, too. Just as Margaret, the alleged reprobate, saved the day in that story, so Hilary is Mary's unlikely saviour at St Bride's. Hilary's disdain for authority, whether it is the college's or de Putron's, is made quite clear:

> "Oh, hang Mary de Putron," said Hilary heartily, tugging down her jumper. "I got sick of all this de Putron racket after I'd been here a week. Who does she think she is, anyway? Don't you pay any attention to her". (BTH, 2002, 157)

Mary whines that de Putron '"was the one person I ought to have been nice to"' (BTH, 2002, 158) in order to gain a place in the hockey team. Hilary reminds her that she doesn't '"have to be a hypocrite any longer"' and that she can '"get in the team on [her] own merits"'(BTH, 2002, 158). Such disdain for hypocrisy encompasses not only Mary's sycophantic attitude towards de Putron, but the general phenomenon of courting authority for reasons of self-interest; what, in 'Conscript' (CP, 262), is called 'The requisite contempt of good and bad'. Hilary's sexuality may be 'other' to the cultural norm but she has an integrity that others could learn from. Realising that Mary needs her protection against the likes of de Putron, the lust Hilary felt at Willow Gables evaporates so that 'Mary's unspoilt innocence, which by rights should only have added a poignancy to the final surrender, became a thing of beauty, worthy of reverence' (BTH, 2002, 174).

Unlike *Trouble at Willow Gables*, in which Hilary's sole intention was to seduce Mary, *Michaelmas Term* plays down her predatory sexual nature. In this novella the two girls do become intimate – though Mary is not coerced into the relationship and there are no evocative physical scenes as there were in the earlier story. According to Rowe, 'the author can no longer be bothered to describe lesbian encounters in any detail' (BTH, 2000, 91), though there is evidence to suggest that Larkin's concern goes well beyond sexual titillation.

After the hockey trial, Mary drinks Hilary's brandy as a means of drowning her sorrow. As a result she feels '"queer"' and doesn't '"remember ever feeling so happy before"' (BTH, 2002, 172). Further details suggest the alcohol's clouding effect on her sense of sober convention. She describes herself as '"not feeling lady-like"' and is grateful for Hilary's sisterly comfort during which she 'shifted to a more comfortable position' (BTH, 2002, 172–3). For Mary, the experience is '"weird"' (BTH, 2002, 173) though to Hilary '"it all seems eminently natural"'.

Hilary applies the term '"natural"' to an episode that patriarchal morality might construe to be depraved or licentious. This brief exchange is critical because it sheds 'illumination' on how Mary's life has been constrained by the apparently 'natural' values of patriarchal society (BTH, 2002, 173). For example, even though it is a women's college, St Bride's 'had been constructed on a masculine model' (BTH, 2002, 132). Moreover, Mary is ill-treated by Mary de Putron who – as the '"biggest lady in the College"' (BTH, 2002, 156) – exhibits the same bullying manner as Miss Holden in *Willow Gables*. By way of comfort, Hilary offers more than brandy. Her campaign against male oppression can be traced throughout the novella. One example of this is the way she keeps a boyfriend waiting – '"it's only a man"' (BTH, 2002, 158) she remarks – and she seeks 'to minimize his masculine qualities by referring to him scornfully as "that *creature*"' (BTH, 2002, 166). The most convincing humiliation of patriarchal condescension, however, comes in a scene which is set in the University Parks.

It is here that an opportunity arises for Hilary to get even with de Putron for her unpleasant treatment of Mary. When Hilary falls into the river, de Putron's boyfriend, Clive, rushes to her rescue: '"English tradition of chivalry, you know. Couldn't leave this girlie to drown"' (BTH, 2002, 195). His remarks reveal a sexist attitude that construes women as helpless '"girlie[s]"' who require the supervision of men. Hilary turns the situation to her own advantage:

> Hilary's mind was working overtime, and she turned to regard him with childish admiration. "Gosh. You must be awfully brave". With a theatrical start she became aware of her soaked and transparent clothes. "Oh, I say, don't I look a *sight*! I say, you really oughtn't to look, really you oughtn't. I feel most frightfully immodest". (BTH, 2002, 194)

By playing the helpless female who dotes on male heroics, Hilary ensures that Clive's sexual interest is aroused to the extent that de Putron is humiliated as her male companion is transfixed by Hilary's 'soaked and transparent' clothes. As in his later poems, Larkin ridicules misogynistic attitudes by parodying certain character types. We can see this here as Hilary flirts with Clive in a 'theatrical' way so that when she 'regard[s] him with childish admiration' she knowingly gulls his expectation of naïve female conduct. Hilary's performance is successful and Mary notes that a continuation of the act would guarantee de Putron's '"social ruin"' (BTH, 2002, 203). Hilary's reluctance to comply, however, suggests her pride in being detached from settled sexual identities: '"And what about my social ruin? Everyone'll say, Hilary's gone queer"' (BTH, 2002, 203). Hilary's response signifies a reversal of conventional assumptions. In her scheme lesbianism is '"natural"' and heterosexuality is designated '"queer"'. The scene is important because it implicitly acknowledges that a character who deviates from cultural norms can triumph over those who adopt conventional attitudes which are customarily endorsed as just and proper.

Elsewhere in the text are glimpses of manly behaviour far more offensive than Clive's patronising manner. On the way to a public house Marie and Philippa meet 'Soldiers [who] utilised unchristian words and gestures as they passed'. When they arrive at the first hostelry they are 'confronted by a notice saying that unaccompanied ladies [are] not served'. Having finally made it to the bar they witness 'a labourer . . . after a series of thickening, phlegmatic coughings . . . spread a viscous gob stringily across the floor with the sole of his boot'. This ordeal over, Marie is interrupted by 'the lecherous advances of a member of H. M. Armed Forces' (all BTH, 2002, 226). All of these examples show the base nature of a construction of masculinity which Larkin criticised throughout all of his writing. What the pub scene also represents, though, is the (Jungian) means by which Philippa is to be cured of her belt fetish – '"a kind of descent into Hell to rescue [the] soul"' (BTH, 2002, 223). Carl Jung's teachings were introduced to Larkin by John Layard in a series of Oxford seminars. Larkin was particularly interested in Jung's ideal 'state of union' (Thwaite, 1992, 53) between the masculine and feminine sides of the psyche and he compiled dream-records to analyse his own psychological progress. There is a Jungian undercurrent in the poems, though it appears for the first time here in a confused and comic form. Like her creator, Marie 'would enter [in her book] the night's dreams, with copious notes and illustrations' (BTH, 2002, 181) and 'During [the girls'] conversation the names of John Barnyard [i.e. Layard], Carl Gustav Jung [and] Sigmund Freud . . . were freely bandied about' (BTH, 2002, 182). Margaret's dream 'that she sometimes [had] . . . about racehorses' (BTH, 2002, 181) may have been modelled on one of Larkin's own dreams, which corroborates a reading of 'At Grass' (CP, 29) in Chapter 4.

Michaelmas Term at St Bride's is important because it opens windows onto new vistas of understanding which disrupt conventional attitudes towards a range of issues including sexual politics and questions of power and identity. In pursuing these concerns it shares with *Trouble at Willow Gables* a debt to Woolf and Edward Thomas. Woolf's name is used for Marie and Philippa and the use of a dinner party as a means of social union echoes a similar device in *Mrs Dalloway*. Stylistically, too, the novella employs abrupt scene changes reminiscent of Woolf. This is most apparent when the narrative cuts from a snapshot of Clive's drinking exploits to Marie's activities in Part III (BTH, 2002, 216–7). Edward

Thomas has a similarly pervasive influence on the text. Throughout the story his *Oxford* (1903) is a constant companion to Marie who imagines she '"is the nursling of a great tradition in a fair city"' (BTH, 2002, 158). Prior to the Woolfs' drinking session, however, his nostalgic volume is invoked in an ironical way. The reverence that Thomas feels for Oxford is utilised to applaud not the hallowed college architecture but the alternative culture of the public house:

> The callow freshman who in his first year thrills to the names of Christ Church, Magdalen, Oriel, Merton, Queen's, New, Corpus Christi and Lady Margaret Hall, will in his third have transferred that delight to the royal thunder of the Black Horse, the Nag's Head, the Royal Oxford, the Apollo, the Mitre, the Eastgate, the King's Arms, the Wheatsheaf; the appreciation he reserved for Christ Church Staircase, for New College Chapel, for Magdalen Tower, St John's Gardens, or the river at Folly Bridge will have mutated into an appreciation of the snuggery at the Turf, the Hogarth reproductions at the Eagle and Child, the pastoralism of the Trout, and the barmaids at the Lord Napier. This is the true mark of an Oxford education: the eye that sees the beauty of the Carpenter's Arms, the romantic garishness of the Northgate Tavern, the steely glitter of vice at White's, sees them, and pronounces them good. (BTH, 2002, 225)

It is this tension between traditional and subversive cultures that occupies *Jill*, where Larkin uses the university city, together with the tugs and pressures of wartime, as an apt setting for John Kemp's development from idealistic dreamer to less deceived realist.

Jill

In later life Larkin was dismissive of *Jill*'s artistic merits, complaining to Barbara Pym: 'Jill [is] dreadful? Filleted of any shred of interest' (u/p postcard note, 2.x.77); but as a discerning novelist herself, Pym sang the book's praises. In her correspondence with Larkin Pym speaks of his poetry and prose in the same breath. Writing to Larkin in 1964, she praises *The Whitsun Weddings*, published that year:

> [It has] Quite a lot of new ones and a favourite I'd seen in some anthology ('Faith Healing') . . . now all together in 'handy form' for reading in Lyons or in bed . . . I shall try to give it to a fortunate friend, also Jill. (u/p letter, 7.iv.64)

In a later passage she points out the imaginative continuity which exists between Larkin's prose and his poetry, and is delighted to find in the novel 'the occurrence of the name "Bleaney" (see *Jill* p. 73). It was a great pleasure to hear you reading Mr Bl. on the Third some weeks ago' (u/p letter, 7.iv.64). Pym's comments suggest that the similarities between Larkin's fiction and his poetry are worth further investigation.

Alienation from bourgeois values characterises John Kemp's journey to Oxford. Acknowledging the novel's socio-historical aspect, Motion describes John's state as 'frightened, inexperienced and – by reason of his coming from a northern industrial town – exiled from his environment, kind and class' (Motion, 1982, 40). In the novel's opening section Larkin uses a mix of social-realist techniques to convey John's despair and displacement. The omniscient narrator moves in and out of John's consciousness, so that we see the hostile environment confronting John whilst at the same time experiencing it through his eyes. For the most part, a third person narrator recounts John's exploits in a linear manner, though indirect free speech and focalisation are also employed to promote a sense of ironic detachment. This acts as a precursor to the adoption of different personae – such as Mr Bleaney, Arnold and the women in 'Wedding-Wind' and 'Deceptions' – in the later poems (CP, 102, 117, 11, 32).

The description of the train journey with which the book opens is figurative of the social journey that John attempts. The pathetic fallacy of the first paragraph implies that John's rite of passage will be beset with rebuff and disappointment. Successive details conspire to create a strong sense of John's alienation from his environment. Significantly placed 'in the corner' of the carriage, John observes the 'opaque clouds' which 'thicken' around him and alert us to the turbulent emotional weather that he will encounter at Oxford (*Jill*, 21). The trees which stand out 'as in spring' and the 'still green' hedges that 'from a distance [look] like . . . flowers' (21) constitute propitious, though misleading, signs. Just as the convolvuli is 'sickly yellow' (21) when viewed at close quarters, so the idyll of college life will sour when John reaches Oxford. His impending estrangement from the culture he is about to encounter is alluded to further by the 'blackened bridges' (21) which he sees through the window. As if to underline their significance as conduits, or means of access, we are told that the 'waters were spanned by empty footbridges' (21) signalling John's slim chance of passing smoothly from one social milieu into another.

The 'swirls of the cleaner's leather . . . on the glass' (21) suggest John's clouded view of the future but anticipate, too, how other characters are separated from what they yearn for most. In 'Here' it is material 'desires', though in 'An April Sunday brings the snow' it is a dead father lying 'Behind the glass' (CP, 136, 21). An early speaker 'watched from windows in the failing light / For his world that was always just out of sight' (1941, CP, 258). Inside the carriage John's view is equally unpropitious. The picture of Dartmouth Castle which 'looked at him from the opposite wall' suggests an alternative, romantic world which finds no echo in the external scene that is 'cold and deserted' (21). The world of romance suggested by the castle is presented as an artistic construct whose relationship to reality is unclear. After his bungled attempts at eating sandwiches, John immerses himself in *A Midsummer Night's Dream* – a choice of reading that signifies a subconscious desire to escape from the strictures of social decorum into a more liberating, fantasy realm.

Motion has shown how food in the novel, and more precisely the manner in which characters eat, functions as an index to their social and sexual ease (see Motion, 1982, 45–6). Evidence to support Motion's case can be gathered from Larkin's undergraduate essays. In one of these Larkin comments on Langland's literary use of food:

> food is mentioned only when someone has not enough, or when someone has too much. Clothes have a similar significance of social standing for him, whereas with Chaucer they are eloquent of character and taste as well. (u/p essay, *c.* 1943)

Larkin's marginal comment – possibly for the benefit of Bruce Montgomery, to whom he had lent the essay – reads 'good PAL' and 'v. good PAL' next to this paragraph. Larkin's approval of his own gloss on the metaphorical import of eating suggests that we should be alert to the significance of food in *Jill*.

John's first meal is taken on the train: conscious that it was 'bad manners to eat in a public carriage' he bolts 'a few of his sandwiches' (22) in the toilet. When an elderly lady persuades him to eat with her he does so with 'his eyes fixed on the dirty floor' (23). In contrast to Warner and his smart friends at Oxford – who consume their food with gusto – John's appetite is always a nervous one. According to Motion, John's paranoia with food parallels a similar frustration in his social and sexual encounters. Thus, when a female passenger 'licked the tips of her fingers' (23) John writhed in humiliation, indicating, perhaps, that eating styles serve as a metaphor for the way that characters perceive their sexual identity. A striking example of the food motif occurs prior to John's abortive meal with Gillian: '[John] prepares a feast for her which is the wartime, rationed equivalent of the meal Porphyro offers Madeline in Keats's "The Eve of Saint Agnes"' (Motion, 1982, 46). Lawrence Lerner has also noted the relevance of food to *Jill*'s aesthetic structure, describing the book's two worlds as 'the world of those who eat carefully and that of those who eat carelessly . . . and this difference is . . . a matter of social class' (Lerner, 1997, 6). Accordingly, when he returns to his seat John looks on enviously as his travelling companions eat their lunches in a relaxed manner. His social unease is clear and the fact that one of the passengers, the clergyman, 'was reading and annotating a book' (22) echoes Crouch's sterile approach to learning which will unsettle further John's future life.

Some commentators have suggested that Larkin includes in *Jill* material that is extraneous to the artistic effect. Accordingly, for David Timms, the book is too '"poetical"' and he claims that 'detail is so fine as to be pedantic, and not at all illuminating. It may flesh out John's background for us to know that his mother tied his sandwiches "firmly, but not tightly"; but we are no better off for knowing that the apple eaten by the clergyman who shares John's railway carriage as he travels to Oxford is russet, nor that it is peeled with a *silver* pen-knife' (Timms, 1973, 44). However, rather than being extraneous, the details are integrated into the passage's structural logic. The lines that Timms quotes illustrate how Larkin refines the food motif. For instance, the fact that John's sandwiches are bound together with humble 'white paper' contrasts sharply with the 'packet in a napkin' (22) that the old lady offers him. Her gesture constitutes an invitation to join bourgeois society with its preference for genteel napkins rather than serviettes. Other seemingly trivial items also assume a significance within this symbolic context: the elderly lady's 'steel brooch' and the clergyman's 'silver penknife' (23) function as markers of social distinction. However, their status is undercut as the *silver* knife is subtly linked to the 'beautiful girl['s] . . . coarse-looking rolls and cheese in *silver* paper' (my emphasis, 22) signalling how glistening outsides can be unglamorous within. In 'What Are We Writing For?', written under the pseudonym Brunette Coleman, Larkin encourages attention to detail: 'It is detail that does it. Detail is a queer thing, but it is better to have a little too much of it than too little' (BTH, 2002, 265). Moreover, the thematic connections and oppositions constitute the novel's 'dialogism' which, for Bakhtin, is an essential feature of the novelist's art (see Lodge, 1990, 86). In criticising the 'poetical' elements of the book, Timms ignores the extent to which this enriches *Jill*'s structural patterns. Larkin's ease at manipulating voices, attitudes and signs in his novels provided a fertile soil from which to cultivate the colliding of positions and voices in the 'major' poems.

At the end of the opening scene John glimpses a fleeting rush of scenes from his carriage window. The technique is one that Larkin employs throughout his career: the watchful, poetic narrative of 'The Whitsun Weddings' (CP, 114) appears in embryonic form in this impressionistic scene. Like the poem, the novel conflates urban and pastoral in a momentary synthesis of random detail. Just as John's train 'clattered by iron bridges, cabbages and a factory painted with huge white letters' (23), so the later train passes 'short-shadowed cattle, and / Canals with floatings of industrial froth'. The texts share, too, the device of syntactically isolating a particular object, thereby investing it with heightened metonymic significance. Thus, in 'The Whitsun Weddings', 'A hothouse flashed uniquely' whilst in *Jill* 'A signal-box' is detached, grammatically, from its surrounding context (23–4). If the poem transforms an ordinary train journey into a synthesised collage of visions, the description of changing landscapes that John sees offers important clues to his predicament. John's 'train knew his destination' suggesting a fate already sealed by the 'regular pattern of beats' (23), and the eclectic mix of scenes that pass reminds us of the poem's similar reworking of randomness. Ultimately, however, though the snatched glance of 'two horses by a gate' (23) prefigures the cinematic still of 'someone running up to bowl', the prose lacks the sense of overarching coherence that characterises 'The Whitsun Weddings':

> He got to his feet and stared at the approaching city across allotments, back-gardens and piles of coal covered with fallen leaves. Red brick walls glowed with a dull warmth that he would have admired at another time. Now he was too nervous. (23)

These lines recall the journey 'Behind the backs of houses', but because he is 'too nervous', John is unaware of any 'frail / Travelling coincidence' that he might be part of. Instead of reconciling differences in moments of epiphanic insight, John 'did not bother to read' the letters painted on the passing walls and in contrast to the all-embracing sky of the poem, John's sky is 'smoke dirtied' (23). Larkin uses similar signifiers in both works, though the result in *Jill* lacks the poem's uplift. 'The Whitsun Weddings' draws to a close with the frisson of impending climax as 'the tightened brakes [take] hold'. John completes his journey by swinging 'violently over set after set of points' as if to suggest the trauma of his redirected life. John is bound for Oxford, though the fact that 'all the nameplates had been removed in time of war' (23–4) implies that he has reached a point when destinations are uncertain. In this, his predicament is typical of many young men confronted with the confusions of post-war Britain. John's wistful reflection on the 'wagon from near his home' implies that 'his heavy suitcase' – which we later learn is 'so heavy . . . [it] . . . forced him to take a taxi' (24) – is symbolic of his inability to escape the baggage of his past life and class. Mary Burch is in a similar predicament in *Michaelmas Term at St Bride's*; she 'had a suitcase to carry and was not sure of the way' (BTH, 2002, 131). 'Maiden Name' (CP, 101) invokes the same metaphor in 1955 to suggest a wife weighed down by the 'depreci- ating luggage' of her married name. These characters are burdened as they confront new codes, conditions and cultures. The novel's sharing of images and techniques with *Michaelmas Term*, 'The Whitsun Weddings' and *The Less Deceived* suggests the important continuities in Larkin's writing.

Contrasting social and sexual values are explored in the relationship between John and Christopher Warner. Differences between the two are highlighted when John has the misfortune to find that Warner has '"taken possession"' (27) of John's room prior to his arrival. John's unease with Warner's friends stems from his belief that rules must be adhered to and that authority should be respected. John is equally aghast to learn that Warner has taken no heed of the bursary's 'list of domestic articles' (32), choosing instead to 'borrow' these things from his room-mate. Such a scheme serves him well: on several occasions, Chris is seen 'holding a kettle' (27) or carving 'a large slab' (29) of cake, indicating his ease at social eating. However, if eating and drinking convey Chris's social and sexual confidence, for John they suggest his inadequacies. Fruitlessly, John 'spent an afternoon among the shops buying . . . things' (32), after which he goes for tea and cake with his mother. This signifies John's detachment from the stereotypical modes of male and female conduct which surround him. Chris is the conventional depiction of dominant masculinity: he has 'a swagger in his bearing' and his 'square, stubbly jaw' (27) anticipates the caricature of manhood found in 'Poetry of Departures' (CP, 85). Elizabeth, too, is an embodiment of socially constructed femi- ninity: her lips, which are 'much thinner than they were painted' (29) suggest artificiality. John's alienation is that of the working-class boy at odds with a superficial bourgeois milieu. In the words of 'Strangers' (1950) he knows little of 'teashop behaviours' and 'Leaving the right tip' (CP, 40). His 'sense of his alien surroundings' (28) – Elizabeth remarks that he has come '"Quite a distance"' (29) – signals his estrangement from orthodox prescriptions of gendered behaviour. Elizabeth imagines that she might be 'speaking to a foreigner' (29).

The plight of isolated characters who are derided for their outsider status is evoked throughout Larkin's literary career. In *A Girl in Winter* Katherine's unspecified origins and low social rank make her vulnerable to prejudice and abuse. Social and linguistic detachment is repeated in 'Like the train's beat' (CP, 288). In *Jill*, John copes with his estrangement in a way that mirrors the importance the Coleman texts had for Larkin.

If John feels alienated from Chris's bluff masculinity and bourgeois values, he feels even more alienated from girls, seeing them as an enemy to be conquered rather than as potential partners. John's reaction on first seeing Elizabeth illustrates this:

> She was powdered carefully, had a reddened mouth, and her golden hair was brushed fiercely up from the sides of her head, so that it formed a stiff ornament, like a curious helmet. (28)

Elizabeth is wholly unattainable for John, so that, like the author of the Coleman texts, his only means of entering her world is by creating a fantasy situation which grants him the control that he lacks in reality. The ideal construction of femininity that John effects is different from the conventional attributes that Elizabeth displays. Before we consider his alternative models, however, we should look at the way in which John himself is constructed by 'the printed directions' of his education (CP, 42).

The first major stylistic change in the novel occurs when the narrative voice slips from John's consciousness to that of his old schoolmaster, Crouch. As a failed university teacher, he preys on the Kemps' working-class reverence for education, telling John's father (a figure taken straight from the novels of D. H. Lawrence) that university is not just a sausage-machine for teachers but a stepping stone to the higher professions. Crouch's attitude to education is that learning can be acquired mechanically, recalling Gradgrind's instruction of 'the little pitchers before him, who were to be filled so full of facts' (*Hard Times*, 1854, 48). Keeping 'some sort of a copy of every important work in the language' (65), Crouch coaches John in the same learn-by-rote manner that he had settled for. Thus, by lending John his 'meticulous notes' (68), Crouch dampens, rather than liberates, any imaginative insight his pupil might aspire to. Simon Petch suggests that there is something Frankenstein-like about the way that Crouch 'creates' his man (Petch, 1981, 27), and this accords with the novel's imagery: 'Mr. Crouch felt strangely as if a mechanical man he had painfully constructed had suddenly come to life' (83). Elsewhere, too, we learn that he thinks of himself as 'a judge' (69), a 'particular guardian' (75) and a 'sculptor' who 'would mould passivity' (72). Like an earlier 'Schoolmaster', this one acts like 'a god' who 'would never fail' (1940, CP, 248). For Crouch, John's education is an exercise in social engineering so that, like Eliza Doolittle in *Pygmalion* (Shaw, 1916), he is fashioned by a dogmatic authority. Once his experiment is over, Crouch despises the attitudes in John that he helped to develop. Reflecting on their association, he says of John: '"You don't feel that reading a poem means any more to him than adding up a column of figures"' (84). Education is as much an agent of social manipulation as conventional gendered identity, and John is processed by both during his journey into adulthood. In particular, John's cramming is the result of the wider uncertainties of wartime. Arguing that John should sit the entrance examination earlier than usual, Crouch remarks: '"In five years' time it may well be that Oxford and Cambridge will be nothing but ruins"' (78). Alan Sinfield's observation that wartime 'enhanced opportunity for social mobility through education' (Sinfield, 1989, 234) reminds us that John's education is shaped by specific historical conditions.

If Crouch's tutoring of John is characterised by the need to remember and record, it is the act of forgetting that characterises Warner's hedonistic behaviour. Warner's memory is appalling: unable to recall his sickness after a night's drinking, he misses appointments with his tutor, whose education he has no respect for, seeing him instead as 'a personal friend who insisted upon talking tediously about literature' (45). Warner is arrogant and boorish, yet he provokes admiration from his circle. Whilst Eddy recounts Warner's sixth form revelling, 'Christopher sat smiling softly, like one who is being praised' (57) and, as elsewhere in Larkin's oeuvre, behaviour which flouts established practice is re-evaluated as worthwhile. In one of a series of identity-seeking poses, John is drawn to a life that is free from the responsibilities of convention. Whilst, at first, John is livid that Warner has appropriated his china, later in the novel he 'rewrites' the episode in different terms:

> It was queer that already the affair of the tea-things was beginning to fade in his memory, falling into perspective as one of the harmless things Christopher did without thinking. He had never seen a person so free from care. (48)

John's admiration for Chris leads him into a fantasy realm in which the two men share a male camaraderie: 'He imagined himself saying in the future: "D'you remember that time we went to the Bull, old boy. In our first term?"' (61). In his effort to be accepted John adopts the gestures of archetypal male pub-talk, though the pose cannot be sustained: John 'felt that unless he flung nets of words over Christopher he might escape' (62). As in the poems, language, the most fundamental of human structures, is often incapable of defining our deepest wants, which are 'untalkative' ('Here', CP, 137). The 'nets of words' cannot sustain John's illusory friendship and his disappointment is compounded as he realises the stock postures of male behaviour don't suit him. This can be seen in his attitude to drinking beer, a traditional 'masculine' ritual. Throughout the scene John drinks 'reluctantly' (64) because of the 'vile taste' (62) and Eddy finishes his beer for him before luring Chris off to get '"tight"' at the King's (64). In addition to his social alienation at Oxford, John shares with many of the poems' male speakers an estrangement from a version of 'masculinity' that is culturally prescribed.

There are other occasions when John tries to develop his own personality by adopting the traits of others. Whilst attending lectures 'he decided to be Mr. Crouch, nodding his head wisely at intervals and making a few microscopic jottings, to be copied and expanded later' (96). In a novelistic context, this donning of masks and styles is clearly signalled by the narrative, though in the poems, changes of voice can be much more subtle and unexpected. Nevertheless, John's numerous experiments provide a prototype for the tonal shifts in 'Church Going', 'The Whitsun Weddings' and 'This Be The Verse' (CP, 97, 114, 180). If John's experiment with role-playing constitutes an act of self-deception, for Larkin it functions as an artistic device which is used repeatedly in later work. The adoption of different personae allows him to revolve and refine experience through a variety of perspectives and it is this *dialectic* that drives many of the poems.

The way that John moves from the real world to a fantasy realm is signalled by a change from a prosaic style into an evocative, lyrical mode. At times mundane discourse is overlaid with symbolic intensity:

> "I want a bow-tie."
> "One bow-tie."
> This gave John a sudden vision of the bow-tie, lying in a pool of light at the bottom of a lift-shaft, very tiny and distinct. (98)

The isolated tie, which is seen 'in a pool of light' at the end of a darkened shaft suggests John's struggle with questions of definition and self-image. Curiously, in expressing the struggles of finding his own personality, Larkin used the same imagery in a letter to Sutton: 'I am sitting *in a pool of light* hollowed out from the darkness' (my emphasis, u/p letter, 25.iii.43). Implicit here is the sense of having to wrest identity out of an oppressive enclosure, a theme which recurs in *In the Grip of Light* (1947). In 'Träumerei', for instance, oppressed subjects are 'shut in / Like pigs down a concrete passage' (CP, 12) – lines which apply equally to John's imprisonment by conventional codes and attitudes.

John escapes his pressures by assuming a series of postures, though it is in the letters to Jill that he gains the fullest respite. In providing a 'means of retaliation' (129) from Warner's offensive habits, the letters make him 'drowsily content' and induce a 'complete absence of worry from his life' (132). This relaxed state improves his appetite: 'Often he forgot about mealtimes and failed to appear in the Hall; later he would feel hungry and buy some bread from the College kitchens, hurrying back to his room to eat it and to start a fresh letter' (133). Whereas John is too nervous to eat with real people on account of his class and personality, with Jill he feels more liberated. Writing to her he re-invents himself as a dominant character whilst Chris is redrawn as '*pathetically dependent on* [John] *for his weekly essay*' (130). More disturbingly, he incites – in the letters' fantasy flights – acts of vandalism against college property, telling Eddy to '*go into the Union there and smash the first glass door you see*' (134). Such impulses might be interpreted as a means of getting even with traditions that have tyrannised John's life in reality. But if he seeks revenge on certain social institutions, what is the significance of conveying these frustrations to Jill, a 'character' who, as 'a hallucination of innocence' (135), seems utterly detached from vindictive tirades?

To answer this we must consider John's conception of Jill. 'He liked to think of her as preoccupied only with simple untroublesome things, like examinations and friendships, and, as he thought, each minute seemed to clarify her, as if the picture of her had been stacked away waiting in his mind, covered with dust' (135). Jill is as much a part of John's personality as the lout who desires to trash the Union. That she 'had been stacked away waiting in his mind, covered with dust', signals how the pressures of traditional 'masculinity' have obscured her presence. Moreover, John makes Jill his *sister*, rather than his girlfriend, thereby ensuring that their 'relationship' is not based on sexual fantasy but on the need to rediscover his feminine self. Archival evidence suggests Larkin's own desire to indulge 'girlish' traits. In 1962 he told Rosemary Hewitt: 'One of the nice things about being a girl is that you can wear all the nicest colours & precious stones & smell of the most beautiful flowers – you are much luckier than men who go about in perpetual camouflage' (u/p letter, 25.iv.62). Larkin's interest in Jung led him to rediscover, through dream analysis, his anima principle, such that his character would develop 'a state of union' between 'masculine' and 'feminine' impulses (Thwaite, 1992, 53). Tellingly, Larkin once remarked to Sutton: 'the prospect of being . . . *a complete man* . . . fills me with terror' (my emphasis, u/p letter, 29.vi.42).

John's narratives about Jill convey a desire to escape the construction of maleness that Christopher represents. As he prepares to write about Jill's school exploits John reflects on how the project inspired him. It was 'as if . . . he had given a cursory rub to some old portrait to which the dust was clinging thickly' and he muses further that 'her face was glowing in his mind' (135). These images resurrect, in John's mind, a 'female' dimension to his personality that has been long neglected. He no longer aspires to Chris's stock 'masculinity', but connects, instead, with a 'feminine' alter-ego: 'It was as if he had been talking to her from a public telephone-box, talking interminably, and then had looked up to see her listening in the next compartment, smiling at him through the glass' (135). At the start of the book, the obscured glass of the train carriage had concealed something from John, forcing him back on the awkward social gestures of the young male; now, Jill is 'smiling at him through the glass', suggesting his new-found connection with his 'female' self. As well as providing refuge from the construction of manliness that Christopher signifies, John also discerns in Jill a detachment from conventional notions of femininity: 'Her face was not like Elizabeth's, coarse for all its make-up, but serious-looking' (135). Unlike Elizabeth's *made up* face, Jill is 'serious-looking' and this anticipates Larkin's challenge to traditional roles for women in the later poems. Accordingly, if *Jill*'s 'Coleman passage' grants John respite from Christopher's repellent masculinity it also allows him to celebrate the autonomies of an exclusively female world. Reflecting on the significance of his fictitious sister, John concludes that 'his invention put out more flowers than he had expected' (136) and there is a steady growth, in Larkin's later work, of this profound sensitivity towards the plight of girls and women.

Late in the novel, Patrick and Eddy discuss John's possible seduction of Gillian:

> "What you do is call for her – "
> "No, damn it, Pat, that's no good; surely *he picks her up* at the Green Leaf where *she can't get away*. What he does is come along and say: 'Sorry, Elizabeth unavoidably detained but here's unworthy self in her place – '"
> "All right, then. Then at tea you *put in the groundwork*. Then after that suggest walking round to see Eddy – "
> "Say you've left your cigar-piercer on my grand piano," cackled Eddy, scratching himself.
> "And then you can *get to work* – sport the oak." (my emphasis, 187)

The major feature of this conversation is its use of derogatory expressions which demean Gillian as a person, recasting her as a sexual object to be pursued and used. In the terms of Eddy's plan, John '"picks her up . . . where she can't get away"' and later on he '"put[s] in the groundwork"' before '"get[ting] to work"'. These phrases might cause offence to some readers (see Jardine and Greer in Regan, 1997, 3, 5) but the novel's objective is to condemn rather than to endorse such crude male bluster. This is clear from the way that John re-articulates the episode in a different register:

> He seriously could not connect what they said with any desire of his own, yet he knew it was a chance for all that, a chance like a piece of

bread thrown among a weaving crowd of gulls and one sleek-headed, quick-beaked bird swooping it off with a slight deflection from its course. (188)

Whilst John agrees with their broad assessment of the situation – namely that he cannot afford to miss the chance of meeting with Gillian – his lyrical reflections, which are reminiscent of Woolf's poetic prose images, reveal a sensitive nature which is at odds with Eddy's coercive 'masculine' attitude to relationships. John reaches the same conclusion as Patrick and Eddy, though the fact that he 'could not connect what they said with any desire of his own' distances him from orthodox sexual politics which prompts men to '"sport the oak"' before '"get[ting] to work"' on girls. Many of the poems show the same tendency of employing different personae to address a single problem. Carey has shown how two selves, one hyper-female and the other hyper-male, co-exist in 'This Be The Verse' (CP, 180). The opening is brash and 'male', in recognising the certainty of inheriting unwanted traits. However, the second stanza perceives the situation through a more intellectual lens. As Carey suggests, the phrase 'deepens like a coastal shelf' is aimed at an educated reader who understands technical terms. Whereas the 'message' of the poem is unchanged, the means of articulation undergoes a stylistic shift. This technique has its roots in Larkin's fiction where the use of extended character discourse and focalised narrative are contrasted. Carey identifies in the poems instances of Larkin's male and female sides which variously collude, clash and subordinate themselves to the other (BTH, 2000, 51–65). Similarly, throughout *Jill*'s aesthetic structure, there is a gesture away from conventional models of gendered behaviour, which are repellent and restrictive, both for women and for men.

If John's retreat into Jill's feminine world signifies a rejection of Christopher's flawed model of masculinity, so his stroll through the market prompts him to re-embrace the values of his working-class roots. At first he delights in the *otherness* of the scene so that 'to step into it from the streets outside was to enter an unexpectedly different world, a world he found he liked' (197). However, the passage is evocative of unpretentious human behaviour and John is seized by the familiar sights and sounds that recall his own modest upbringing. In its portrayal of a working community the following lines convey a human dignity similar to that which is depicted in 'The Explosion' or 'Dublinesque' (CP, 175, 178):

> They straddled round as they stood, talking patiently, exchanging traditional unquestioned comments on things that affected their daily lives. As he slipped past them he heard them say things their parents must have said, things that women like them said in every country,

and looking at their fat or withered faces, their hair tucked into old hats, and the worn purses in their hands, they seemed to him the oldest thing in the city he had seen. (197)

As in *Michaelmas Term at St Bride's* the quotidian detail of workaday lives is privileged against the more acclaimed splendours of the ancient city. When John wanders around the market he shows an appreciation of the thrift common in working-class communities. For example, he decides not to buy cigarettes as he is 'alarmed at the price' and he knows how to choose a good lettuce 'because of experience at home' (197). John's empathy with communal continuities anticipates the 'Regenerate union' of 'Show Saturday' (CP, 199–201) which reveres fellowship above wealth and capitalist enterprise.

The clearest indication that (at this point in the novel) John is re-embracing his working-class origins occurs when he returns from the market in order to dine in college: 'He was too nervous to eat and almost immediately after leaving Hall began to feel hunger' (197). In view of the metaphorical framework already noted, John's inability to eat whilst inside the college, and the hunger he feels when released, signifies a renewed allegiance to his own kind. 'Story' (1941, CP, 257) is an early blueprint for John's strained social mobility. The poem's subject grew 'Tired of a landscape known too well' though eventually he recognises he 'lived his dreams' in a 'mirage'. Like the 'Story' character, John also sees the hollow nature of 'his wished-for lie' (CP, 257). The railway motif is re-invoked to suggest John's new-found pride in his social roots:

> as he watched, an express train hurtled past twenty yards off on the shining rails, and the long stretch of coaches racing away awakened nothing like regret in him, as they once would. He was glad to see them go; glad, simply, to be where he was, and to see them go. (194)

Painfully aware of how the train brought him on a social journey at the start of the novel, John is less interested in social mobility at the end, preferring, instead, 'to be where he was'. The covered market passage hints at the balanced attitude to life that John now holds: 'As he left the shop he noticed from his reflection in the window that his hair was just breaking prettily out of place, half-way between wildness and precision, and this pleased him' (197). The line echoes 'Like the train's beat' (CP, 288) in which the airgirl's hair is 'wild and controlled' suggesting the tugs of rebellion and constriction. John's condition 'half-way between wildness and precision' implies the synthesis of contrary perspectives advocated in Woolf's novels.

As the novel draws to a close, John prepares for the final stage of his enlightenment that will confirm the folly, not only of aping Chris, but also of constructing a fantasy around the real girl, Gillian. When news breaks of the bomb-blast in Huddlesford, Whitbread advises John to return home:

> "I should go and see for yourself."
> "Yes, but – " John was conscious of being badgered towards action he did not want to take.
> "Well, hang it, man," exclaimed Whitbread, "you've got to *know*!" (205)

Whitbread's pragmatic suggestion that John should discover the facts about his parents' welfare contrasts sharply with Eddy's encouraging him in an unlikely affair. In the scheme of the novel, John has begun a movement away from fantasy and towards reality, a process accompanied by hard lessons about the social milieu he once courted. Accordingly, Whitbread exposes Chris's social posturing:

> "I get sick of his sort. It's not as if he were any real class, either: now, someone of consequence, from Eton or Harrow, say – I can respect them. Someone of breeding. Money makes a difference, and it's no use saying it doesn't. But these fellows like Warner, trying to jump into the class above them . . . " (207)

Some critics have seen Whitbread as mean and opportunistic, with his Crouch-like approach to making contacts and his dull, relentless study habits. The character is based on the imaginary 'Yorkshire scholar' whom Larkin and Norman Iles impersonated at St John's College. According to Larkin he was 'a character embodying many of our prejudices' (Larkin, 1983, 19) but in the novel Whitbread's advice to John is sound. He points out the shallowness of Warner's set, yet he is not fool enough to think that real class boundaries can be easily crossed. Such practical advice is an important factor in John's return to reality in subsequent scenes.

It is during the return trip to Huddlesford, though, that John reappraises his attempts to separate himself from his class and culture. Significantly, the direction of travel is the reverse of that in the opening section and John sees himself 'leaving a region of unreality and insubstantial pain for the real world' (211). Subsequently, in a passage which recalls how the Coleman stories changed conventional categories of meaning, John reinvests his past with a fresh significance:

> The very things that in the past had most irritated him about them –
> his father's deliberate way of hooking on his spectacles: first one ear,

then the other; or the noise his mother made when she swallowed – these very things turned suddenly round and became emblems of their most lovable qualities. (211)

Familial ties are also rekindled when John stumbles through the debris near his old home. Here, John sees the error of wanting to detach himself from his parents' culture: 'Any attempts at a personal life he had made seemed merely a tangle of hypocritical selfishness: really he was theirs, dependent on them for ever' (214). But if the worth of his social identity is at last acknowledged, the war has dashed, irretrievably, any links with the continuities of the past:

> Dozens of places he knew well had been wrecked: the local dingy cinema, a fish shop; great gouts of clay had been flung against posters. As he walked he looked at the ruins, tracing the effects of single explosions on groups of buildings, great tearing blows that left iron twisted into semi-interrogative shapes . . . The wreckage looked like ruins of an age over and done with. (215)

At the start the passage functions metonymically, the familiar landmarks – a 'dingy cinema, a fish shop' – suggestive of a pre-war, communal existence which has been destroyed. Commenting on 'New Year Poem' (CP, 255), Regan notes how that poem 'recreates a wartime setting where continuing normality prevails against sudden disruption' (Regan, 1992, 72). Here, however, 'normality' is overturned by wartime conditions, which unsettle roles and identities as much as physical landscapes. Larkin's 1940s poems show a similar concern with wartime experience, though the passage connects with *The Less Deceived* as well as *The North Ship* and *In the Grip of Light*. The 'great gouts of clay . . . flung against posters' precedes the imagery of 'Essential Beauty' and 'Sunny Prestatyn', which also gain their éclat from posted images. Just as these poems smear the notion that adverts provide ideal blueprints for life, so in *Jill* the mud-bespattered hoardings suggest the ruined aspirations of peacetime. The 'interrogative shapes' of the debris suggest a questioning of known destinies in the face of a traumatic upheaval. Whilst the novel documents John's personal estrangement from social and sexual codes, it also addresses the wider sense of displacement caused by war.

Ultimately, Larkin's first novel addresses not only the difficulties of social mobility in wartime Britain but also the human need to create order through art. Looked at in this way, John's striking of fictional poses is a construction of 'how life should be' ('Essential Beauty', CP, 144). However, if John conceived Jill to be 'serious' and 'innocent' as a foil to the orthodox sexual politics of Elizabeth and Christopher, his interest in

a 'real' Jill – Gillian – alerts him to his own involvement with the coarse-
ness of male desire:

> When he thought of Christopher in his dressing-gown, legs strad-
> dling, his hand steadily working the razor and talking reflectively
> about what was going to happen, he knew with a sickening certainty
> that he could never sustain that position . . . (170)

Terrified that he might succumb to Chris's brand of male sexuality,
John wants a relationship with Gillian 'away from his present surround-
ings' (171) where Christopher's stock 'masculine' attitudes predominate.
Even as John stumbles towards his fateful encounter with Gillian he has
to '[force] himself towards the event' (234) as if to suggest his discomfort
with the orthodox rituals of male courtship that are termed 'uncorrected
visions' in 'Breadfruit' (CP, 141). After John kisses Gillian, Christopher
knocks him out and 'The moral' of this episode, for Janice Rossen, 'seems
to be that women like Gillian are unattainable for men like John Kemp'
(Rossen, 1989, 79). However, Christopher's punch, rather, signifies the
suppression of alternative models of gendered behaviour by conventional
constructions. The botched kiss with Gillian is an expression of John's
'male' desire which prevails, much to his disgust, over his 'female' connec-
tion with Jill. As he recovers from the brawl in the College sickroom, John
recognises that, despite the humiliations that his male desire has caused,
his 'feminine' side is still in touch with Gillian:

> Somewhere, in dreams, perhaps, on some other level, they had inter-
> locked and he had had his own way as completely as in life he had
> been denied it. And this dream showed that love died, whether
> fulfilled or unfulfilled . . . . The difference between them vanished.
> (242)

The book closes in a similar way to the poem 'Dockery and Son'; the
latter affirms that choices made between opposing paths are ultimately
futile: 'Whether or not we use it, it goes, / And leaves what something
hidden from us chose' (CP, 153). As John's journey towards being less
deceived reaches its conclusion, he realises that whether he had taken 'this
course, or this course . . . still behind the mind, on some other level, the
way he had rejected was being simultaneously worked out and the same
conclusion was being reached. What did it matter which road he took if
they both led to the same place? He looked at the tree-tops in the wind.
What control could he hope to have over the maddened surface of things?'
(243). These lines suggest that any blueprint for life is merely a construct,
whether it negates or endorses customary norms. *Jill*'s final message

appears to be that any desired absolute is doomed; in the words of 'Poetry of Departures' – to be 'Reprehensibly perfect' (CP, 86).

As well as having a meaningful structural aesthetic of its own, *Jill* provides many of the narrative and thematic tropes of Larkin's later poetry. The ploy of colliding voices and attitudes, the technique of inverting and undercutting conventional categories of understanding, and the use of a complex system of symbols and leitmotifs, all find their way into the 'mature' volumes. Larkin's second novel, *A Girl in Winter*, also seeks alternatives to settled attitudes towards class and culture. In that text, however, Larkin transforms the quest for different identities to a more searching indictment of orthodox sexual politics.

2

A Girl in Winter and the Unfinished Novels

A Critique of National and Sexual Politics

In *Jill* John is frustrated by the scripts for masculinity that he is obliged to enact: only in his fantasies does he acquire 'feminine' personality traits that assuage the social and sexual identities that imprison him. However, *A Girl in Winter* employs a female consciousness for the entire novel, thereby highlighting the cultural strictures that impinged on real women in the 1940s. Commentators have viewed *A Girl in Winter* as being more obscure than *Jill* and Larkin himself conceived the book as a prose poem, writing to Sutton that it would bear similarities to the styles of Woolf and Henry Green. There is no point, then, in criticising the novel for lacking the social realism of *Jill*.

Describing the 'variety and confidence in [*Jill*'s] characterization' and Larkin's 'near-infallible ear for dialogue on several social levels', Alan Brownjohn reflects that these 'are talents present, but not developed' in *A Girl in Winter*. Brownjohn concludes that *A Girl in Winter* 'somewhat resembles certain of those early Larkin poems in which the technique is already highly accomplished and the substance remains elusive' (Thwaite, 1982, 115, 119). Similarly, in judging the novel as typical of the social-realist tradition, Timms objects to Larkin's use of the 'occasional redundant simile, as when Katherine's vacillating emotions are compared at length to a flock of birds' (Timms, 1973, 51). Roger Day also gauges the book by Edwardian criteria, claiming that 'the characterisation is sometimes thin: Mr and Mrs Fennel are never more than cardboard figures, and Jack Stormalong whom the author evidently despises, is frankly hardly credible' (Day, 1987, 24). However, some critics have looked beyond the traditional requirements of character development to locate more positive qualities. Commenting on a passage which deals with Katherine's thoughts, Petch notices how it 'develops into a series of similes whose purpose is to illuminate each other. As the passage develops it leaves Katherine behind' (Petch, 1981, 34–5). Petch goes on to suggest that detailed characterisation, in the social-realist tradition, was never intended:

> The ordered pictorialism of many of the metaphorically suggestive descriptive passages – and the opening chapter of *A Girl in Winter* itself has the quality of 'a formal painting' (Bayley, 1974, 654) which belongs to the landscape it describes – shows us the narrator moving beyond the central character to a more direct enunciation of his own perceptions . . . we can see Larkin outgrowing the need for another mediating, fictional consciousness . . . In future the brief assumption of a mask was to replace the extended treatment of a single character, and such masks as were required could be incorporated within poetic forms. (Petch, 1981, 38)

Petch sees the visual element as critical in *A Girl in Winter* and Whalen also refers to this concrete, visual aspect of Larkin's prose, suggesting that it could have been prompted by the influence on Larkin of his painter friend Sutton, whose advice Larkin regularly sought. Trevor Tolley similarly focuses on Larkin's pictorial scene-setting in his treatment of *A Girl in Winter* and traces this influence to Woolf's *Orlando* (1928), which, like the former work, makes extensive use of weather as a signifier for emotional climate (Tolley, 1991, 27). *A Girl in Winter* is only 'elusive' if we ignore its gestalt or perceptual structure of signs and symbols, which articulate a rejection of settled assumptions about class and sexual relations. Motion explains how Larkin's second novel achieves its effects:

> *A Girl in Winter* is deliberately vague; where Jill is unwaveringly – sometimes excessively – naturalistic and realistic, A Girl in Winter is 'a Virginia Woolf – Henry Green kind of novel' (Haffenden, 1981); and where Jill incorporates its symbolic structures into an empirical framework, A Girl in Winter matches its actual observations with well-advertised symbolic intentions. (Motion, 1982, 55)

Like Woolf, Larkin also grew tired of the predictable patterns and limitations of conventional fiction, and sought to experiment with progressive techniques. However, though the 'empirical framework' is less defined than it is in *Jill*, Larkin resists a total departure from the traditional strategies of social realism. As well as an affinity with the modernist style – moments of epiphany; the omission of the mechanics of narrative – *A Girl in Winter* owes a debt to a Lawrentian mode in which symbolic fabrics are woven into the plot to link together episodes that might otherwise seem superfluous.

Whalen attributes Larkin's imagist dimension to Lawrence, who also made extensive use of metonymy and synecdoche as a means of conveying the denatured tendencies of the modern age (see Cooper, 1999, 25 and BTH, 2000, 108). *A Girl in Winter* also employs such tropes to evoke the manner in which precise cultural factors delineate the lives of Larkin's principal characters. One of the most striking aspects about the symbolic passages in *A Girl in Winter* is the extent to which female characters are perpetually jostled by patriarchal manoeuvres: Katherine Lind, Jane Fennel and Miss Green must all clear a path for themselves through hostile male territory. In this, they recall the exploits of the Coleman heroines, though their plights also anticipate the marginalisation endured by female protagonists in many of the later poems.

Beside unease with conventional gender politics, we can locate in *A Girl in Winter* a dissatisfaction with wider social establishments. The novel punctures the myth of wartime endeavour and its post-war spirit of social cohesion. Several scenes unsettle the apparent consensus in a poignant manner, though it is in the Sutton letters that Larkin hones this disenchantment with subversive attitudes. Reflecting on how 'the tone of England is generally optimistic, and everyone is talking about post-war reconstruction' (u/p letter, 30.ix.43), Larkin is cynical about such hopefulness, remarking that 'Some one [sic] had better construct a few jobs I reckon' (u/p letter, 30.ix.43). At other times Larkin suggests that his being at odds with the prevailing positive mood provided the vital inspiration for his work:

> The post war [sic] world will I think be rather nasty but not as nasty as war, and in any case a nasty world is as good as a nice one to an artist, as long as he has means wherewith to live and practise his art. (u/p letter, 8.ix.44)

In *Jill* and the Coleman fiction, Larkin had transmuted into art his unease with an authority culture, but in *A Girl in Winter* and the unfinished novels, this indictment of establishment norms becomes even more pronounced. Much of Larkin's disillusionment is bound up with a deep-seated resentment of the war. Larkin encouraged Sutton in his thoughts of desertion, wishing him 'all luck in any kind of anti-army activity' (u/p letter, 29.vi.42), and later he shunned the VE Day rejoicing, claiming 'the only sense in such a day is to think of people still serving who may soon be coming home' (u/p letter, 8.v.45). Larkin's sympathy for the marginalised innocents of war would almost certainly have been fuelled by his reading of Wilfred Owen. In a review written in 1963 Larkin eagerly embraced Owen's anti-war perspective, enthusiastically commenting that it was right that 'the war should be shown up, that the carnage, the waste, the exploitation should all be brought home to innocent non-combatants' (Larkin, 1983, 160). Owen's intolerance with the generals of World War I is matched by Larkin's impatience with the warmongers of World War II; Larkin confides in Sutton that he tires of 'Churchill blathering' (u/p letter, 8.v.45) and in the same letter expresses his indifference to upbeat post-war sentiment:

> all day I have had a headache and felt despondent . . . I have the sense of being seven-eighths below the surface, like an iceberg. Every house has its flag and a good deal of bunting is strung across the main streets . . . as for what I feel, a sense of foreboding broods on me . . . I feel more as if the war was starting than ending. (u/p letter, 8.v.45)

The iceberg simile is reminiscent of how ice signifies a sense of isolation in *A Girl in Winter*, and Larkin's feeling that war is beginning rather than ending may be due to his perception of life as a continual battle against capitalist oppression. He moaned to Sutton: 'I object to being forced to spend all my life performing a job like checking notes or making bicycles for people I shall never see. We are all rats in a big machine that feeds us' (u/p letter, 7.xii.42). Larkin was still 'struggl[ing]' with 'The unbeatable slow machine' thirty-one years later in 'The Life with a Hole in it' (CP, 202). Similarly, railing at London's inhuman scale he is outraged by its 'enormous demands – demands that any of which keep 10,000 men busy 8 hrs a day in supplying' [sic] (u/p letter, 7.xii.42). According to Larkin, the supply-and-demand logic of modern life has a 'panic-streak in it all' (u/p letter, 7.xii.42), a sentiment no doubt born of his own over-worked and unfulfilling job as Wellington librarian, an experience he recalls in *Required Writing* (1983): 'I drew the line at cleaning the floor, but I stoked the boiler and kept it going through the day, served the children, put up the papers and so on' (Larkin, 1983, 51). Disgruntled at his working conditions he whined: 'I have never felt anything but degraded as the librarian in this hole of toad's turds' (u/p letter, 26.vi.46) thereby presaging the reptile metaphor of 'Toads' and 'Toads Revisited' (CP, 89, 147).

Larkin's principal gripe about modern industrial society is the way it severs human beings from their natural environment: 'I am flooded with waves of horror at "everyday life" as revealed by "the office" – the absolute insulation of all necessary contacts with natural forces' (u/p letter, 17.viii.42). If Larkin absorbed his rejection of wartime heroics from Owen, his distaste for modern capitalist practices came from Lawrence, a writer who, he told Sutton, should 'be read out in churches' (Thwaite,

1992, 57). Whalen has interpreted many of the major poems as attempts 'to unwrite the lies of the industrial-commercial state' and explains Larkin's fascination with *Lady Chatterley's Lover* (1928) (Whalen, 1997, 151) in terms of its critique of modern industrial society and its assessment of limiting gender stereotypes. These themes recur throughout *A Girl in Winter* and the unfinished novels. Whalen focuses on major poems such as 'Poetry of Departures', 'A Study of Reading Habits' and 'If, My Darling' (CP, 85, 131, 41) though his conclusion that Larkin 'unwrites a stereotypical picturing of the male as hero by subverting the role requirements of both the chivalric and the Bourgeois Male' (BTH, 2000, 119), is one equally applicable to Larkin's later fiction, which began in 1947 with *A Girl in Winter* and ended in 1953 when he finally abandoned *A New World Symphony*.

A Girl in Winter

A Girl in Winter opens with a description of prolonged wintry weather that symbolises the bleak emotional climate pervading the novel. Of particular significance is the marginalisation of human endeavour in this early passage. Lacking any clear indication of identity, we know only that 'people told each other there was more [snow] to come' (*A Girl in Winter*, 11) which suggests both the human necessity to order and predict and also the perpetual human struggle against an indifferent environment. The hopeful speculation that 'it *seemed* that they were right' (my emphasis, 11) implies that human pronouncement is little more than a placatory construct, which is imposed on a chaotic environment at odds with human design. Human activity's peripheral role is highlighted by the snow's gathering 'where only birds walked' (11) and such ferocious conditions actively hamper human purpose:

> Villages were cut off until gangs of men could clear a passage on the roads; the labourers could not go out to work, and on the aerodromes near these villages all flying remained cancelled. (11)

The snow isolates and alienates on a physical level. The chill which paralyses the landscape, however, is a metaphorical one, with material conditions as the cause of the blight.

Symbolising man-made divisions of meaning, 'the fences were half-submerged like breakwaters' (11), ominously predicting how human structures will soon be engulfed by more powerful forces. 'To look at the snow too long had a hypnotic effect' which draws away 'all power of concentration' (11) – human understanding is smothered by an elemental realm that the blanket of snow signifies. It is recognised, however, that 'Life had to be carried on' even in the face of such potential futility:

> Nevertheless, the candles had to be lit, and the ice in the jugs smashed, and the milk unfrozen; the men had to be given their breakfasts and got off to work in the yards. (11)

The passive constructions and the detached perspective suggest a mechanical, involuntary routine. The lighting of the candle and the smashing of the ice symbolise the human need to illumine and impact upon an environment which freezes out concern for the human predicament.

The end of the first section introduces Larkin's favoured motif of the railway line, which, though the lines 'were empty . . . led on northwards and southwards till they began to join' (11–12). Their being empty is unpropitious, though their leading to 'the cities where the snow was disregarded, and which the frost could only besiege for a few days' (12), sets the novel's subsequent human activity against the backdrop of an indifferent universe.

Like *Jill*, *A Girl in Winter* deals with the alienation of a central character, though here the isolation felt is much more extreme, arising from the protagonist's gender, social class and historical placing. By virtue of her being foreign and in humble employment, Katherine is doubly sidelined from the dominant cultural norms of wartime Britain. The novel's title succinctly suggests the predicament of someone who is gripped in a cold and hostile environment, though Larkin's original title stressed even further the futility of rebellion against the status quo. *The Kingdom of Winter* emphasises the powerful position of those who can shape Katherine's life; the word 'Kingdom' may allude to the United Kingdom, whose wartime jingoistic fervour would have frozen out attitudes which ran counter to the national interest. Katherine's unease with the dominant contemporary ethos underwrites the imagery, symbolism and signification of *A Girl in Winter*.

The novel's elaborate arrangement of literary devices is consistently suggestive of Katherine's social predicament. From the outset, her environment is rigidly defined by the strict patterns of a capitalist work ethic. In the library, it is Katherine's 'business to keep in order . . . the books in smooth, unbroken lines' (14). Like the lines of men in 'MCMXIV ' (CP, 127), the library books must also appear smart and orderly at all costs, 'the date-stamps adjusted, the files of tickets at the counter pushed into tight columns' (14). Military precision over the cataloguing signifies the general climate in which the need to conform and comply is paramount. The Head Librarian, Mr Anstey (whose name is a thinly-veiled anagram of 'nasty'), actively promotes the stultifying and oppressive atmosphere. He is described in Dickensian terms, his 'ratchet-like voice' causing his employee, Miss Feather, to 'danc[e] before it like a leaf in a storm' (13). The imagery signals conflict between natural and mechanical processes, and gothic language enhances his sinister presence: Katherine reports to Anstey's office which 'was in a dark passage ending in a twisting iron staircase' (15). Although he chides Katherine for sloppiness, his own room is 'very untidy' (16) unlike Katherine's meticulous shelving. At work Anstey is only interested in rigid protocols and his view that he just 'happens to be dealing with books instead of houses or perambulators' (19) suggests his aloof attitude to library administration. He acquired the job as a result of the war when his predecessor had '"to go into the army"' (37). Thus, his 'theatrical gesture of resignation', his need to 'put on his distant expression' and his 'third manner . . . of the judiciary' (20) imply that he is simply playing the part of librarian. Reluctant to delegate to Katherine for fear of what increased democracy might bring, he acts like 'a guardian of traditional secrets' and 'he seemed unwilling to let her pick up any more about the work than was unavoidable. Therefore any odd job that was really nobody's duty fell to her' (25). Wartime conditions have exacerbated social injustice by promoting incompetents like Anstey to positions of authority. Katherine's lack of status as 'temporary assistant. . . marked. . . off from the permanent staff' denies her a voice in the library's patriarchal hierarchy, and exposes her to various indignities – 'from sorting old dust-laden stock in a storeroom to standing on a table . . . to fit a new bulb. . . while old men stared aqueously at her legs' (25). Their voyeuristic leer represents Katherine's objectification by controlling male impulses. At the same time, however, the phrase hints at another of the later poems' themes: men's hopeless enslavement to sexual desires from which they are powerless to break free.

Anstey excuses Katherine from work so she can accompany a colleague to the dentist. Miss Green's dental affliction symbolises the painful conditions of employment which both women endure. Rather than sharing in any worker solidarity, the two last spoke 'nine months ago' when Miss Green welcomed Katherine 'in offhand nasal tones' (26), and their cold personal relations exacerbate their plight. Even the description of the city centre conveys Katherine's angst in symbolic terms. Echoing the overbearing nature of bureaucratic structures, the 'two sides of [the square] were taken up by the Town Hall and Municipal Departments'. The fact that 'the branches of the leafless trees' are under the prospect of the 'high-pillared façade of the Central City Library' implies how man-made institutions stifle nature. 'The green was covered in snow' (31) signals further impersonal bureaucracy's smothering tendency. Recalling Joyce's

'After the Race' (*Dubliners*, 1914), the traffic's meaningless cyclical routines reflect the stagnant processes of the city: 'There was one-way traffic round the square, and she watched the taxis and saloon cars go by at a distance, the noise of them sharpened on the cold air like a knife on a whetstone' (33).

In 'The Dead', '"snow is general all over Ireland"' (208): Gabriel has to '[scrape] the snow from his goloshes' (174) and outside the Dublin houses 'snow [lay] on the branches of trees'. As in *A Girl in Winter* snow delineates human interest in Joyce's story. It forms 'a bright cap on the top of the Wellington Monument' (189) and on other statues there 'lay patches of snow' (212). Joyce's use of snow and cold weather to con-textualise human intrigue and to signal icy human relations is strikingly similar to Larkin's in *A Girl in Winter*, though the link between the two texts goes beyond shared imagery. Like *Dubliners*, *A Girl in Winter* eludes many of the categories of traditional realism. Neither work quite satisfies 'the criteria of intelligibility and coherence normally demanded of the classic readerly text' (Lodge, 1977, 125). At the same time, though, neither book is a wholly modernist text. What differentiates them from, say, *The Waves*, or *Ulysses* (1922), is the way that their 'metaphorical similarity is still subordinated to metonymic contiguity' (Lodge, 1977, 129–30). They adhere to conventional notions about characterisation and plot, even if their commonplace and anticlimactic experiences make it difficult to ascertain with any degree of certainty what they are 'about'. Nevertheless, the significant moments of intensity in both *A Girl in Winter* and *Dubliners* imply a degree of counterpoise between orthodox realism and a subtly evocative mode where signs and motifs interrelate.

Such a mode is apparent as Katherine contemplates an urban scene: 'The traffic circulated under the porticoes of the high buildings, the cars sounding their horns like ships lost at sea' (38). The novel conveys how those who are trapped in unfulfilled lives search endlessly for something better and, as in *The North Ship*, the sailing motif signifies questing after a utopia which social and economic forces curtail. To the very end, Katherine's life is constricted by establishment practices: the wartime cur-few makes her evening stroll 'against the police regulations' (24), and a good-natured offer to give directions results in a racist snub when a child 'shrank from her foreign voice' (27). There is little evidence in all this for what Tom Paulin calls 'a rock-solid sense of national glory' (Regan, 1997, 161). Evidently, Larkin's novel espouses a dissident outlook that Paulin's critique fails to take account of. Katherine's isolation on the grounds of race, sex and social standing prompt a rendezvous with a pen-friend. Utilising a similar technique to that used in 'An Unwritten Novel' (Woolf,

1944), present events are left far behind in a speculative survey of various potentialities:

> Would there be a letter? Robin surely must have had time to write by now, if he wanted to. Perhaps he was not greatly interested to hear that she was in England again. Of course, he wouldn't be as excited at the prospect of meeting as she was . . . It might be that he was stationed in some inaccessible spot – Ireland, perhaps – which letters took days to reach, or possibly he was busy on a scheme or battle-course that left him no time for writing . . . It was all very tantalizing. (28)

Katherine's isolation is experienced by many protagonists of modernist fiction whose piecing together of broken fragments conveys a greater sense of lived experience than traditional realism.

Katherine's alienation has a metaphysical dimension; not just isolated from her tangible world, she is also cut off from any 'pre-existent reality beyond [her] own self'. Lukács continues: 'the hero . . . is without personal history. He is "thrown-into-the-world": meaninglessly, unfathomably. He does not develop through contact with the world; he neither forms nor is formed by it' (Walder, 1990, 160). While *A Girl in Winter* is clearly much more rooted in the realist tradition than later works by Joyce or Woolf, the gaps in Katherine's personal circumstances – which make her colleagues 'uncertain who she was' (14) – suggests a tilting of the novel towards modernist tendencies: though Larkin's novel grew out of wartime conditions, it is by no means limited to them.

Ironically, in having to deal with a real-life event, Katherine is forced to temporarily abandon the fictional constructions about the Fennels which sustain her existence. During the bus journey to the city centre, Katherine recognises the imperfections of the dominant culture. Like Kemp in his railway compartment, Katherine is also aware of a deceptive filter through which she perceived events. Recognising that she was 'entering on a fresh stage of some more important journey . . . [she] rubbed a space clear on the window as they moved off'. Once the mist has been cleared she sees in the street life outside a communal alternative to the divisive capitalist model:

> In some of the little shop-windows candle-ends were burning to melt the frost from the glass. They were all very much alike, selling tobacco and newspapers, or bread and canned food, or greengroceries. But they made a living from people dwelling in the many poor streets around them, who went no further for their shopping.

The shared endeavour of ordinary communities contrasts with the icy relations that exist between employer and employee in other parts of the city. Katherine contemplates how the bourgeois Fennels construct a sanitised version of history which ignores the suffering of the excluded: 'They only noticed things that artists had been bringing under their noses for centuries, such as sunsets and landscapes' (29).

As with Larkin's poetry, certain passages from *A Girl in Winter* function by challenging the reader to reassemble disparate items into a meaningful context, which is never definitive or fixed, yet which is akin to the endless revolving of possibilities by the central character in an attempt to create meaning. Such passages include Larkin's eclectic lists, in which items serve as signifiers for attitudes and lifestyles, which have been juxtaposed to provoke unexpected insights. This metonymic process is typical of realist fiction, which implies further that *A Girl in Winter* is not the kind of modernist text that Lukács describes. The process is observable during one of Katherine's bus rides. Staring through the window Katherine saw a connection between the tired elements of urban life and the Fennels, whose lifestyle seems far removed from such scenes. The 'bare-ankled girl' (30) is as much a victim of social forces as those who pawn their goods; both have been seduced by the invidious nature of consumer-capitalism. The image of a bomb-damaged house is the logical and tragic outcome of an acquisitive regime. The link Catherine makes between these images and the Fennels suggests that it is the complacent, middle-class attitudes of people like them that have caused such despair and alienation. Concrete realist detail simultaneously places Katherine in a precise social and historical setting and provides what T. S. Eliot would call an *objective correlative* for an emotional response which transcends realist detail (see Eliot, 1919). The very presence of such realist elements, however, imbues the novel with a stylistic counterbalance to the modernist traits identified earlier.

Katherine's need to revolt against social injustice has been evident since her early contempt for Anstey, whom she looked at 'as if he were an insect she would relish treading on' (19), but it becomes more urgent as she takes Miss Green to the dentist. An unswerving disciple of the orthodox work ethic, his chant of "'I don't work on Saturday mornings'" (41) implies a ruthless compartmentalising of life, similar to that which encouraged the library's rigid cataloguing methods. In search of relief from Miss Green's toothache – itself symbolic of a wider malaise – the two women pass from the care of one tyrannical patriarch to another, whose surroundings are similarly associated with corruption and decay. Reminiscent of a Graham Greene novel, the room has an 'unlit gas fire' with a chair 'bolted to the floor' (42), signifying the patients' powerlessness in a hostile environment. As in the opening section, the description is highly pictorial, so that colours convey a jaundiced atmosphere. The 'sticky-looking, brown wainscoting' and the 'dusty yellow' wallpaper connote sickness rather than health and the instrument of relief is a 'crooked . . . drill' (42) which instils as much confidence as 'the knot [that] ran round the short, endless course' (43) – evocative of meaningless cyclical processes. The dentist's inability to hear properly (see his endless '"pardons"' and his terse rebuttals ['"You aren't going to fill it, are you?" / "Fill it? No"' and '"I must have gas" / "I can't give you gas"' (43, 45)]) implies an automatic reliance on the orthodox medical practice of supplying as little information as possible, and recall the way Katherine was prevented from learning too much in the library. Like Anstey, the dentist is representative of an establishment culture which is not used to being challenged. Thus, Katherine's request for gas is an act of defiance against orthodox protocols, and traditional boundaries are transgressed: 'Her own voice sounded unnatural, raised to penetrate his deafness' (45). The context implies that 'natural' is synonymous with meek acquiescence, the expected behaviour for young women of low social status. Exasperated by her stubbornness, the dentist asserts '"It's the law – the law of *this* country"' (46), reminding Katherine of her inferior foreign status. The set-piece ends with 'Katherine . . . almost feel[ing] the pain exploding beneath the anaesthetic' (48). Katherine's mental outrage at an inflexible regime is externalised in Miss Green's physical pain which conveys the less tangible, though equally felt, social injustice. The dentist's act of removing 'the wet and bloodstained roll of cotton wool' along with 'the rubber gag' (48), symbolises how women during this period were silenced by the dominant male culture, which relegated them to the 'natural' practices of wives and mothers. Ironically, it is this orthodox role that Katherine herself adopts at the end of this scene. In helping Miss Green through her ordeal she felt that 'all the responsibility fell on her that otherwise Miss Green's mother would have borne' (52) and later, once she has made Miss Green comfortable in her room, 'Katherine [felt] that she was telling [Miss Green] a fairy-story before sending her to bed' (58). The book criticises patriarchal society for restricting women to such roles, as does 'The Literary World' (CP, 38) where male success is pathetically dependent on indefatigable female domestic management:

> [Mrs Tennyson]
> (apart from running the household)
> Brought up and educated the children.
> While all this was going on
> Mister Alfred Tennyson sat like a baby
> Doing his poetic business.

Section two of the novel looks forward to 'Next, Please' (CP, 52) as Katherine contemplates an apparently flawless future. Katherine hopes that her pen-friend will be a soul mate, but their letters are no more 'than an interminable business correspondence' (68) and the gap between Robin and her ideal image further stresses her need to reconstruct reality: 'she had assumed he was a variant of the red-hair, freckles and projecting-teeth English face. In this she had been wrong' (72). Meeting Robin at Dover, she found him 'not at all as she had pictured him' (77); the sea imagery suggests a fundamental opposition in their outlooks. Seeing her at the quayside, Robin observed 'that it was a perfect day for seeing across to France' but she 'remembered how she fancied she could see large patches of weed dark through the lucid water, but dare not try to explain this' (75). Robin's seeing *across* to France, in clear weather, suggests his confinement to the surface, whereas Katherine's awareness of what lurks below the waves hints at a more profound sense of understanding. As in *The North Ship*, the metaphorical use of ships and the sea pervades the novel. During her voyage Katherine 'walked to and fro across the sharp shadows on the deck, noticing how the deck and all the ropes had been drenched in sea-water and then whitened in the sun' (67). In his demystification of cultural signs, Roland Barthes has explained the full import of the image of the ship:

> the ship may well be a symbol for departure; it is, at a deeper level, the emblem of closure. An inclination for ships always means the joy of perfectly enclosing oneself, of having at hand the greatest possible number of objects, and having at one's disposal an absolutely finite space. To like ships is first and foremost to like a house, a superlative one since it is unremittingly closed, and not at all vague sailings into the unknown: a ship is a habitat before being a means of transport. (Barthes, 1957, 66)

Similar signification explains Katherine's mental state. The 'sharp shadows' suggest a clarity of vision whilst on board, and the drenched ropes which are 'whitened in the sun' imply a closeness to the elements, which, throughout the trip, promise to embrace Katherine in their 'illimitable strength' (72). Conveying the transient nature of the glimpse into wholeness that the journey provides, when 'the boat shuddered to a standstill . . . [she] looked over the rail at the bare stones of the quay, terrified' (73). Elsewhere in the novel, travel and the brief insights it brings are brought to our attention. When Robin's father drives them to London, Katherine experiences the brief sense of cohesion enjoyed by the speaker of 'The Whitsun Weddings' (CP, 114): the fleeting 'glimpse of a straight road' followed by 'the baker as he went from door to door' momentarily 'filled [Katherine] with a sense of relaxation' (78). As in the poem, these epiphanies have the power to synthesise disparate elements and to invest mundane human experiences with new worth. At a later stage in the journey, 'Only infrequently did [Katherine] see things that reminded her of landscape paintings . . . and . . . Everything seemed enshrined beneath the sky' (80). The clichéd representation of the English countryside as conventional landscape image is superseded by the poignant perception of many scenes that are conflated by the car's motion. This unity, which pervades seemingly diverse forces, sustains Katherine during her stay with the Fennels.

From the first moment of her arrival Katherine is revolted by the Fennels' oppressive conventionality. Full of old-fashioned attitudes, the house is like 'a museum' (103), and the '"Private. No Landing Allowed"' (87) sign on the river bank implies an insular, Little Englander mentality. The way in which Robin disposes of a moth is a metaphor for the genteel, yet ruthless, treatment of those excluded from the Fennels' bourgeois world. Mrs Fennel's instruction not to crush it but to deal with it '"firmly but gently"' insinuates that Katherine might be similarly dealt with if her presence disrupts settled social rituals. The unwanted moth had 'flown into the creeper' (89) suggesting Katherine's shame at being similarly excluded from society. As in the dentist's surgery, concrete details serve a symbolic purpose: they are directly related to contemporary social issues. Watching Robin play tennis, Katherine noticed that 'There was something mechanical about it', with his 'cross-drives [which] were largely a matter of habit' (100). His style is 'fast' and 'unvarying', and at the end of the match he took care to 'screw his racquet into its press' (100–1). Robin's too-rigid conventionality is also evident during Katherine's punting lesson. Unable to master the orthodox method that Robin prefers, she can only '[make] paddling motions . . . with a half-nervous, half-excited laugh, foreign and gleeful, that she thought might attract him' (87). Later, Jane tells her to ignore Robin's advice and aim merely to '"drive the boat along"' (126), signifying the importance of steering her own course, unconstrained by the narrow channels of existence navigated by Robin and his family. Jane's dissatisfaction with her role is made clear when Katherine accidentally breaks the Fennels's china. Jane brushes the mishap aside as '"the kind of thing that makes life worth living"' (106), and Katherine's intention to get out her grandmother's silver because it was '"meant to be used"' (108) indicates respect for present circumstances over outdated traditions.

Her capacity to perceive hidden connections in the disparate flux of life prompts Katherine to recognise that Robin's 'gracious carriage of the personality . . . was not natural', and she is convinced that 'behind it was a desire to see her'. The unlikelihood of such a connection, however, causes Katherine to escape from surface reality altogether:

> after this period of order, her thoughts broke their pattern once more and recommenced rocking to and fro, so that she became too tired to follow them any more and sank into half-consciousness. At this, half-effaced impressions rushed upon her, details of the journey and passengers, the shine of the sea, the lifting of the waves that was the slumbering of strength, the gulls at Dover, and above all her surprise that after so many miles and hours and different vehicles . . . she should at last be lying in this house, surrounded by strangeness on all sides to a depth of hundreds of miles, and yet be feeling no anxiety of any kind. (91)

Reminiscent of Clarissa Dalloway's drifting away from her regulated social chores, Katherine rejects the 'order' and 'pattern' that Robin imposes on the world. Her envelopment in her natural surroundings implies that individual consciousness can merge with elemental processes. The transcendent soaring of the spirit that the gulls signify, and which make Katherine feel 'no anxiety of any kind', is similarly Woolfian in expressing the need to escape a limited existence.

Katherine experiences her visionary moments during a journey in which she is removed from the constricting social forces of fixed locations. When Robin sees that Katherine was '"tired after [her] journey"', Jane cryptically remarks that '"we were tired after our lack of journeys"' (92), a reference to how women's prospects are hampered by patriarchal structures which limit their activities to domestic subservience. After her arrival Robin 'motioned that Jane should pour out a cup of coffee for [Katherine]' (93). Details such as she 'resembled a doll' (137), and acts like 'a discontented schoolgirl on perpetual holiday' (116), further suggest her inferior social status. Describing her previous employment, Jane's use of passive constructions – '"it was decided I ought to do something"' and '"When I was considered to know enough"' – imply how other people have planned her life, especially her father who '"got [her] into an office of a friend of his"' (151). When she was made redundant she just '"messed around"' in father's office and '"hadn't anything definite to do"'. Like Katherine in section one, Jane is forced into traditional female roles, and so when she is ejected by her male employers, she 'came back to "help mother"' (152). Despite their different nationalities and social class, both Katherine and Jane are excluded by wartime patriarchal culture. Ironically, Katherine is annoyed that her fellow sufferer continually resists a friendship with Robin, whose sex and class are her persecutors. Jane observes how patriarchal society values achievement above all else: '"They've got this desire to – well, it's hardly that; I mean it seems quite natural for them to peg along and do things, they don't give it a second thought. But I don't see any *point* in it"' (153). This opposition underpins poems such as 'Dockery and Son' and 'Toads' (CP, 152, 89) where conventional lifestyles are questioned. *A Girl in Winter*'s entire symbolic framework, together with the outsider status of the narrative consciousness, provokes a deep sympathy for Katherine who suffers as a result of hostile attitudes towards women and foreigners in the 1940s.

The narrow-mindedness of Robin and his friend, Jack Stormalong, run dangerously close to fascist attitudes. When Katherine speculates that '"families with a foreign side are more interesting"', Robin curtly reminds her '"That's what the Jews think, isn't it"' [sic] (158). For Roger Day, Jack Stormalong is 'hardly credible' as a character (Day, 1987, 24), though his 'flat' presentation is a necessary part of the novel's purpose. Jack's surname is suggestive of blundering insensitivity and his 'military face' and 'sense of his own authority' caricature him as jingoistic warmonger who offers 'peace but not friendship on certain terms' (159). Jack is not a fully rounded character in the social-realist tradition; rather, he parodies the shallowness of the colonial hunter-type who has '"seen a tiger with as many as eight bullets in it"'. Given Larkin's concern for animal welfare and Jane's dry put-down of Jack's enthusiasm for killing ('"You can't help feeling scared. That's where the fun comes in." "I think it would go out, with me," said Jane' [169]) and bearing in mind the decentred narrative voice, the likely intention is a wholesale indictment of colonialism, a theme in Larkin's work which many critics have ignored. *A Girl in Winter* contains elements that are far removed from the depiction of Larkin by, for example, Jardine, who insists on reading his work as being ingrained with reactionary sexual politics and entrenched nationalist tendencies.

The novel suggests a triumph of the feminine over the masculine, the visionary over the factual and the rebel over the conformer. As at the end of section one in *To the Lighthouse*, the nurturing female encompasses the rational male view within its own vision. Tiring of Jack's tales of predatory male behaviour in the colonies, Katherine seeks refuge by the river where she is met, unexpectedly, by Robin:

> As they proceeded downstream, sending ripples towards either bank, the trees fell behind and fields opened around them. On one side the bank had been built up with bricks, now grown dull and mossy after much weather, and an iron ring fastened in them was rusty and disused. The water was the colour of pewter, for the afterglow had faded rapidly and left a quality of light that resembled early dawn. It had drawn off the brightness from the meadows and stubble-fields, that were now tarnished silver and pale yellow, and

> the shadows were slowly mixing with the mist. In this way the edges
> of her emotions had blurred, and they now overlaid each other like
> twin planes of water running over wet sand, the last expenditure of
> succeeding waves. There was no longer any discord in them: she felt
> at peace. (171–2)

Echoing Lawrence's prose, the landscape serves a symbolic purpose.
Away from the stuffy house the 'fields opened around them' and the river-
side wall, formerly 'built up with bricks' is now 'dull and mossy'. The
imagery recalls the opening section of *Trouble at Willow Gables* and
suggests the triumph of nature over man-made containment. The 'rusty
and disused' state of the 'iron ring' symbolises the couple's escape from
the shackles of restrictive bourgeois codes. Whalen has shown how Larkin
compares money, often unfavourably, with natural coin in *High Windows*
(BTH, 2000, 108) and attributes this to the influence of Lawrence's
poetry, particularly 'Money-Madness' and 'Aristocracy of the Sun'
(Whalen, 1997, 152). In the passage above, the 'tarnished silver' country-
side affirms its superior worth to the Fennels's monetary wealth.
However, Katherine feels no bitterness towards Robin ('the edges of her
emotions' being 'blurred') and the Woolfian imagery at the end suggests
that whilst their world-views have clashed, reconciliation is still possible
– the natural force of 'succeeding waves' washes away artificial divisions.

Responding to the epiphany of the boat ride, Robin comments, in a
hopeful tone, that '"If we'd lived in prehistoric times, before England was
an island, I could nearly have taken you home"'. Robin detaches himself
from the anti-European mentality which has alienated Katherine.
Moreover, his observation that '"The Thames used to flow into the
Rhine"' (172) promises union, not merely between two individuals, but
also between two countries torn apart by conflict. Wartime, however, on
both a personal and a public scale, prevents the connection.

Reflecting Katherine's new sense of pragmatism, the winter weather at
the start of section three is neither 'romantic [n]or picturesque' (177) and
her new desire to 'remember . . . the Fennels, plainly and without embroi-
dery' contrasts with how, earlier, 'she had told her friends that Robin was
passionately, simply madly and passionately, in love with her' (180).
Katherine deals with the unsatisfactory relationship by 'suppressing as far
as she could every reference to her former life' (181), though a negation
of the past is difficult to achieve:

> Nearly everything she possessed was a reference back to the days
> before she left home: her leather motoring-coat, for instance, was a
> relic of her student days. There had been a fad about dressing in
> accordance with the machine-age. (182)

The 'motoring coat' recalls the obsessive car imagery associated with Jack. Descriptions of how the 'dark crimson sports car roared hoarsely' and his use of 'a new kind of juice' (158), testify to an unhealthy single-mindedness which applauds efficient modernity above all else. When she arrives at Dover, Katherine's conception of an idyllic England is spoiled by the traffic: 'It was difficult to see it. The main roads were full of cars' and Robin's eagerness to drive – '"Could I take a turn, dad?"' (80) – imply a passion to override nature. Katherine is also influenced by 'the machine-age' (with its associations of arrogance and self-righteousness) and this prepares for her sympathetic view of Anstey as a victim, rather than an agent, of establishment culture.

When Katherine returns Miss Parbury's handbag she cannot resist reading the letter it contains. Her 'eye fled from sentence to sentence, trying to break into the meaning' (187). Again, her ability to see beneath the surface is apparent: 'Once more she read through the shrouded sentences, feeling somewhere the meaning striking like a muffled drum'. Subsequently, the 'drums deepened' (188) and as in *The North Ship* they symbolise the dawning of an epiphanic moment. Katherine's attempt to construct a plausible framework for the life of a stranger allows her to '[glimpse] the undertow of peoples' [sic] relations, two-thirds of which is without face' (199–200). Alienated by the material conditions which kept her subservient in the library, Katherine is now appalled by the emotional exploitation which suffocates Miss Parbury's life. The resigned tones in which Miss Parbury recounts tending to her mother ('"Once I was ill for a week and we had a nurse in. We had to, you see"' [197]) suggests how conventional emotional attitudes minimise life's potential in the same way as material forces erode the will. Katherine rails at conventional filial responsibility: '"it would be better if she were in a hospital," she added, rebelling against this conspiracy to make Miss Parbury into a tragic personality', and she later claims '"When you make kindness a duty, everybody resents it – it's such a mistake, I think"' (198). Acutely aware of Anstey's troubled personal life, Katherine empathises with her former adversary:

> she could not hate him as simply as she had done, now that she had come across this part of him that had no bearing on her. For her conception of him as a hostile cartoon she had to substitute a person who had and could evoke feelings, who would undertake the support of an old woman, and on whose account she had seen another crying.

Like Katherine, Anstey is also a victim; this complicates the notion that a dominant patriarch is exploitative of a socially inferior female. Reading Miss Parbury's letter, Katherine finds that Anstey's emotional entanglements erase from her mind the 'hostile cartoon' of Dickensian overlord 'to substitute a person who . . . could evoke feelings' (204–5). Katherine's awareness that an apparently unsympathetic character has redeeming features subverts conventional perceptions. On the same theme, Terence Hawkes explains how art 'defamiliarizes' what seems 'natural':

> According to Shklovsky, the essential function of poetic art is to coun-
> teract the process of habituation encouraged by routine everyday
> modes of perception. We very readily cease to 'see' the world we live
> in, and become anaesthetized to its distinctive features. The aim of
> poetry is to reverse that process, to *defamiliarize* that with which we
> are overly familiar . . . (Hawkes, 1983, 62)

Hawkes is referring to poetry but his observation applies equally well to the poetic mode of writing in *A Girl in Winter*. The early presentation of Anstey as the stereotypical tyrant is subtly rewritten, as he becomes an individual with real feelings who is bullied by convention to 'undertake the support of an old woman' (205). Anstey's happiness is prevented by his allegiance to orthodox attitudes that Katherine identifies as '"duty"' and '"kindness"' (198). By revealing this side to Anstey's character, Larkin's second novel is much more radical than it first appears. Not only does the outsider suffer at the hands of an exploitative employer, but that employer himself is so conditioned by bourgeois ideals that he also suffers. Consequently, Katherine feels little satisfaction when she squashes Anstey in the manner she had always wanted. Outraged at finding that Robin has left messages for Katherine, Anstey repeats the capitalist mantra of segregating work and leisure:

> *It is not my policy*, Miss Lind, to take cognisance of what members
> of my staff do when they leave this building after their working hours.
> I don't consider it is anything to do with me and frankly I do not give
> a twopenny damn, provided their work is done properly and they
> keep their affairs clear of mine . . . (209)

Given Anstey's aversion to mixing public and private concerns, it is ironic that Katherine confronts him at work with his personal problems:

> She hardly knew she had said it till she saw its effect on him. It had
> exploded like a depth-charge. He sat in his chair as stiffly as a
> corporal who has been told to remain seated by a field-marshal. (211)

Military imagery emphasises the extent of Anstey's shock yet also signifies the war's role in creating tragic circumstances. In the same way that the dentist could only treat patients by being cold and aloof, Anstey can only cope by artificially compartmentalising his life. By forcing a confrontation between Anstey's two selves – worker and vulnerable lover – Katherine exposes the limitations of the patriarchal-capitalist ethic that excludes emotion from the work place.

Symbolism cements the link between Katherine's and Anstey's suffering – Anstey's expression when confronted with his relationship with Veronica Parbury, Katherine reflects, was 'as if he had broken a tooth', a simile which recalls Miss Green's ailment in section one. If Jane suffered by virtue of her sex and position, Anstey's rigid adherence to traditional attitudes to caring have diminished his personal happiness.

Realising that each one of us is prone to the disappointments of imperfect lives, Katherine concedes that neither rejection nor acceptance of life's injustices matters: 'there would be other Miss Greens, Miss Parburys, Mr. Ansteys; all this was inescapable, and it did not matter if she accepted it or not. It accepted her' (216). Katherine's only solace is that nature's embracing power sanctifies fragmented lives by giving them a meaningful context:

> the dark soared up like a cathedral . . . covering not only these miles of streets around her, but also . . . the shores, the beaches, and the acres of tossing sea that she had crossed, which divided her from her proper home. At least her birthplace and the street she walked in were sharing the same night, however many unfruitful miles were between them . . . the same winter lay stiffly across the whole continent. (224)

The final phrase recalls a line from *Dubliners* – 'snow was general all over Ireland' (*Dubliners*, 220) – and Katherine shares Gabriel's perception of icy human relations which are peculiarly subsumed by the snowflakes in 'The Dead'. In contrast to Katherine's understanding, however, Robin has learned very little by the end of the book. Re-entering Katherine's life he remains contemptuous of her work, sneering at her '"marvellous job"' which he mocks as '"Very learned"' (228). Like Katherine, he resigns himself to the paralysis of wartime, though whereas she strives for higher knowledge and 'had made some discovery about herself' (225), he continues in his superficial ways. Using the confusion of the 1940s in order to '"Get as much fun as possible"' (230), his main concern is that Katherine is mixing with the kind of '"decent people"' (232) who share his narrow outlook on social and sexual politics.

When Katherine gives in to Robin's sexual demands, she sees them as 'an unimportant kindness, that would be overtaken by oblivion' (243) though their bungled lovemaking develops into something more meaningful: 'He closed the door quietly, smoothing his hair. A snowflake had clung to his shoulder but quickly melted' (244). Again, the imagery is reminiscent of 'The Dead'. Gabriel arrives at the party with snow 'on the toes of his goloshes' (175) and in Joyce's story the image is emblematic of personal coldness. Similarly, in *A Girl in Winter*, the melted snowflake symbolically suggests that Robin has the potential for human warmth that he formerly lacked. His attitude towards bourgeois culture undergoes a similar change:

> 'This war, it's mucked everything up. All happened so naturally, but my God it's made a mess of things . . . Broken the sequence, so to speak. I mean, I knew pretty well what I was going to do, my career and so forth. All gone to blazes. Of course, if I come through, I suppose I can go on – but the funny thing is, I don't much care now. Awfully difficult to explain to one's parents'. (246)

The disruption of war forces Robin to reappraise settled assumptions. Oscillating between rebellion and conformity, he finally gains a new perspective on bourgeois culture:

> 'I'm sorry to burble like this. But it's not worth while. Obviously it's the only worth-while thing, a career and getting a family, increasing and multiplying, whatever that means. But when you don't feel it . . . ' (247)

Robin's '"burble"' contrasts starkly with his old 'guidebook style' – he knew '"all the dates"' (93) during his tours with Katherine. Like Lucy Honeychurch in E. M. Forster's *A Room with a View*, who abandons her Baedeker in order to see '"the true Italy"' (37), Robin recognises the limitations of a too-prescriptive world-view. The last paragraph describes what Booth has aptly termed the 'negative sublime' in Larkin's work (BTH, 1992, 168); it evokes an awareness that Katherine and Robin now share:

> There was the snow, and her watch ticking. So many snowflakes, so many seconds. As time passed they seemed to mingle in their minds, heaping up into a vast shape that might be a burial mound, or the cliff of an iceberg whose summit is out of sight. Into its shadow dreams crowded, full of conceptions and stirrings of cold, as if icefloes were moving down a lightless channel of water. They were going in orderly slow procession, moving from darkness further into darkness, allowing no suggestion that their order should be broken. . . Yet their passage was not saddening. Unsatisfied dreams rose and fell about them, crying out against their implacability, but in the end glad that such order, such destiny, existed. Against this knowledge, the heart, the will, and all that made for protest, could at last sleep. (248)

This looks forward to *The Less Deceived* in its recognition that the dreams that sustain us are only illusions, yet given the human need for 'such order' this grants human existence some dignity in a world at the mercy of wider forces. More immediately, the passage coincides with the thematic and stylistic concerns of *In the Grip of Light*. The reference to a 'lightless channel' and the travel 'from darkness further into darkness' anticipates that volume's concern with subjects who are oppressed by restrictive cultural pressures. The novel's closing lines convey the unpublished volume's ironical import. In 'Träumerei' 'light is cold' and the dreamer is 'shut in' by 'walls [which] have killed the sun' (CP, 12). This fading of light chimes with the novel's sense of being gripped by dark, as opposed to enlightened, social forces. The characteristic imagery of *A Girl in Winter* and *In the Grip of Light* – light, snow, ice and cold – are reinvoked in later poems as a means of signifying degrees of aloofness and social exclusion.

A New World Symphony

Writing to Sutton in 1946, Larkin confided that he wanted 'to write a <u>long</u> book . . . [with] . . . plenty of things happening . . . and . . . a gold line round everyday objects' (u/p letter, 1946). Larkin had already begun the traumatic struggle to write more novels in 1945 (see BTH, 2002, xxvii) and versions of two late attempts (*No For An Answer* [c. 1948–9] and *A New World Symphony* [c. 1949–53]) are now published. A glance at Booth's reconstruction of *A New World Symphony* confirms its commonplace, if not dreary, subject matter, but the above comment implies a desire to imbue seemingly unpropitious material with aesthetic worth. The story is set in a provincial college which, like Leicester University, was a former asylum and the main character, Augusta Bax, bears a striking resemblance to Monica Jones who taught in that institution. Both women are strong-willed academics with bad teeth and Monica's keen dress sense is matched by the 'hangerfuls of clothes . . . doubly loaded' in Augusta's wardrobe (BTH, 2002, 373). Booth declares that:

> *A New World Symphony*, like *No For An Answer*, is very much a work of social realism. The meticulously nuanced opening conversation . . . is far removed from the mischievous artifice of his Brunette mode, and equally distant from the inward 'poetic' elements of *A Girl in Winter*. (BTH, 2002, xxxvii)

Despite generic differences between the unfinished novels and Larkin's Coleman prose, they both challenge orthodox constructs of social and sexual conduct. Booth attempts to isolate Larkin's artistic phases – he talks about the 'neat mid-century division between a pre-1950 novelist and a post-1950 poet' (BTH, 2002, xli) – though he suggests that the works raise the same questions about gender and identity that exist elsewhere in the oeuvre:

> A *New World Symphony* shows Larkin evading the autobiographical risks of focusing on a young male protagonist and returning to his attempt to 'be that girl'. (BTH, 2002, xxxvi)

Like 'I see a girl dragged by the wrists' (CP, 278) *A New World Symphony* also overturns familiar assumptions about identity and gender, five years after that poem was written.

In the opening passage gender stereotypes are used to parody familiar characteristics, though an amusing disruption of settled gender codes is also attempted. Augusta Bax, a university lecturer, is shopping with her mother, 'a provincial businessman's wife, sufficiently freed from house-running to play golf, play bridge, entertain and be entertained'. Identified in relation to her husband's profession, Mrs Bax is a lady of leisure who is comfortably supported by her husband's income. The women shop for clothes, though any stereotyping that such activity suggests is subtly disrupted: Mrs Bax 'seemed . . . to be holding a perpetual kit-inspection on life, and to be finding it a disgrace' (BTH, 2002, 367). Military imagery associates her with conventionally designated 'masculine' aggressiveness, and her judgement on life anticipates her later distrust of the status quo. Customary expectations about femininity are ruptured throughout the tour: mother and daughter had 'a raffish air about them' and browsed 'as if they were two gallants, sneering, hostile, potentially dangerous' (BTH, 2002, 368). Given Larkin's affinity with Joyce, the phrase recalls a story in *Dubliners*. The focus of 'Two Gallants' is on two archetypal 'masculine' cads, Lenehan and Corley, who exemplify the art of extracting money and sex from local women. Their male bluster is aptly summarised by an example of the pair's banter: '"you know how to take them"' quips Lenehan, to which Corley responds, '"I'm up to all their little tricks"' (*Dubliners*, 51). Joyce's denouement chastises the mens' posturing, though Larkin subverts conventional gender constructs further by granting his female characters the gallants' arrogant swagger. The portrayal of 'hostile [and] potentially dangerous' (BTH, 2002, 368) women buying clothes is highly comic, but it has the effect of unsettling orthodox attitudes towards gender differences, and prepares for the women's more serious rejection of patriarchal cant that they encounter later. The ferocity with which they are prepared to fight in the sex war with men is made clear:

when she and her mother were together and striking the same chords it was only the fiercest, most immovable temperament that could withstand them . . . A third person, a man especially, felt himself being jeered out into the open, until his exasperation swiped out at them; and then their combined retaliations landed on him like a mallet, driving his face into the mud, never, as far as they were concerned, to be entirely clean again. (BTH, 2002, 369)

After the shopping trip 'Mrs Bax was subdued enough . . . to be loosed on Butterfield' (BTH, 2002, 369) implying that he is about to enter a lion's den of feminist stridency. Prior to his arrival, however, Augusta shows her mother around the bedsit to 'exemplify . . . her independence, her capability, which had long roots in Mrs Bax's approval'. Mother and daughter are a united sisterhood, so that even smoking a cigarette together becomes 'a joint declaration of independence' (BTH, 2002, 374). Given the novel's unfinished nature it is hard to know how to respond to this early passage. However, in the light of proto-feminist tendencies that occur elsewhere in Larkin's fiction, the surface humour may cloak concerns about gender and identity that run counter to the 'derogatory remarks about women' in the *Selected Letters* (Jardine, cited in Regan, 1997, 5).

Chapter Three is more serious in tone, especially in tracing Augusta's rejection of passive femininity which would have been 'natural' in the 1930s. As in *A Girl in Winter*, the dispirited female protagonist is focalised so that we empathise with her plight. Selected memories of childhood injustice explain Augusta's rebellion against her upbringing. When the Bax family celebrate Guy Fawkes Night 'her father liked [Augusta] to applaud rather than take part' (BTH, 2002, 394), and as she grew older 'Augusta should be in by nine, by nine-thirty, by ten'. The narrative voice assumes Mr Bax's domineering tone: 'She should not put that filthy stuff on her lips, and she should take that other stuff off her nails, too. And what was this book he had found lying about?' Like Jane in *A Girl in Winter*, Augusta is coerced by a tyrannical patriarch; it is hardly surprising that 'She was not a father's girl'. The inherent contradictions of a bourgeois upbringing are made clear in a passage that recalls Forster's novels in its application of the term 'muddled' to unsound moral principles:

John Bax's ideas of bringing up a daughter were muddled, for he believed that a girl should be a good mixer, dancer, moderate drinker and able to take care of herself, while at the same time feeling that it was his duty to keep her away from the Tubby Roberts crowd, and stop her soaking gin at the Yacht Club . . . (BTH, 2002, 395)

'The Dance' condemns dancing as 'That muddled middle-class pre-
tence' (1963–4, CP, 154) but for her father, suitable accomplishments for
Augusta are either social or decorative. Mr Bax disapproves of her stud-
ies on the grounds that 'A University education costs a fortune' and 'would
take her out of the marriage market for three critical years' (BTH, 2002,
397). Once again, Larkin's fiction illustrates how women's prospects are
compromised as they are required to fulfil the 'appropriate' roles of wives
and mothers. Whilst Larkin is not directly identified with Augusta, the
main character's situation certainly has its roots in his own predicament.
Like Augusta, Larkin had a domineering father and was born in August;
like her too, he felt pressurised by the institutions of marriage and respon-
sible gender roles as conceived in the late 1940s.

Augusta's persecuted childhood allows her to indulge Mrs Bax's defla-
tion of Butterfield's ego in chapter two. When he arrives at Augusta's
bedsit, he boasts how his teaching has '"done the state some service"'
(BTH, 2002, 376), though Mrs. Bax cuts him short, showing a keener
interest in the hall flowers. Similarly, after he has explained how depart-
mental politics have put a professorship within his reach 'Mrs Bax was
. . . non-plussed by this long avowal'. Augusta's wry comment that her
superiors' in-fighting resembles '"a little Greek tragedy"' (BTH, 2002,
380) ridicules the male ego's pretension to high drama. Whereas Mrs Bax
was described in 'masculine' terms, Butterfield's bitching about a col-
league further disrupts settled gender stereotypes:

> "he's bald now, but in those days he had thin curly hair, with the
> hint of a bald spot like a saint, most inappropriate, yes. He had a
> biggish head and rather pale, staring eyes."
> "And pink, frilly lips, like a stimulated carnivorous orchid,"
> Augusta enunciated deliberately, as if spitting out lemon-pips. (BTH,
> 2002, 384)

Writing to her mother about common-room politics she confesses to
overhearing 'words like "development" and "tendency" floating out of
their discourses so [Butterfield] probably fancies he's doing himself a bit
o'good. Silly as I tell him 'cos *I* know what they talk about: gardening. He
ought to mug up about cow-parsley and sow-thistle' (BTH, 2002, 391).
Augusta's acute perception of (male) college politics suggests that those
whom it traditionally excludes (women) are better placed to recognise its
hollow nature.

The enduring concern with identity and role-playing occurs elsewhere
in the novel. Augusta has the respectable accomplishments of a middle-
class young woman. Her mother 'trained her' to 'get out of a car without
showing her thighs [and] talk politics to different sorts of people' and Amy

is open about her daughter's constructed role: 'a lady behaved at all times in a ladylike manner, a ladylike manner being *acting* like a lady' (my emphasis, BTH, 2002, 396). Like Estella in *Great Expectations*, Augusta is groomed in social etiquette for the express purpose of gulling certain attitudes. At college, her life continues as a calculated pose:

> She went nowhere, played nothing, declared no allegiance or enthu-siasm: none the less she became distinguished in a small way by always wearing gloves and stockings, and going to Evensong on Sundays, and buying a big three-branched candlestick to put on her writing-desk. (BTH, 2002, 398)

Recalling Hilary in the Coleman novellas, Augusta is able to assume any number of poses in the pursuit of her purpose. During her school-days 'She could mimic the mistresses['] . . . "voices"' (BTH, 2002, 397) and in college she similarly exploits her different personae: 'By *setting up* as an eccentric – vague, wispy, slightly-distracted but exquisitely-bred – she gained a reputation in College many envied' (my emphasis, BTH, 2002, 399). After leaving college, Augusta advances her career through skilful play-acting, becoming tutor to the daughter of a novelist, Melibee Vane, who was 'deceived by Augusta's competent pose and fancied she could do almost anything. In fact, she could do almost nothing'. At the university she 'had a formidable surface power as a candidate' (BTH, 2002, 404), a quality that gained her a lecturing job. Writing to her mother (in a section not published by Booth) she recounts, with great incredulity, how Apegrin – a rival applicant – had 'cut his throat . . . by pulling Butterfield up on a point of information in a way so tactless it might have been recorded and sold as the Way Not To Do It' (u/p sec-tion, Fragment 2, 30). Later in the letter, Augusta confides that the appointment 'was in the bag when [Butterfield] pushed my chair in so lovingly for me' (u/p section, Fragment 2, 31). Augusta turns to her advantage the conventional sexual politics which conspired against Katherine Lind in *A Girl in Winter*. Significantly, she describes her appointment with Vane as '"a Jane looking for her Rochester"' (BTH, 2002, 400), recalling Jane Eyre's efforts to survive by assuming different guises. Fragment 1 ends with a passage – omitted in Booth's edition – that confirms the novel's interest in alternative identities:

> For the most part Mrs Bax was genuinely tired of her husband, as if she were a man tiring of a woman: she didn't even want to be angry about him: there was nothing she wanted except to be allowed to target him absolutely, to let him fall clean out of her mind. It was certainly an unfeminine characteristic, and Amy never quite admitted it to herself. (u/p section, Fragment 1, 18)

Contravening the tenets of patriarchal realism, Amy Bax is the active party in jilting a partner, a typically male activity. By reversing archetypal gender traits, the politics of conventional sexual relations are comically subverted.

In a later scene, this reversal is serious rather than comic. Augusta's colleague, Julie Farmer, is brusque and patronising towards an enthusiastic male student: 'Julie was firm. "Well, restrain your curiosity till next week. We'll go into it then. Good-morning"' (BTH, 2002, 414). The use of positional authority by a woman over a man serves as a corrective to Anstey's harsh treatment of Katherine and suggests that *A New World Symphony* is as disruptive of orthodox gender roles as the Coleman fiction and the completed novels.

In Chapter Five Butterfield assesses his life and career. Like Augusta, Butterfield was derided by his father who told him he had '"the brains of [a] lead pencil"'. Whereas Augusta, as a girl, felt more at liberty to reject her father's chauvinism, Butterfield, as a boy, feels constrained by the male success ethic. Consequently, 'every success he gained he deposited at his father's feet, like a knight slaying bigger and bigger dragons' (BTH, 2002, 430). Staring at the professorial application form, he ponders his latest challenge:

> He tried imagining what (in a successful application) should come next: Assistant Lecturer 1923–1926: Lecturer 1926–1929: Fiddle Reader in Godsknowswhat at, probably, Manchester, 1929–1930: Assistant Professor, Idaho State University, 1930–1933: Faddle Lecturer on the Seventeenth Century, University of Oxford 1934–1939.

The listing of such unlikely positions as 'Fiddle Reader' and 'Faddle Lecturer' parodies academia's preoccupation with titles; the formal style projects an image of conformity though, in reality, Butterfield longs to opt out of the labelled roles of adult existence. Rejecting the orthodox form-filling as 'this solemn rigmarole' (BTH, 2002, 426), he humorously contemplates an alternative application which makes no reference to pretentious readerships: 'He might as well send them a postcard saying '"Count me in" . . . everyone knew him . . . [he'd] been there for years' (BTH, 2002, 426). Butterfield's irritation with his application form foreshadows how Larkin's later poems chafe at orthodox procedures.

Academic appointments are not made on the basis of loyal service or sound teaching – '[Butterfield] was the most popular lecturer in the College' (BTH, 2002, 440) – but in accordance with who will fit most easily into settled college hierarchies. The new Principal, Welsh, fits the bill perfectly. Like the career academic in 'Naturally the Foundation . . . ' (CP, 134), he has travelled the globe to augment his curriculum vitae:

> even from Tasmania he seemed to sense who commanded the situation, and before closing asked for a £100 rise in starting salary and first-class fare home. This was conceded with a slight, pleasurable thrill: he sounded the man they wanted. (BTH, 2002, 434)

Welsh's academic qualifications are unremarkable though he is politically astute, using machiavellian tactics to promote the new formalities of chapel attendance and gown-wearing. Butterfield 'doubted if [these customs] would improve the quality of the students any more than calling the cook a Domestic Bursar would improve the quality of the cooking' (BTH, 2002, 436). As an old-school university teacher Butterfield is appalled by academe's increasing preoccupation with research: he reflects that 'The University world was divided into scholars and teachers: well, he was a teacher and not ashamed of it. All young lecturers cared about nowadays was rushing their names into print: their students could go hang' (BTH, 2002, 431). Nevertheless, Butterfield still dreams of scaling the career ladder:

> Five years from now he might be sitting in a leather chair, wearing a smoking jacket, rapidly correcting the galleys of his book, surrounded by long envelopes typewrittenly addressed to *Professor Butterfield*: he ran over the shapes of titles in his mind – *Prolegomena to the Study of*, *The Life and Letters of*, *The Relation to his Century of*. The fringed standard lamp would beam down. A tap at the door: a cosied teapot, a boiled egg: "Your tea, Professor Butterfield." He grinned, right elbow cupped by his left hand, right hand tickling the hairs that grew from his ear: that wouldn't come under four-and-a-half guineas a week. On the pavement opposite a little boy began defacing a house-agent's advertisement. (BTH, 2002, 432)

Butterfield is concerned with the trappings of office rather than the substance. His detailed reverie about room service contrasts with the vague and incomplete book titles in his mind. He longs for the decadence of professorial life though his fixation is part of a wider set of social pressures. Reminiscent of the trashing of the poster in 'Sunny Prestatyn' (CP, 149), the boy's 'defacing' of a 'house-agent's advertisement' signifies the dead end of material satisfactions. The message is clear: instead of finding fulfilment as a professor, Butterfield would miss the less remunerative though more worthwhile pleasures of teaching. Accepting that he will not be promoted he reappraises his life:

he unexpectedly heeled over into a kind of contentment. If his life was settled in failure, it was at least settled. Undeniably he enjoyed himself . . . his half-dozen honours students existed life-size in his attention; he liked them, stood them dinners: they brought him their gossip, and drinks. It was borne in on him that he had become a figure, a character. (BTH, 2002, 440)

The passage overturns the ideological framework that an acquisitive and competitive society constructs. The phrase 'settled in failure' disrupts the customary perception of 'failure' as a state of disappointment and loss. For Butterfield, 'failure' signifies 'contentment', underlining his refusal to feel the 'requisite' despair at being rejected by the system. *Trouble at Willow Gables* also explores the consequences of spurning conventional expectations, and it recurs in 'Conscript', 'Places, Loved Ones', 'Wild Oats' and 'Dockery and Son' (CP, 262, 99, 143, 152). Butterfield's manner of re-evaluating established values echoes the subversive effort of 'Movement' novels. In John Wain's *Hurry on Down* (1953), Charles resents being judged by middle-class codes: 'He did not fit into their world or speak their language, and after a perfunctory attempt to fit him into their prim, grey jigsaw puzzle they had disliked and rejected him' (*Hurry on Down*, 16). What lies at the heart of Butterfield's estrangement from establishment culture is the conviction that life can be egalitarian and harmonious:

As most popular man on the staff (among the students) and accepted antagonist to the Principal, he began being pointedly democratic. He had always nodded to everybody out of nervousness: now he never passed a gardener without a few minutes' discussion of whatever happened to be growing nearby, or a cleaner without a reference to dust or sciatica. (BTH, 2002, 440–1)

If Augusta cynically adopted the system's invidious methods to advance herself, Butterfield's 'pointedly democratic' sense is oblivious of a world at odds with his own principles:

As time drew on (and the war broke out without snapping any essential thread) he added check shirts, silk bows, a bludgeon of a walking-stick. If he could have stood it he would have smoked a cherrywood pipe. In the year of the invasion of Europe he bought rather a wide-brimmed hat. (BTH, 2002, 441)

Refusing to allow the war to invade his own plans – the parenthesis indicates the relegation of its importance for him – Butterfield detaches himself from the dominant concerns of 1940s Britain. His dandyish indulgence 'In the year of the invasion of Europe' aligns him with non-conformist idealism when social forces sought to unify popular opinion. Thus, despite its unfinished and comic nature, one of the book's most notable features is the extent to which characters subvert established attitudes, imposing, instead, their own conceptions of 'how life should be' (CP, 144).

No For An Answer

No For An Answer also overturns conventional ideals, though critics have emphasised instead its reliance on biographical events. For Booth, the text 'fictionalises Larkin's domestic situation at Christmas 1947' (BTH, 2002, xxxiii), a time of exceptional gloom for the writer. Not only had his father recently died, but his mother had been ill and a union with Ruth Bowman was becoming increasingly likely. Parallels between the ill-fated Bowman–Larkin liaison and Sam and Sheila's situation are not hard to find. Motion describes Wagstaff's plight in terms of Larkin's:

> His dilemma is the one Larkin himself had been confronting ever since beginning the novel. Sam thinks that if he marries he will re-create his parents' unhappiness; if he doesn't marry he knows he will feel sexually deprived. (Motion, 1993, 226)

However, the 'novel' aspires to social commentary as well as biography. Sam and Sheila are 'the socially-determined products of . . . their material social conditions' (BTH, 2002, xxxiv) though Booth ignores the extent to which the text probes the basic assumptions which underlie their 'socially-determined' lives. In his introduction, Booth offers little in the way of close textual analysis, though he discerns in the tale 'Larkin's irresponsible masculine imagination [that] subverts his moral judgements' (BTH, 2002, xxxv). On the contrary, however, it is the text's 'moral judgements' that subvert the 'masculine imagination'. As with *A Girl in Winter*, this 'novel' also challenges the orthodox principles of patriarchal culture so that marriage, wartime heroics and capitalism are all systematically undermined.

Fragment 4 opens with Sam Wagstaff's girlfriend, Sheila Piggott, discussing Christmas and her love life with her mother. As with Larkin's earlier prose, realist details are imbued with symbolic functions: 'Every so often [Sheila] glanced at the clock, then went on sorting her Christmas cards, the smallest at the front, the largest at the back. There were forty-seven of them, and she did hope she would reach fifty by the time Christmas was over' (BTH, 2002, 279). Sheila's obsession with time and her scrupulous ordering of the cards, as if they were units of factory production, suggests a mercenary outlook at odds with the season. Just as she quantifies the number of cards she wants to receive, so her relationship with Sam is based on material considerations. Sheila views Sam as 'her father's partner's son, and she had grown up within the unspoken idea that eventually the children might, someday . . . '. Sheila's mother speculates that '"He's a worker . . . [who will] . . . get a position very soon"' further signifying the importance of social status for the Piggotts, who seem oblivious to Sam's personal attributes, relegating him to the status of income-slave who will '"never earn what some men do"' (BTH, 2002, 280).

Sam is involved in an accident in which he knocks over a bicyclist. The incident is reported in Booth's edition but an unpublished section revives the vivid motoring metaphor of *A Girl in Winter*. Prior to the crash, Sam's consciousness is focalised:

> Sam Wagstaff liked driving, and liked driving fast. It engrossed him
> . . . At the softest touch the car surged forward like a powerful current.
> It was a post-war model, made by his firm. Except for a dead turkey
> in the back seat, Sam was alone. (u/p Fragment 1, 1)

Sam's penchant for 'driving fast', and his surging forwards 'like a powerful current' suggests the gathering pace of consumer-capitalism in the economic resurgence of the late 1940s and early 1950s. The injured cyclist is the human cost of the drive for mechanised 'progress'. Sam is no more certain of his role in the new capitalist world order than the Larkin of the Sutton letters who saw 'a panic streak in it all' (u/p letter, 7.xii.42). After the accident 'Sam felt no freedom' (4) – a state of mind which survives in Fragment 4 (BTH, 2002, 281) – and reflecting on the mishap, he had an 'itch to ring up authority, to stride into an office of justice, to settle on the spot whether or no he was to blame' (BTH, 2002, 283). If Sam is uncomfortable with his complicity in a decadent regime, Sheila's mother is quite at ease. Questioning Sam as to the bicyclist's identity she uses her influence, as the powerful entrepreneur's wife, to 'buy' his innocence: '"Now who was he, did you know him?" asked Mrs Piggott, leaning forwards like a counsel' (BTH, 2002, 281). To get their way, the family employ an iniquitous network of suspect allegiances prompting Mrs Piggott to '"get [Stan] to speak to the Super down at the club"' (BTH, 2002, 282). In every sense, the novel's aesthetic concern is to disentangle itself from unjust and immoral practices.

At the rugby club dance Sam is uncomfortable with his friends' 'respectable' middle-class behaviour. Arriving at the dance, Sheila is angry with Sam over his shoddy dressing. Appeals to '"Do your shirt up,

Sam"' and '"make yourself decent"' (BTH, 2002, 284) are part of the bourgeois creed of a dress code consistent with one's class and social standing. To adapt the words of 'Self's the Man' (CP, 117), when he meets his friends Sam is struck by the contrast between his life and theirs:

> Many of his friends were married by this time, and the others seemed to find no difficulty in having girls occasionally. He felt a little annoyed at being in neither class. The thought crossed his mind occasionally that he ought to have a serious bash at Sheila. (BTH, 2002, 285)

By drawing on Marx and Louis Althusser, Terry Eagleton has shown that the most extreme form of ideological persuasion is brought about not by coercion, but by the agent's having so internalised the edicts of dominant thought that complicity with the system is automatic (see Regan, 1998, 244). Thus, Sam's friends exert a group pressure on him, such that he perceives marriage and sex as 'tabled . . . rites' (CP, 42) that he 'ought' to take part in. Moreover, the blunt, colloquial terms in which he considers having 'a serious bash at Sheila' signifies that courtship has been reduced to a strategy of convenience, which is, of course, exactly how Sheila herself sees it. Beneath the collusions of image, metaphor and sign, the unifying structural principle is a critique of precise social and material conditions. The unfinished novel demystifies the 'natural' processes of marriage, money-making and all the other practices of bourgeois living which post-war society instilled in the collective consciousness.

At the dance Sam learns of the awful compromises that marriage could bring. When Sheila remarks '"[The Gassoways] had another scrap last week"', Sam's rejoinder – '"I'd just break her neck"' – boasts a rebellious intolerance of the give and take of matrimony. However, Sheila's comment that he '"wouldn't hurt a fly"' illustrates the self-deluding nature of his excessive boast. Whether he likes it or not, Sam is not immune from the powerful influence that society exerts. As Sheila points out, his threatened violence – and the disruption of social codes it represents – is unlikely to be carried through. As in the Coleman texts, conventional morality is reversed: Sheila's 'compliment' on his essential decency 'displease[s]' Sam and 'brought the accident to his mind again' (BTH, 2002, 286). Sam is troubled by the extent to which he is being drawn into a bourgeois existence which – as the car accident conveyed – is founded on harmful cultural and material forces.

Porky, the ex-serviceman, is described in terms which extend the novel's subversive theme. As '"a man who's had a tough time"', Porky has suffered at the hands of the '"little yellow bleeders"' during the war.

Another of Sam's friends, Ben, remarks how '"He didn't ask for it – he got it"' (BTH, 2002, 287) and, in accordance with the structural principles detected elsewhere, the phrase hints at how servicemen are abused in the same way as workers within capitalist society. After getting drunk he is thrown out of the dance hall on the grounds that '"behaviour like that lets the whole club down"' (BTH, 2002, 298). Porky's excessive drinking is related, presumably, to his horrendous past, though he is viewed as a social embarrassment rather than as a casualty of war. Sam sympathises with Porky, and his perception of him as 'a piece of machinery left twelve months on waste-ground' (BTH, 2002, 290) indicates how capitalism superannuates human beings. Reflecting on his accident, Sam reappraises certain values:

> Ten years ago, he could not help thinking, Porky would have been among his friends at the bar or dancing with a girl he had hopes of. Now many of the friends had gone, those that were still here had privately abandoned him . . . Sam had an acute perception of the damage of time . . . It was replaced by thoughts of the accident. (BTH, 2002, 291)

The precision of the phrase 'the damage of time' poignantly suggests how wartime experiences have deprived Porky of the usual pleasures of youth and turned him into a social outcast. Once again, Sam's flashback to the accident – and all it represents – reveals his guilt at being an accomplice to the decadent cultural forces that have caused Porky's suffering. The description of Porky 'pondering like a labourer brooding on some injustice' (BTH, 2002, 289) suggests that his predicament is similar to that of the worker who has also been manipulated by a dominant order.

The connection between the plight of the worker and the soldier is made clear later when Sam is driving along the Banbury Road. Just as he is pressurised into adopting the conventional trappings of marriage and a career, so he assumes an oppressive role as the son of an industrialist: 'Sam returned home . . . past a camp of German prisoners: two men in black battledress were tending a bonfire. They straightened as Sam's car sped past' (BTH, 2002, 306–7). As in *A Girl in Winter*, the car's speed symbolises the relentless onslaught of capitalist–imperialist values; the soldiers who stand to attention represent Sam's complicity in a world order which subjugates the weak and the conquered. The fragment disrupts the complacent attitude which reveres mechanised 'advancement' and the hierarchical divisions that ensue from military victory.

Though we should not rely on biographical detail to support our reading of these texts, it is worth noting that Larkin suffered acute personal strain whilst writing the unfinished fiction. Undecided about the direction of his relationship with Ruth Bowman, Sydney Larkin's ailing health also affected his work at the end of the 1940s. Accordingly, *No For An Answer* fictionalises reality as Sam is under increasing pressure to get married:

> According to Sheila's code, Sam had been pushing her increasingly into a false position; when she thought about it, she felt people might think she was a fool. That was insufferable. What she felt was, Sam had used his position as old friend of the family to treat her as a regular girlfriend without having any of the responsibility entailed . . . Some allowance should be made for ex-airmen, but not all that much. (BTH, 2002, 303–4)

Concern for what 'people might think' suggests the societal pressure to conform to the bourgeois ideal of *responsible* behaviour. Whereas Porky is physically chastised at the dance, Sam is reprimanded by the subtle coercions of 'Sheila's code' of traditional sexual politics.

What then, of Sam's relationship with his father? Samuel Wagstaff senior is a ruthless capitalist who kept 'Questions of policy . . . above Sam's head' and 'talked . . . about efficiency, management, and push'. His addiction to the work ethic makes him see business as 'a test of endurance, of ingenuity, of will-power . . . like keeping three plates spinning on three billiard cues' (BTH, 2002, 310). The downside of his philosophy is that he fails to seize the moment. When he is worried that renovations will not be finished on time, his business partner, Stan, highlights his flaw: '"In six months' time, the roof'll be sound, the furnishings'll be dry, the rooms'll be aired, the garden'll be dug, the – the floors'll be scrubbed, – " here he glared at Samuel – "and you'll be in bed, dead. Well, it's your own fault"' (BTH, 2002, 335). Wagstaff's controlling nature relates him to the Father in *Night in the Plague* in which both men's obsessions are put into perspective by Death.

Sam felt that 'he could never live up to Samuel Wagstaff's standards' and as 'an ordinary son' (BTH, 2002, 308) he distances himself from his father's business empire. His desire to 'use the business to give himself money and a good time' (BTH, 2002, 310) runs counter to the old man's prudence and suggests Sam's wish to escape what a poem refers to as the 'intensely sad' effects of accumulated wealth ('Money', CP, 198). A consideration of Samuel's physical appearance is critical in understanding the full extent of Sam's revolt against his father's values. He 'had a savage face' with a 'moustache scored under his nose' and 'His lips had been a thin bar of irritation'. This is a caricaturing of a certain notorious fascist, but the comparison of his mouth to 'a sunken crater of past annoyance' (BTH, 2002, 309) strongly associates the memory of a parent with images of wartime destruction. According to Adam Piette, the symbolism of bomb damage and air raids gave Larkin 'a splendid opportunity to annul the pre-war, to unspend . . . childhood' (Piette, 1999, 9). Whether Samuel Wagstaff was inspired by Sydney Larkin or not, Larkin's contempt for capitalist-imperialist endeavour is inextricably linked with the destructiveness of war and the extent to which his own father admired the economic policies of Nazi Germany in the 1930s.

As far as fiction was concerned, Larkin realised that his over-reliance on biographical detail was his chief flaw. Reflecting on his novel-writing, Larkin admits that 'they were just too hard for me . . . novels are about other people and poems are about yourself. I think that was the trouble, really. I didn't know enough about other people, I didn't like them enough'. In lamenting his 'failure' as a novelist Larkin jokingly suggests what may have been his motivation for writing novels in the first place:

> I could never write a third novel, though I must have spent about five years trying to. I felt a bit cheated. I'd had visions of myself writing 500 words a day for six months, shoving the result off to the printer and going to live on the Côte d'Azur, uninterrupted except for the correction of proofs. It didn't happen like that – very frustrating. (Larkin, 1983, 49)

Describing the novels as conduits to sumptuous living was both jocular and disingenuous. Perhaps a more accurate account of Larkin's decision to stop writing novels can be found in material written in 1950, a time when Larkin's novel-writing crisis was at its most intense.

Dubbed 'a Shavian dialogue' by Motion (1993, 190), and built around a version of 'Fiction and the Reading Public', *Round the Point* (1950) is a debate between two characters, Geraint and Miller, concerning the reasons for Geraint's lack of novel-writing success. As well as the debate's relevance to Larkin's literary impasse in the early 1950s, the protagonists' opposing positions correspond to the collision of conventional and unconventional views pervasive in Larkin's prose since the Coleman texts. Geraint is a serious writer for whom writing should 'find out the truth about life' (BTH, 2002, 478). His literary ambitions make him view readers with élitist distaste: 'whereas [Life] runs through them like a couple of pints of beer the writer transfixes it for what it is in imaginative terms' (BTH, 2002, 479). Though he seeks to distance himself from autodidacticism – the 'stupid Stockport bank clerk, forming his style in the evenings on Pater and Ruskin' (BTH, 2002, 475) – his arguments rely on the patronising supposition that his perceptions are superior to those of ordinary mortals. Ultimately, Geraint's principal failure, like Larkin's in the novel fragments, is believing that 'A writer's work should embody what life has taught him' (BTH, 2002, 480). Subsequently, Miller, who is a believer in the common touch, takes considerable delight in debunking the clichés for success that Geraint holds dear.

Miller begins his assault by breaking the customary links between sign and signified. Responding to Geraint's frustration at being unproductive, he tells him that he is 'deficient in a writer's qualities' and that these are 'Stupidity. Complacency. Insensitivity' (BTH, 2002, 475). For Miller, such qualities are to 'be found in every well-known man of letters, particularly in the "great" category'. Miller's case is necessarily argued in comic tones, though, as elsewhere, it has the effect of rupturing orthodox notions of what is valuable and what is not. Sweeping aside the need to produce serious art, Miller prioritises a good read over moral issues advising Geraint to get 'a certain feeling for the yahoo's point of view' and to 'meet your reader on all fours' (BTH, 2002, 476). Just as important as the plot is the requirement that the writer actually enjoys what he does: 'No one will enjoy reading what you did not enjoy writing' (BTH, 2002, 478). Despite Larkin's remark that 'Deprivation is for me what daffodils were for Wordsworth' (Larkin, 1983, 47), the novel fragments' 'anatomising of [Geraint / Larkin's] dreary experiences' (BTH, 2002, 482) would hardly have been inspirational for the writer, and would doubtless have impeded the books' completion. Accordingly, Miller finishes hectoring Geraint by identifying a 'hash up [of] certain events in [Geraint's] life' (BTH, 2002, 480) as unsuitable material for novels.

The first debate shows us that Larkin's enduring artistic instinct – to question and subvert conventional beliefs and established ideals – is best served by the dialogic interplay of opposing voices. Larkin wrote a competent, if derivative, play which, like 'Church Going', 'Toads' and 'Poetry of Departures' employs the debating method in obvious ways (CP, 97, 89, 85). 'Lines on a Young Lady's Photograph Album', 'Deceptions', 'The Whitsun Weddings' and 'This Be The Verse' rely on a more subtle colliding of attitudes and personae (CP, 71, 32, 114, 180). Larkin never abandoned his prose skills, but incorporated them into a poetry which allowed this dialectic impulse to flourish. If *Round the Point* provides clues as to why Larkin stopped writing novels, his second debate, *Round Another Point* (1951), corroborates the pervasive interest in sexual politics in his fiction.

From the outset, Geraint argues aggressively against marriage, seeing it as 'a confession you can't get women by any other means' and is 'just the end of you, socially, intellectually, [and] financially' (BTH, 2002, 487). He develops his case against 'the matrimonial mouse-wheel' (BTH, 2002, 490) by disputing Miller's claim that marriage is recommended by 'Nature' and 'Society'. For Geraint neither of these has a stake in the moral high ground: 'Nature advocates bubonic plague and syphilis. Society advocates war and lynching-parties' (BTH, 2002, 495). The anti-establishment stance on sexual politics in the fiction and the Sutton letters is still a major concern for Larkin in 1951.

Anticipating the 'debates' of later poems, Miller counters the assumption that marriage is synonymous with sacrifice and suffering. He argues that it can also be tolerant, balanced and enjoyable:

> realise this: the ordinary fellow LIKES the recurrent intimacies of marriage, they LIKE each other's familiar presence, they LIKE buying a house and furnishing it and having a place where they can tell the rest of the world to go to hell. They LIKE having children, they LIKE guiding their first tottering steps, and buying cricketbats and fishingrods and partyfrocks [sic]. (BTH, 2002, 496)

Thus, whilst the debate addresses an unresolved conflict – between celibacy and marriage – for Larkin it also provides a clear outline of the issues contested throughout the fiction. Subversive attitudes towards national as well as sexual politics characterise not only the later poems but also the early poems, which many critics find vacuous and uncertain.

To read the fiction in its entirety is to recognise that Larkin can no longer be caricatured as a reactionary writer with sexist and racist tendencies. The aesthetic structure of the novels – both finished and unfinished – reveal an artistic consciousness which questions and challenges conservative beliefs. In the unpublished letters to Sutton in the early 1940s, and in certain episodes of *Jill* and *A Girl in Winter*, Larkin is in fact creating a subversion of dominant protocols. The later fiction displays a bitter impatience with traditional mores, despite its encumbrance with Larkin's personal angst.

3

Auden, MacNeice and James Sutton

The Construction of a Subversive Aesthetic in the 1940s Poems

The imaginative and symbolic landscape of *The North Ship* is similar to that of *A Girl in Winter*; it also shares the latter's rejection of establishment values and conventional ideals. However, modern commentators have largely ignored the volume's specific attitudes to social and political realities. Prompted by Larkin's hints in the Introduction to the 1966 edition, Philip Gardner describes *The North Ship* as 'dominated by the influence of Yeats' and goes on to condemn the volume as not 'having proceeded out of a *particular* experience' (Gardner, 1968, 89). Timms also identifies the volume's 'lack of particularity, which makes [the poems] insubstantial' and his overall impression is that *The North Ship* 'will not bear the very close critical reading that is appropriate to Larkin's mature work' (Timms, 1973, 28, 22). Other critics have similarly gauged *The North Ship* by the standards of Larkin's later output: for Lolette Kuby the volume is 'immature' (Kuby, 1974, 160) while to Brownjohn 'the later Larkin *is* [there], though writ very small' (Brownjohn, 1975, 6). Petch claims that *The North Ship* 'hardly foreshadows . . . either the interests or the methods of Larkin's later work . . . Everything is impressionistic, and nothing is analysed in any depth' (Petch, 1981, 19–20). For Whalen *The North Ship* poems are 'quite pale' (Whalen, 1986, 29), whilst to Roger Day they show a 'vagueness of the emotions' (Day, 1987, 29). Motion is more specific about their failings: the poems are 'almost all languorously drooping in their rhythms and uninventively romantic in their references. They frequently borrow direct from Yeats . . . Their mood is invariably gloomy without justification, their time of day dawn or dusk, their weather cold, rainy and windy, and their symbolic details monotonous' (Motion, 1982, 33). Everett also criticises the volume's 'extreme unsociability' (Hartley, 1988, 142). However, some judgements are more positive: Rossen suggests that *The North Ship* 'often *appears* to be a Yeatsian pastiche' (my emphasis, Rossen, 1989, 25), implying that occasionally the volume rises above this, and Booth holds that 'in a minor way, [the poems are] distinctive and original' evincing at times 'the authentic voice of Larkin himself' (BTH, 1992, 64–5).

Not all commentators criticise *The North Ship* for the absent 'true voice' of the later Larkin. Swarbrick warns against the 'tendency to overlook [*The North Ship's*] most immediate circumstances which contribute to its opaqueness and sense of threat' (Swarbrick, 1995, 23), citing Larkin himself: 'one had to live through the forties at one's most impressionable time and . . . a lot of poems I wrote . . . were very much of the age' (Hamilton, 1964, 72). Regan illustrates an element of social awareness in the early poems and the projected volume, *In the Grip of Light*. He ascribes this partly to Auden, though he also sees in the early poems a 'general sense of dissatisfaction and unfulfilment associated with wartime Britain . . . In comparison, the later poems in *The North Ship* might well appear oblique and withdrawn' (Regan, 1992, 69). Elsewhere, however, Regan highlights the shared content of *The North Ship* and *Poetry from Oxford in Wartime* (1945), which 'ought to remind us that *The North Ship* is itself a wartime collection of poems, however derivative or immature they might appear' (BTH, 2000, 123). Appraising a selection of Larkin's 1940s poems in the light of archival evidence clarifies Larkin's symbolic framework during this period. As well as addressing wartime frustrations, Larkin's 1940s poetry overturns a more widespread set of conventions in a way that most commentators have failed to recognise.

Rather than searching the 1966 Introduction for *The North Ship*'s sources, we might look for its genesis elsewhere in Larkin's musings. The volume undoubtedly contains elements of 'Yeatsian pastiche' (Rossen, 1989, 25), but its combination of the lyric with the politically orientated is typically Audenesque. Larkin's youthful obsession with Auden is well-known – praising *Look, Stranger!* in 1941, he tells Sutton: 'When I read stuff like this I tend to fold up and die' (Thwaite, 1992, 28) – and in 1960 Larkin identifies the features of his idol that he particularly admires. He dismisses Auden's later work as 'too intellectual' when compared to his early writing which 'put poetry at the service of the working-class movement'. Enthusing about 'this tremendously exciting English social poet', Larkin remembers him as 'concerned with the historic necessities of the age' and as 'so committed to [his] period'. The subjects of his commitment are 'the Depression, strikes, the hunger marchers . . . Spain and China', and Larkin reads in Auden 'a sense that things needed a new impetus from somewhere'. These remarks reveal Larkin's interest in a poetry of radical political idealism and Larkin recognised in Auden something 'akin to the healer and the explorer' (Larkin, 1983, 123–4), referring to *Letters from Iceland* (1937) as an example of Auden's subversive 1930s style. Auden's exploration of unorthodox social and political territory in *Letters from Iceland* is adapted by Larkin in *The North Ship*. Later, Larkin enquires: 'Auden has always been brilliant at prose parody – did he write "Hetty to Nancy"?' (Larkin, 1983, 126). It was MacNeice, and not Auden, who wrote the spoof schoolgirl correspondence in *Letters from Iceland*, in order to articulate social and sexual tensions. The adoption of a female pseudonym was a strategy that also fascinated Larkin, and he utilised it in both the Coleman fiction and in *Jill*. Auden and MacNeice's influence on Larkin can also be seen in 'Last Will and Testament' (CP, 250), which Larkin and Noel Hughes wrote for *The Coventrian* as a farewell to King Henry VIII School. The poem is light-hearted in tone but the original by Auden and MacNeice is highly critical of 'city-crowded Europe' and the impending 'war's eruption' (LFI, 1937, 228–9). The subversive attitudes of *Letters from Iceland* provided one of the major sources for Larkin's critical idiom in *The North Ship*.

The Journey North

In the Foreword to *Letters from Iceland*, Auden states the work's intentions: 'Though writing in a "holiday" spirit, its authors were all the time conscious of a threatening horizon to their picnic – world-wide unemployment, Hitler growing every day more powerful and a world-war more inevitable'. Describing Iceland as having 'the most magical light . . . on earth' where 'modernity does not seem to have changed the character of the inhabitants', Auden conceives of the island as a 'classless society' where 'they have not – not yet – become vulgar' (LFI, 1937, 10). 'Journey to Iceland' offers that country as an alternative to the insidious urban decadence of the south:

> And each port has a name for the sea,
> The citiless, the corroding, the sorrow.
> And North means to all: 'Reject!'
> (LFI, 1937, 23)

If the journey northwards grants Auden and MacNeice an escape from convention, leaving home also 'make[s] one reflect on one's past and one's culture from the outside' (LFI, 1937, 139). Topics for scrutiny include traditional attitudes to sexuality, the work ethic, and an increasingly mechanistic way of life. In 'A Letter to Christopher Isherwood', Auden tells his friend that 'the sex life' on Iceland is 'Uninhibited' and that 'There is little stigma attached to illegitimacy' (LFI, 1937, 27). Living in Britain under restrictive homosexuality laws, Auden would have found Iceland's tolerant views liberating. Elsewhere, MacNeice fictionalises his Icelandic experiences in a parody of a schoolgirl's letter in which he challenges the conventional sexual politics of marriage. Hetty reflects on a friend's warning against the institution:

> She is afraid that I will become servile. I tell her that Robin is much too vague for anyone to be servile to him but she maintains that that makes him all the more dangerous and that I shall have to spend my time running after him with his season ticket. M. says only unintelligent women ought to get married. She would prefer me to have a career like yours, darling . . . (LFI, 1937, 166)

As in Larkin's fiction, the parodic style is profoundly disdainful of the way that women's independence is curtailed by marriage. Larkin's specific references to 'Hetty to Nancy' in 'What's Become of Wystan?' (Larkin, 1983, 126) and the tale's resemblance to Larkin's own girls' school stories – both stylistically and in its subversive sentiment – suggests that 'Hetty to Nancy' was a model for the Coleman fiction. In *Trouble at Willow Gables* the Headmistress is uncompromisingly authoritarian in her treatment of the girls and Hetty also describes a Head who wants 'everything to be right and tight in her own little hive and doesn't care a hang for the girls' lives as individuals' (LFI, 1937, 191). At the end of Larkin's novella, the sexual frisson that Margaret derives from horse riding is strikingly similar to Hetty's experience 'when . . . you plop up and down in the saddle to a perfectly regular rhythm' (LFI, 1937, 188). Both writers use schoolgirl fiction parodically to criticise repressive authoritarian culture and the journey north represents a release from social and religious constriction. Accordingly, Hetty is 'blunted and crippled by . . . early religious instruction' and regards 'Iceland [as] one of the few places where you don't feel it in the air when it's Sunday (LFI, 1937, 192). Booth claims that Larkin's Coleman novellas were inspired by the girls' school novelist, Dorita Fairlie Bruce (BTH, 2002, xvii) but it is equally likely that Larkin acquired the genre's subversive potential from MacNeice.

All of the contributions to *Letters from Iceland* underline the need to exchange city pressures for a natural existence in the north. Nowhere is this more apparent than in MacNeice's poem 'Letter to Graham and Anne Shepard':

> we must mortify
> Our blowsy intellects before we die,
> Who feed our brains on backchat and self-pity
> And always need a noise, the radio or the city,
> Traffic and changing lights, crashing the amber,
> Always on the move and so do not remember
> The necessity of the silence of the islands,
> The glacier floating in the distance out of existence . . .
> (LFI, 1937, 30)

A similar realm of sublime liberation is evident in *The North Ship* where the instinctual seeks to conquer the artificial. 'Never were hearts more eager to be free, / To kick down worlds' proclaims the speaker of 'Love, we must part now' and, dissatisfied with the fruits of contemporary human endeavour, he continues: 'we are husks, that see / The grain going forward to a different use' (CP, 280). Repeatedly, *Letters from Iceland* calls for a utopia which puts human potential to a 'different use' where 'European . . . fanatical patriotism' (LFI, 1937, 27) becomes 'a different rhythm, [when] the juggled balls / Hang in the air' and where 'we can take a breath, sit back, admire / Stills from the film of life, the frozen fire' (LFI, 1937, 32). The imagery chimes with that of 'Is it for now or for always' in *The North Ship* (CP, 296) where 'suns [are] like a juggler's juggling-balls'. 'Letter to Graham and Anne Shepard' reappraises the tired maxims that govern our lives:

> Among these rocks can roll upon the tongue
> Morsels of thought, not jostled by the throng,
> Or morsels of un-thought, which is still better,
> (Thinking these days makes a suburban clatter).
> Here we can practise forgetfulness without
> A sense of guilt, fear of the tout and lout . . .
> (LFI, 1937, 33)

In *Letters from Iceland*, as in *The North Ship*, gulls, breezes, rocks, ice and waves symbolise how nature gives solace to those maddened by human codes and institutions. In 'Letter to Lord Byron' the speaker has 'had the benefit of northern breezes' (LFI, 1937, 198); in MacNeice's 'Epilogue' 'the gulls . . . weave a free / Quilt of rhythm on the sea' (LFI, 1937, 252) and in 'Iceland' the 'glacier's licking / Tongues deride / Our pride of life' (LFI, 1937, 226). Any interpretation of *The North Ship* must take into account Larkin's adaptation of the symbolic framework used by Auden and MacNeice in *Letters from Iceland*. Rather than being 'insubstantial' (Timms, 1973, 28), *The North Ship*'s use of such a framework allowed Larkin to articulate the same political questioning that inspired his mentor in 1937.

As well as the quest for alternative models of social organisation, *Letters from Iceland* also calls for a more tolerant perspective on personal identity and gender roles; *The North Ship* is similarly intent on disturbing settled assumptions about sexual politics. For some critics, searching Larkin's work for progressive views on sexuality is anathema. Incensed at the 'derogatory remarks about women' in the *Selected Letters* (1992), Lisa Jardine assumes that such posturing adequately summarises Larkin's beliefs. Regan, however, criticises Jardine for 'simplifying the relationship between the letters and the poems, and for seeming to make "political correctness" the only criterion of value' (Regan, 1997, 5). Far from being politically *in*correct there is evidence to show that even in the 1940s Larkin was steadfastly opposed to misogyny and chauvinism.

Larkin's sympathetic concern for women's marginalised status was considerable and is expressed at various points in his unpublished papers. Nowhere is it so poignant as in an autobiographical fragment in Workbook 5, where Larkin resents his father's attitude towards his daughter. According to Sydney, Catherine was 'little better than a mental defective, who was showing regrettably few signs of marrying and clearing out'. Larkin recalls how his sister was persecuted for her 'qualities of . . . fantasy-spinning' that had so 'infuriated [his] father till he made her life a misery'. Catherine led 'a pallid existence until she took up art, and even then day-classes at midland art schools did not lead to the excitements they should have' (u/p fragments, 1945). In the letters he wrote to her from Oxford in 1941 Larkin's own attitude towards Catherine was respectful and supportive. They document the rapport that existed between Larkin and his sister on a range of issues such as politics, literature and the war.

The letters acknowledge a shared student solidarity between two artistic natures: 'the university,' Larkin imagines, 'is no more composed of sensitive undergraduates than the Teachers' Assoc. is composed of sensitive teachers' and in the same letter he implores Catherine to visit him as he is anxious about his studies: 'My exam is June 12th. Can't you possibly get here for a day – even by car or something?' (u/p letter, 24.v.41). Larkin attempts to unite their two circles of friends: 'If you ever meet a WAAF in Loughborough College called Betty Williams I am very friendly with her brother David' (u/p letter, 28.x.41). In another letter Larkin respectfully sets his sister's training college on a par with Oxford, in the salutation 'Hail, and all hail, from one seat of learning to another' (u/p letter, 15.x.41). Larkin vigorously encouraged Catherine in her studies. Commenting on her full timetable he tells her 'you have plenty to occupy your mind' and he admires her tenacity in 'ceaselessly adapting [her] personality to the different subjects and classes' concluding that she is 'very clever to be able to do it' (u/p letter, 14.xi.41). Larkin not only urged success for Catherine, sending her 'Best wishes for [her] esperriment [sic] in the modern theatre' (u/p letter, 28.x.41), he also gratefully received her views on his writing, recording Catherine's opinion of 'Ultimatum'[1] as '"sincere" and "passionate"' (u/p letter, 18.ii.41) and he involves her in his enthusiasm for Oxford discussion. Telling Catherine that he had 'joined an elementary psychology group under John Layard', Larkin writes to her as an intellectual equal in an exposition of Layard's creed: 'every rise in moral, social, and spiritual-God values is accompanied by an equal fall in animal, individual, and natural instincts' (u/p letter, 15.v.41). Larkin's discussion of this with his sister is significant in terms of understanding *The North Ship*, which is preoccupied with the marginalised status of women and with the flight from artifice to nature.

The most striking feature of Larkin's brief correspondence with his sister is the way that he confides in Catherine a subversive attitude towards the war. Reflecting upon 'the sudden appearance of Hess' he informs Catherine that he is only 'mildly' interested (u/p letter, 15.v.41), and he delights in reporting Norman Iles's 'constant prayer' that we should '"hurry up and lose"' (u/p letter, 24.v.41). Throughout, there is a feeling that brother and sister are in collusion against the dominant pull-together ethos of wartime Britain. The extent of this shared dissident politics is particularly evident when Larkin complains of the new 'condition of residence' for wartime students:

> This is merely part of the govt's scheme to reduce Oxford to a Combined Technical College and Officer Cadets Training Unit, and which is causing much annoyance. I enclose a leaflet for you to peruse at your leisure. (u/p letter, 24.v.41)

The leaflet was issued by the University Labour Federation and it is utterly hostile to the government's proposed wartime strategy for education in the early 1940s (see Appendix, p. 185). Years later, it 'was on Larkin's instructions that the Brynmor Jones Library built up its Labour Archive, with the Fabian Society Library as chief treasure'. As Clive James notes, this sits oddly with the popular perception of Larkin as 'a rabid reactionary' (James, 2001a, 111–12). Larkin's sending of the leaflet to Catherine stresses his desire to include her in a debate that is highly crit-

---

[1] The poem calls for 'the need for emigration: / . . . For on our island . . . / There are no tickets for the Vale of Peace'. The speaker instructs that 'we must build our walls, for what we are / Necessitates it, and we must construct / The ship to navigate behind them' (CP, 243). There is a sense here of a shared cause in standing against hostile forces and the maritime imagery anticipates *The North Ship*'s charting of new social principles.

ical of establishment practice. Just as Larkin gives his fictional women, Augusta Bax and Katherine Lind, a political voice, so, in his letters, he encourages his sister to take a stand against perceived injustice. It is no accident that Catherine shares the same name, albeit with a different initial, as Larkin's protagonist in *A Girl in Winter*.

Much has been made of how Larkin presented different 'selves' in his letters, depending upon who the recipient was, though much of the anti-establishment rhetoric that he wrote to Catherine is similar to the rejection of convention contained in the letters to Sutton. These letters are shot through with subversive views on a variety of topics, and now it is possible to scrutinise the other side of this important literary correspondence.

Sutton's wartime letters to Larkin sustain a friendship which is threatened by war. One letter refers to the dire communication problems: 'I write under difficulties. I lay on my side on the bed & write round the respirator case on my chest. I think of you in red trousers & envy you' (u/p letter, 1941). The two friends nurtured each other's self-esteem throughout this traumatic period. Sutton assured Larkin: 'I have faith in you as a writer if that's any good to you. You certainly improve like merry hell' (u/p letter, 25.iv.41), and after reading one of Larkin's letters, Sutton remembers it 'like a meal divine, the holy wafer in which one partakes of Christ' (u/p letter, 19.vii.41). For his part, Larkin recalls their banter on artistic matters: 'Ah, if only we could get together again and you stuff my poems in your cavernous pipe, and I put my feet through your canvases two at a time as of old' (u/p letter, 5.viii.42).

Sutton's letters corroborate Larkin's sense of a collaboration: 'We have the same type of makeup [sic] more or less & it is natural that a writer should be able to paint a bit & a painter write a bit' (u/p letter, 1941). Larkin's fiction has an affinity with the pictorial and Sutton's letters show how he was influenced by his friend's bookishness. Reading *Lady Chatterley's Lover*, Sutton is struck by 'The vivid impression of decline of England & the evil of the modern industrial spirit & its power to crush Connie & Mellors' (u/p letter, 16.iv.51). Like Lawrence's characters when they are confronted by forces threatening communality Sutton is oppressed, and he objects to his military involvement claiming 'The War is terrible' (u/p letter, 3.viii.41) and 'The Army deadens me' (u/p letter, 41), telling Larkin that he 'want[s] to desert to be with friends (= you) again' (u/p letter, 19.vii.41). Throughout the correspondence, Sutton allies Larkin to his own revulsion from the war, advising his friend that 'it would be wrong for you to join up' (u/p letter, 14.iv.41) and that 'The Army is often painful for a sensitive or thoughtful man' (u/p letter, 41). This anti-war feeling is discussed in quasi-religious tones: 'The first day or two in the army are pure hell' (u/p letter, 14.iv.41) and Sutton preaches 'by god we've all got to be born again, we not the least. I don't feel very proud to be English, no suh!' (u/p letter, *c.*1950). Sutton promoted his friend's subversive attitudes by unwittingly providing prototypes for Larkin's master images in the 1940s:

> I have a feeling you won't like the Army. At first it is like being plunged into ice cold water . . . After about 3 months it goes stagnant & you have a sensation of being suffocated, you are in the water all the time & can't get out. (u/p letter, 1941)

This is reminiscent of how entrapment and limitation are expressed in terms of being submerged or frozen in *The North Ship* and *A Girl in Winter*. As an artist, Sutton was acutely conscious of the power of symbolism, and he discusses its significance frequently, claiming to 'draw in symbols to a large extent' (u/p letter, 1941). A sketch of himself – in the throes of drowning beneath naval vessels – is particularly poignant:

In unpublished letter (18.v.42)

Sutton evokes the pointlessness of soldiering by constantly referring to adverse weather: 'Today has been hell-cold, it has snowed & we have been arsing about in the wide open spaces watching tanks in action & being snowed on' [sic] (u/p letter, 30.x.41). Sutton's descriptions of war's numbing effects inform the imaginative landscape of *A Girl in Winter* and *The North Ship*, texts which consistently utilise wintry conditions to express hardship and exclusion.

Sutton's wartime correspondence was an influential source for Larkin's symbolic framework in the 1940s. Sailing towards an unknown destination, Sutton records: 'There is a lot to say about this voyage but we are not allowed unfortunately but it is an adventure . . . & until I have to become a real soldier for self preservation I shall more or less enjoy it' [sic] (u/p letter, 3.viii.42). In the same year he describes the ship which carries him to war as 'a marvel, every part essential . . . man can feel himself the greatest god on earth . . . but this is prevented by masses of men & huge mechanical things' (u/p letter, 1942). There is an impression here of cutting loose from what is expected and customary, yet also of being under threat from large, impersonal forces that sideline human strivings. Sutton's wartime travels and their mode of expression gave Larkin the motifs and symbols for his own quest in *The North Ship*, a quest for an alternative ideology to that which ill-treated his friend and turned him into 'a real soldier' in the name of patriotism and duty.

If the literary devices in *A Girl in Winter* and *The North Ship* are similar to those of Sutton's letters, these texts also share with the correspondence a disruption of conventional models of sexuality and gendered behaviour. Temperamentally unsuited to the machismo culture of army life, Sutton informs Larkin that 'the sensitive part of one is hurt too much amonst [sic] these people'. Distancing himself from the soldiers' coarse sexist attitudes towards girls, Sutton continues: 'Crumpet talk is disgusting revolting . . . in the mouths of crude bastards such as you often get [in the army]' (u/p letter, 14.ix.41). Just as Sutton challenges fixed assumptions about war service, so he rejects a construction of masculinity that demeans women. Another letter explores Sutton's discomfort with 'the pose of being manly' and he emboldens himself, as well as his reader, to 'Be yourself first you won't be any the less manly & probably more manly'. Sutton longs to escape the version of maleness that army life encourages: 'At Oxford I am more myself. In the Army I appear more manly on the surface but am merely twisted & chaotic inside' (u/p letter, 30.x.41). For Jung, 'men have – carefully guarded and hidden – a very soft emotional life, often incorrectly described as "feminine"' (*Collected Works VII*, paras 296–301); this sense of exploring beneath the surface mask of human personality is highlighted in another passage that echoes the language and imagery of Larkin's early publications. Advising Larkin on characterisation, Sutton lectures:

> to have a well founded character one must mirror all the life beneath the surface as well as above. One must realise that 9 tenths of an iceberg lie beneath the surface so essential to the tenth part.' (u/p letter, 6.viii.44)

Sutton's interest in aspects of character usually kept hidden would have fuelled Larkin's advocacy of alternative models of personality and sexuality. Rejecting the army's definition of 'manly' as too narrow, Sutton destabilises the 'natural' model for sexual relationships:

> Say you look at a woman & think she's pretty but are not attracted to her in <u>anyway</u> (there is more than one way of being attracted to a woman) than this mental feeling ie. not a feeling at all but founded on convention of cosmetics big eyes, small nose small mouth yellow hair . . . [sic] (u/p letter, 19.vii.41)

Sutton's exposé of how sexuality is culturally determined is detached from the dominant male sexual behaviour of the time. A frequent complaint against Larkin is that he was a rampant nationalist and a sexist bigot. However, such a view overlooks the extent to which he shared with Sutton a radical questioning of settled assumptions – about the war, capitalism and gender issues – which impacts on his writing in the form of symbols and motifs, and which appeared in embryonic form in these wartime letters.

In her book, *Reconstructing Women's Wartime Lives*, Penny Summerfield recalls the officially approved representation of masculinity during the Second World War:

> posters depicted soldiers in the thick of battle jumping from aircraft, firing guns and sinking ships, their lifelikeness enhanced by details such as their clothing, sometimes in tatters which revealed muscular bodies, and their resolute facial expressions. (Summerfield, 1998, 120)

This evaluation of masculinity with a strong desire to fight is opposed in 'Conscript' (CP, 262), a Shakespearean sonnet of three quatrains and a couplet. Larkin dedicated the poem to Sutton 'as a token of high regard' (u/p letter, 19.xi.44), though 'Conscript' was written three years earlier in 1941 when Larkin was reading Sutton's poignantly expressed objections to army life. The poem is powerfully alert to the resentment caused by enlisting civilians for military service, and each stage in the subject's 'story' is examined from a range of perspectives.

The first stanza reveres the balanced individual who has 'inherited' an identity that has been lovingly 'tended' like a farmer's field. He is an educated man, a possessor of 'All knowledge' who has a sufficient understanding of both 'good and bad'. However, the stanza is suffused with disillusioned cynicism. As something to be 'inherited', 'The ego's county' suggests self-interest and the need to tend it signals the brittle nature of preserving a selfish ideology. The claim to 'All knowledge' is undercut as the subject learns only 'that [which] the study merited' implying a prescribed curriculum designed to condition and brainwash. In the last line 'The *requisite* contempt of good and bad' (my emphasis) hints, menacingly, at the 'correct' internalisation of a morality which 'good' citizens should possess.

The next stanza continues by blurring the divisions between categories that are traditionally distinct and easily recognisable. Applying the terms 'violated' and 'curtly' to the enlisting officers problematises the identity of the subject's true enemy. 'A bunch of horsemen' conveys the idea of a gangster-like mob rather than fair-minded officialdom and their 'different dialect' signals an ideological conflict between the potential conscript and the state apparatus.

The subject's recruitment is brought about not by physical coercion but by eliciting guilt about identity and duty to nation. The subject is told 'he was to blame' and that 'he must help them'. The finality of 'stated', and the strong assertive tone ('he *was*', 'he *must*') underline the self-righteous attitudes that demand compliance with the patriotic ideal. There is a brusque, attitudinising 'voice' in this stanza which bullies the subject into acquiescence. His 'assent' is 'founded on . . . self-effacement', the genteel bourgeois practice of outwardly respecting what we inwardly loathe, those 'sternly . . . instilled / . . . routines' of 'Vers de Société' which 'shows us what should be' (CP, 181). The subject defers to these to maintain his 'birthright', which rejection of military service might jeopardise. The word 'brave', appearing at the end of the line as a masculine syllable, bears the cargo of dutiful self-sacrifice which pressurises the subject into joining up far more than 'official' reprisals ever could. The next line, 'For nothing would be easier than replacement,' suggesting a possible last minute avoidance of conscription, hints at the interchangeability of different human cogs in the machinery of war. The subject's 'brave' rejection of the possibility of replacement implies an acceptance of individual responsibility, which echoes the sense at the start of the poem that his is the 'ego's county'. This might be seen as a positive affirmation of the individual identity of the human spirit as opposed to the mass conscription of war. Alternatively, there is the possibility that part of the motive is self-interest ('In order not to lose his birthright') and even if a nobler motive is accepted, it is worth asking whether this has intrinsic value, or if it is merely a reflection of a wartime ideology designed to promote self-sacrifice, which may prove to be futile. The implication is that the subject will either die fighting, or feel the guilt of not having lived up to ideals 'tended' in him by establishment wartime thinking. This sense of conflict, not with an external enemy, but with an ingrained set of beliefs, is also addressed in Auden's 'Far from the heart of culture he was used' (*The English Auden*, 258). Auden's poem considers the predicament of the soldier who 'neither knew nor chose the Good'. As in Larkin's poem, there is an acute sense of the subject's subservience to 'Innate assumptions' (CP, 153) that exert a powerful influence over attitudes to war and conscription.

The complexity of the different possible attitudes juxtaposed in 'Conscript' is mirrored by the structure of the verse. The regular iambic pentameter and strong full rhymes in the first two stanzas provide a powerful sense of inevitability. The third stanza ends with a softer, more questioning feminine rhyme suggesting a reflective tone as the question of motivation is explored; in the final couplet feminine endings combine with imperfect (and therefore uncertain) rhyme to produce a troubled resolution. The subject follows 'The details of his own defeat' all along implying complicity on his part – though he only dimly perceives being duped by false ideals, he is still powerless to resist the ideological pressure which results in the tragic consequences of being a dutiful and patriotic soldier. 'So you have been, despite parental ban' also questions the purpose of war: 'That name for which you fought – does it quite fit?' and 'Spring Warning' criticises those who 'follow with their eye / The muffled boy, with his compelling badge' (1940, CP, 236, 237). Jardine criticises Larkin's writing for lacking '"humane"' qualities (Regan, 1997, 5) but these poems are as opposed to patriarchal culture as Woolf's *Three Guineas*, in which the author confronts the antagonistic male:

> you are fighting to gratify a sex instinct which I cannot share; to procure benefits which I have not shared and probably will not share; but not to gratify my instincts, or to protect either myself or my country . . . I want no country. (Woolf, 1938, 125)

Women's alienation from the dominant male culture is also addressed in 'Like the train's beat' (CP, 288). Taking advantage of the clearer vision made possible by a train journey (in 'The Whitsun Weddings' the carriage has 'All windows down' [CP, 114]), the speaker of 'Like the train's beat' observes a foreign girl in the corner of a railway compartment. Arrested by the light on the girl's face and the way that her hair is tousled by the breeze, he becomes fascinated by her foreign speech. Though incomprehensible to him, he still perceives how the girl's presence mysteriously transforms a blighted landscape.

Comparing the girl's rapid talk to the rhythmical movement of the train conveys the girl's natural pulse and the opening simile recalls the traveller's habit of imposing a spoken refrain upon the sound of the wheels on the track – a sound which alternates between being acutely audible and barely discernible. The odd 'flutters' of the girl's speech fail to communicate with the speaker, though, as yet, the 'message' is unclear. Significantly, it is the 'Swift language' that is the subject: it 'flutters the lips' of the girl. This is crucially important as it suggests that the girl is an ideal conduit for whatever 'message' may ensue. As with John Kemp's journey to Oxford, there is a marked sense of the girl being on the fringes of social experience; she sits 'in the corner seat' and her Polish nationality sidelines her still further on what is, presumably, a British train. She is strongly associated with nature; the sun 'Lights her eyelashes' and 'shapes / Her sharp vivacity of bone'. Her 'wild and controlled' hair implies a natural though dignified assurance, but it also signals how something elemental has been restricted by wider cultural forces. At the end of the first stanza the girl connects with the speaker. Just as the 'English oaks' nod to the passing travellers, so the girl 'gestures' with a sweep of her hair. Both tree and girl are denied a 'voice', though the girl's message is as unmistakable as that of the oaks that symbolise the enduring power of nature.

'The train runs on through [a] wilderness / Of cities' and like the speaker of 'Going, Going', (CP, 189), the poem is contemptuous of urban sprawl. The line break after 'wilderness' delays the rupturing of conventional expectation and attention is drawn – in a manner reminiscent of *The Waste Land* (1922) – to compromised, urban lifestyles. The lines: 'Still the hammered miles / Diversify behind her face' suggest a landscape despoiled by industrialisation, which is then calmed, or made 'Still', by the girl's natural grace:

> Before her angled beauty falls,
> As whorling notes are pressed
> In a bird's throat, issuing meaningless
> Through written skies; a voice
> Watering a stony place.

Discussing how women are excluded from the 'dominant masculine ideology', Carolyn Burke notes that 'when a woman writes or speaks herself into existence, she is forced to speak in something like a foreign tongue, a language with which she may be uncomfortable' (see Showalter in Lodge and Wood, 2000, 316). Accordingly, the 'Polish airgirl' of the poem finds a language with which she is comfortable by rejecting formal verbal communication: the final image registers the power of instinctive forms of communication over those that are culturally fabricated. Despite being as 'meaningless' as the 'whorling notes . . . / In a bird's throat', the girl's 'angled beauty' reinvigorates the 'stony place' that modern society, with all its restrictions and regulations, has become. The syntax mimics the way in which natural empathy usurps the straitjacketing of spoken language: the insertion of 'Through written skies' fractures the 'narrative' of the last three lines by separating the subject (the 'bird's throat') from the object and predicate ('a voice / Watering a stony place'). Hearing the bird's notes 'Through written skies' implies the triumph of natural communication over what is 'written' or artificially constructed. For Tom Paulin, the girl speaks a 'language of the passions that Larkin is unable to understand' (Regan, 1997, 169) but the poem's entire aesthetic objective prefers a 'language of the passions' to a language of reason.

Composed in 1943, 'Like the train's beat' has much to say about those who were denied a voice by contemporary authoritarian regimes during the Second World War. Poland became the first victim of Nazi Germany in 1939, though the 'Polish airgirl' is not just a symbol for a persecuted nation – she also represents a woman employed in a specific wartime role. Larkin's poem addresses the precarious position of working women during the war, who remained subjugated by patriarchal attitudes despite having abandoned traditional 'feminine' roles. Advocating that natural instincts should influence human structures, the poem implies how a matriarchal society would redress the confrontational divisions of patriarchal culture.

In 1944 Larkin wrote to Sutton, quoting a line from his own poem 'I see a girl dragged by the wrists' (CP, 278): 'The strongest feeling I have these days is a double one – personal sorrow and impersonal joy. Everything that my personality colours is a balls up – my own affairs and so on. But when I am being "no more, no less than two weak eyes" everything is filled with a blessed light, bells, bugles, brightness and lord knows what. It's an odd feeling, and the split – which seems to widen day by day – is alarming' (u/p letter, 24.v.44). Larkin's 'personal sorrow' stemmed from anxiety over his writing and the ill-defined nature of his relationship with Ruth Bowman, exacerbated by the daily drudgery of his Wellington library job. By reflecting upon a series of symbolic episodes, the poem addresses the 'split' between different states of awareness and locates the frustrations of 'personality' in a wider cultural context that imposes settled notions of identity.

Whilst out walking, the speaker in 'I see a girl' is struck by the image of a girl who playfully struggles with her lover in a snow-covered field. Envying the uncomplicated pleasure that the girl enjoys, the speaker walks on until he sees two men clearing the snow. For a moment the latter image occludes the former, but the contrast between the speaker's misery and the girl's joy finally prompts him to seek solace in spiritual terms.

Significantly, the speaker identifies with the girl's submissive state as she is 'dragged' across the 'dazzling field of snow'. The location introduces the idea of seeing things in a changed or overpowering light. Just as the snow blurred the human divisions in *A Girl in Winter*, so here established perceptions are temporarily obscured. Larkin uses snow as a catalyst for new insights elsewhere in the ouevre. 'Thaw' refers to 'a hospital of snow' (1946–7, CP, 19) and in 'The Winter Palace' snow aids recovery from the 'damage' of formally acquired knowledge (1978, CP, 211). In 'I see a girl' the speaker finds 'nothing in [him] that resists', though his desire to emulate the girl's yielding nature is only recently acquired:

> Once it would not be so;
> Once I should choke with powerless jealousies;
> But now I seem devoid of subtlety . . .

In the past the speaker would have been jealous of the girl's male lover rather than empathising with her compliant state: he was 'choke[d]' by cultural pressures that dictated that jealousy was the appropriate response. Perceiving the scene differently in the present, he is 'now . . . devoid of subtlety', implying that he is aware of the contrived nature of conventional behaviour. The speaker completes his detachment from settled perspectives by 'Being no more, no less, than two weak eyes'. The speaker is free to perceive the world 'As simple as . . . [he] see[s]' without the clutter of conventional modes of perception and response to control his social and sexual identity. The desire to see *simply* anticipates the 'clear-eyed . . . realism' (Hartley, 1988, 299) of *The Less Deceived*, which is also concerned with new angles of vision.

The snow's symbolic import is reinforced in stanza two: it is now 'everywhere, / . . . in one blinding light' and 'Even . . . smudged in her hair'. By changing the appearance of the landscape, the snow encourages new contours of understanding: the 'blinding light' recalls the Platonic notion that over-illumination confuses established belief. The symbolism blurs the distinction between the snow and the girl whose affinity with nature separates her from the detached speaker:

> Nothing so wild, nothing so glad as she
> Rears up in me,
> And would not, though I watched an hour yet.

These lines suggest the speaker's separation from the girl's unbounded joy, but they also convey his failure to be sexually aroused by the girl. Depicting the girl as an impersonal natural phenomenon allowed Larkin to articulate his ambivalent feelings for Ruth Bowman. Motion points out that 'by changing her from real to unreal [he] secures for himself the freedom of solitude' (Motion, 1993, 127). What is clear from the poem is that the speaker is no longer attracted to the active role of getting the girl. His experiences are passive; from 'I see a girl' in stanza one through to 'I watched an hour yet' in stanza two, he reacts to his environment, rather than acts upon it. His feelings are described in terms which reflect an abdication of initiative: 'nothing in [him] . . . resists' rather than 'he does not resist' and 'nothing so glad . . . / Rears up in [him]' instead of 'he is not glad.' The speaker's desire for a passive role is reminiscent of Sutton's rejection of conventional notions of 'masculine' behaviour in his wartime letters.

To fulfil the 'sickly hope . . . to be / As she is' the speaker is thrown back on established structures:

> For the first time I'm content to see
> What poor mortar and bricks
> I have to build with, knowing that I can
> Never in seventy years be more a man
> Than now – a sack of meal upon two sticks.

This recalls 'A tattered coat upon a stick' ('Sailing to Byzantium', *W. B. Yeats: Selected Poetry*, 1991, 128) but echoes, too, other poems in which Yeats utilises construction metaphors. In Larkin's poem, the conventionally masculine building metaphor conveys how the speaker is pressurised to construct himself as 'a man'. Yeats's metaphors suggest the manufactured nature of personal identity: the speaker returns to 'where all the ladders start' in 'The Circus Animals' Desertion' (SP, 1991, 224); in 'Lapis Lazuli' (SP, 196) 'All things fall and are built again'; and 'The Gyres' (SP, 194) includes 'The workman' in its cyclical rebuilding of values and beliefs. These images form part of Yeats's continual need to assemble alternative conceptions of self. Timothy Webb observes that, for Yeats, 'identity was not so much a given or a solid and stable entity as an artificial construct' (SP, xv). In Larkin's poem the speaker has 'poor mortar' with which to build and so he struggles to attain the wisdom of Yeats's 'aged man' in 'Sailing to Byzantium'. Declaring to 'walk on' in stanzas three and four, the speaker continues his quest for an identity, though the imagery is negative. Within the poem's symbolic framework 'Clearing the drifts with shovels and a spade' dissolves the 'dazzling' new perception of stanza one and re-imposes a conventional outlook. The 'ragged men' who 'sweep the girl clean from [his] heart' suggest how the speaker's meditation is interrupted by reality, though their action also implies how societal pressures banish the 'feminine' aspects from his personality. The men 'stand coughing in the sun' after their task signalling their disharmony with nature and stanza five condemns their 'worn-out' attitudes, which are too readily prescriptive of conventional masculine behaviour.

The penultimate stanza tackles the speaker's frustration at being denied the identity he craves:

> To be that girl! – but that's impossible;
> For me the task's to learn the many times
> When I must stoop, and throw a shovelful:
> I must repeat until I live the fact
> That everything's remade
> With shovel and spade;
> That each dull day and each despairing act . . .

The speaker wants to experience life *as* a girl, which will bring him closer to nature and thereby allow him to discard the active role which is conventionally perceived as masculine. These lines also refer to the drudgery of writing that the (male) poet-speaker finds 'despairing'. In *Round the Point* (1950) Larkin describes his ideal creative imagination: 'The writer is feminine: his attitude to life is passive' (BTH, 2002, 479). There is a sense, then, in which the speaker's art, as well as his general existence, is hampered by his gender. Realising that a change of identity is 'impossible' the speaker resents his coercion into attitudes he despises; the browbeaten tone of 'For me the task's to learn' and 'When I must stoop' highlights how traditional male activity repeatedly oppresses the speaker. As before, the imagery of throwing, shovelling and manufacture are deemed to be suitable masculine occupations. Having to 'repeat' his labour 'many times' until 'everything's remade' suggests how the speaker is socialised by repeated exposure to certain actions which renders them 'natural' whereas, in reality, they are constructed by powerful cultural processes. Little wonder that, given the speaker's wish to cultivate other, more receptive traits to his personality, he finds 'each day dull'. Forced into adopting an identity he loathes, the speaker 'Builds' a platform 'from which the spirit leaps' into a Yeatsian realm where an 'image of a snow-white unicorn' provides 'sanctuary' against conventional masculine requirements.

The final stanza suggests that Art provides an antidote to the speaker's frustrations and this is described in a quasi-religious manner, as the 'golden horn' of the Muse 'Descend[s]' into his hand. Larkin over-poeticised and used excessive symbolism at this stage in his career, though the ending remains sensitive to sexual politics. Significantly, the speaker does nothing to receive the Muse's favours – it is 'put into [his] hand' and traditionally, unicorns can only be tamed by virgins. The soul – described as the 'beast most innocent' – signals a welcome release from the rather less innocent beast who 'choke[d]' to ravish the girl in stanza one. Thus, the retreat into aesthetic contemplation is another means of neutralising aggressive male instincts. 'I see a girl dragged by the wrists' is acutely conscious of alternative forms of masculinity, subverting established models and upsetting distinctions between 'male' and 'female' behaviour in its deliberate rejection of orthodox constructs of sexual identity.

In the volume's title poem, 'The North Ship' (CP, 302), Larkin adapted Auden and MacNeice's symbolic framework of *Letters from Iceland*. Here, the simple ballad form of the first section cloaks a serious quest for ideal types of social organisation. The image of the 'three ships' that sail to different points of the compass symbolises the various political structures that are possible. Confronting the elements during the journey (the rising 'wind' and 'the lifting sea'), each ship represents a man-made framework that is imposed on an indifferent natural realm. That 'one [ship] was rigged for a long journey' suggests that one idealistic goal is less attainable than the others. The first ship, however, follows a course that is well-charted and familiar:

> The first ship turned towards the west,
> Over the sea, the running sea,
> And by the wind was all possessed
> And carried to a rich country.

This journey is towards a consumerist destination, the ship's being 'all possessed' by the wind suggesting the possessive attitudes that capitalism invokes. The eastern-bound ship, on the other hand, is 'anchor[ed] in captivity', an allusion to the oppressive nature of Eastern bloc totalitarianism in the early 1940s.

Registering their well-defined routes, the first ships simply 'turned' towards their destinations, though the third ship 'drove towards the north', acknowledging the north ship's challenge in charting new territory. Suggesting hostility to unorthodox practice, the natural environment hinders the progress northwards; described earlier as a 'lifting' or 'running' sea, the now 'darkening sea', with 'no breath of wind' intensifies the sense of marooned isolation in alien waters. Like Auden and MacNeice's travels to Iceland, Larkin's journey north carries the freight of an urgent exploration of alternative culture which, at a time of international crisis, could only have been articulated in the mellifluous manner of 1940s new romanticism. Drifting far out from the known shores of convention is risky: unlike the first ships, which came home 'Happily or unhappily', the return of the north ship is uncertain. The vessel's 'unforgiving' and 'unfruitful' channel through cold waters suggests the frosty reception that new and radical attitudes are often met with. Arriving 'Under a fire-spilling star' in the section's last stanza, the questing north ship has identified an elemental dimension to societal organisation, as opposed to political principles that have been ideologically constructed. The imagery threatens an unbridled destructiveness that ensues from so radical a departure from conventional practices, which, despite their limitations, are known and workable.

Subsequent sections focus on the difficulties which confront those brave enough to seek out alternative cultures. The titles' juxtaposition of numerical compass bearings with the vaguely-termed 'Songs', 'Fortunetelling' and 'Blizzard' signals a clash between rational and intuitive forces. Their opposition illustrates how each world-view vies for control in the quester's consciousness. Alan Ross used a similar technique in 'J. W. 51 B: A Convoy' (*Poems 1942–67*, 1967):

> The Log Book written on a tilting desk,
> Records a position at noon on the 26th
> Of 68° 23′ North, 6° 32′ West . . .

Adam Piette notes that the poem 'reads like a logbook, with precise details of the movements of the convoy.' However, as Ross's poem develops, it becomes 'oddly but convincingly double: a poem of professional record and a poem of tender imagination. The double status of the poem rhymes with the double nature of the men on board' (Piette, 1995, 275):

> Each man waiting was two men,
> The man with Pay Book and number,
> A rank and duty, Sick Berth
> Tiffy, Torpedoman, Tanky
> And Stoker, and another man inside
> With a healthy fear of his own skin . . .

Piette points out how the war's rational impetus has wrought a profound change in identity, such that their inner imaginative life strives to transform the austere world of war into a camaraderie of affectionate nicknames. A similar questioning of rational categories is evident in Larkin's poem. Sceptical of the precise course set by the ship's compass in stanza one, the speaker has a nightmarish vision in which 'all things seem / Sickeningly to poise / On emptiness.' Conventionally thought of as overhead, the stars are now 'under the world'. The cautionary tone of the second stanza recalls Sutton's wartime letters, though Tony Lopez (1999) has noted links with 'The Rime of the Ancient Mariner' (1798):

> When waves fling loudly
> And fall at the stern,
> I am wakened each dawn
> Increasingly to fear
> Sail-stiffening air,
> The birdless sea.

Mindful of how the Mariner's killing of the albatross symbolised humanity's disdain for nature, Larkin's poem cautions against the hubris of trusting in man's designs. The fateful collision between the artificial and the elemental recalls Hardy's poem 'The Convergence of the Twain' in which the 'Immanent Will', in the guise of an iceberg, chastises man's arrogant conception of an 'unsinkable' Titanic (*Poems of Thomas Hardy*, 1977, 216). The poem also echoes Sutton's plight as he sailed to war in 1942:

> Yesterday, for a special reason, we went high up on the ship, usually prohibited, & whereas the men on the deck below got smaller the sea got bigger. The ship too seemed small because you could see the whole of its stern against the water, water both sides & behind fierce & lively & joyous & big . . . (u/p letter, 3.viii.42)

Sutton is concerned with a different angle of perception, 'usually prohibited', and *The North Ship*'s characteristic imagery – as in 'When waves fling loudly / And fall at the stern' – is also discernible. Elsewhere in his travels, Sutton recalls 'an intense feeling of the elemental strength & divineness of the universe' and despite sensing 'an all embracing love like God himself looking over his creation' he concludes that he is 'rather small & humble' (u/p letter, 3.viii.41). Sutton's voyage to war provided the scaffolding for Larkin's frightening yet uplifting vision of nature's magnitude and man's insignificance in the final stanza.

The verb 'strikes' conveys the ice's power to overwhelm and destroy, but also its ability to make death a 'serene breath' which grants unity with nature. Like the 'dazzling' snow in 'I see a girl', the ice facilitates a vision of elemental grandeur so that man's designs must either accommodate nature's principles or face the consequences. The 'dream' in which the speaker draws up a 'bargain' with nature is based on the philosophy that Larkin acquired in John Layard's seminars at Oxford. Enthusing about these sessions to Catherine in 1941, Larkin told her that 'The way of salvation lies not away from the instincts but into them' (u/p letter, 15.v.41) and it is the flight from the reasonable to the instinctual which occupies the third and fourth stanzas.

The ship's northerly course is plotted with mathematical certainty in contrast to the speaker's more intuitive progress. In 'Fortunetelling' a seer's voice informs the speaker that 'a dark girl will kiss [him]' at the end of the 'long journey'. Significantly, she kisses him 'As softly as the breast / Of an evening bird' recalling the 'birdless' sea of section two. Just as the Ancient Mariner sanctified his 'birdless' ship by blessing the water-snakes, so Larkin's speaker is reconciled to nature by a girl linked to the protectiveness of the 'nest'. In the second stanza the seer keeps the speaker's understanding instinctive rather than rational by telling him that the girl 'will cover your mouth / Lest memory exclaim / . . . it is the same / As one who long since died.' As in 'Like the train's beat' the orthodox means of communication and recognition, language and memory, are superseded by the natural empathy between the girl and the speaker. By obscuring the course ahead, the 'Blizzard' of the fourth section reiterates the folly of plotting a rigid course with the intellect. Reminiscent of the fusion of human and nature in 'I see a girl', the snow is 'as tangled / As a girl's thick hair.' Reaching the denouement, the ship, symbolic of the rational and mechanised, charts a clear course of 75° N., whilst the speaker's way forward is mysteriously clarified as his identity is confused with the girl's:

> Some see a flock of swans,
> Some a fleet of ships
> Or a spread winding-sheet,
> But the snow touches my lips . . .

The 'clouds of snow' provoke different meanings though the final line has the assured tone of one whose whole outlook has been unmistakably transformed. What is 'beyond all doubt' in the final stanza is the speaker's union with nature through empathy with the girl. The girl 'winds [the speaker] in her hair' signifying his alertness to the 'tangled' strands of the natural, and this constitutes – in the words of 'Poetry of Departures' (CP, 85) – a 'purifying, / Elemental move' away from the ship's rational code.

The last section, 'Above 80° N.', parallels the two 'voyages' that the poem charts. Evocation of a limitless universal realm seems to signal the end of the quest:

> Farther than Betelgeuse,
> More brilliant than Orion
> Or the planets Venus and Mars,
> The star flames on the ocean . . .

A complete internalisation of nature's principles ultimately eludes human perception. At the end of the quest there exists a greater power beyond the brightest and most distant star. As mythological signs for the hunter (Orion), the lover (Venus) and the warrior (Mars), the symbols represent humanity's prime concerns which are 'outshone' by 'The star [which] flames on the ocean'. The quest's objective is unspecified, underlining how it eludes human definition (though the term 'Betelgeuse' derives from the Arabic 'yad al jauza' meaning the 'Central One' or 'Mysterious Woman'). Larkin's mythological allusions are underpinned by the idea that a 'feminine' impulse is central to all life. At the end, transcendental understanding is circumscribed by the boatswain's refrain: '"A woman has ten claws"'. Framing the visionary with the inebriated sailor's misogynistic remarks signals the gulf between the speaker's ideals and the boatswain's chauvinistic chants which remain within the ship and the limited 'masculine' understanding that it symbolises.

Whilst certain characteristics of *The North Ship* betray the influence of the 'Yeats stolen from the local girls' school' (Larkin, 1983, 28), the abstract surface conceals a highly-wrought symbolic network that is acutely sensitive to social, moral and gender-related concerns. Thematic links with the unpublished letters of Jim Sutton and Catherine Larkin, and with *Letters from Iceland* by Auden and MacNeice, suggest that the poems counter traditional beliefs, but also that they go beyond them in seeking alternative principles for human conduct that are based on intuition and receptivity to nature.

Gripped by Light

The North Ship's complex symbolism makes the poems quite inaccessible, though their obscurity constituted a safe retreat from wartime tensions. Regan describes the volume as a 'poetry of political quietism rather than political commitment' (Regan, 1992, 67) and looks to earlier, Auden-inspired poems written before 1943 for continuities with the metonymic idiom of *The Less Deceived*. 'Midsummer Night, 1940' (CP, 244) and 'New Year Poem' (CP, 255) are 'more firmly located in place and time than those in *The North Ship*' (Regan, 1992, 69) and Regan detects in these poems an outspoken preoccupation with wartime anxiety. This pervades even the social chatter of 'After-Dinner Remarks' (CP, 241):

> All the familiar horrors we
> Associate with others
> Are coming fast along our way . . .

As in several poems from this period, acting metaphors are used to convey revulsion for the contemporary escalation of militaristic activity:

> And so, while summer on this day
> Enacts her dress rehearsals,
> Let us forget who has to die . . .

In other, seemingly less socially engaged poems the same sense of despising the casual acceptance of orthodox role-playing exists. In 'Nothing significant was really said' (CP, 235) the speaker dissents from the consensus that 'The brilliant freshman . . . / Deserved the praise he won from every side' recalling the subject's exploitation by the 'bright unreal path' of a conventional education. As well as signalling enlightenment, the phrase hints at the pointless drudgery of orthodox learning.

Anticipating Larkin's own participation in the theatre of war – an experience he told Sutton would be 'a dose of hell' (Thwaite, 1992, 27, 20.xi.41) – 'May Weather' (CP, 261) pinpoints the stagecraft of wartime propaganda:

> The stage that summer builds
> And confidently holds
> Was floodlit by the sun
> And habited by men.

The ruling class's confident hold over popular attitudes recalls Woolf's explanation of how established 'masculine' culture hypnotises the mind with a 'coarse glare of advertisement and publicity' (Woolf, 1938, 131). The condition of being *gripped* – against one's will – in the light of a coercive power is a common theme in Larkin's 1940s writing and this terminology occurs regularly in his letters. In 1939 he complained to Sutton that 'America is in the grip of the White bands . . . I'd back coloured against white most times' (u/p letter, 39) and in 1942 he advised his friend to 'get out of [the Army's] grip' (Thwaite, 1992, 36). 'May Weather', however, suggests that the 'grip' of wartime propaganda has failed to take hold; an unconvincing jingoistic script is evoked:

> But parts were not correct:
> The gestures of the crowd
> Invented to attract
> Need practice to perfect . . .

Like Woolf's *Between the Acts* (1941), which is also concerned with performance and play-acting, the poem registers despair at society's escalating militarism. It is cynically alert to the way in which official statement was artfully contrived to court support for wartime activity. In 'May Weather', Larkin's distrust of establishment rhetoric recalls George Orwell, who wrote in his diary for 27 April 1942 that 'Nowadays, whatever is said or done, one looks instantly for hidden motives and assumes that words mean anything except what they appear to mean' (CEJL II, 423).

Another poem to condemn the hypocrisies of contemporary political posturing is 'Observation' (CP, 264), which recognises that death is the only time 'When mask and face are nailed apart'. Larkin's youthfully dissident credentials are apparent from the reference to 'a government of medalled fears' in which 'much is picturesque but nothing good'. First published in the *Oxford University Labour Club Bulletin* in 1941, the last line's awareness that 'nothing can be found for poor men's fires' shows concern for the plight of working people during wartime austerity. Neil Roberts uses this poem to buttress his claim that Larkin's rejection for military service on 1 January 1942 was responsible for the tonal differences between the poems written before this date and those which appeared in *The North Ship*. The cynical use of war imagery envisages military call-up as 'Machine-gun practice on the heart's desires' and Roberts argues that Larkin abandoned this socially engaged idiom in favour of an asocial register after being excluded from the war. For Roberts 'I dreamed of an out-thrust arm of land' (CP, 267) is withdrawn because of Larkin's 'multiply isolated consciousness' that ensued from being separated from Sutton and Amis, whose military service provided them with 'the defining experience of Englishmen of [their] generation' (Roberts, 1999, 13). Considering the negative representations of non-combatant males in wartime, Larkin's introspectiveness in *The North Ship* is understandable. Throughout the war, the dominant culture underwrote derogatory constructions of men who did not engage in military activity:

> Posters in which civilian men became visible depicted them . . . as comic figures: little old men staggering under the weight of giant vegetables in the 'Dig for Victory' series; ageing 'gents' lounging in clubs or phone boxes in 'Careless Talk Costs Lives'; self-absorbed swells hovering in front of booking offices or working-class types furiously stuck in railway carriages surrounded by freight in 'Is That Journey Really Necessary?' (Summerfield, 1998, 120–1)

Against this backdrop, 'I dreamed of an out-thrust arm of land' is understandably detached from hostile realities, which are shunned in favour of sand, waves and gulls – imagery characteristic of the retreat from worldly turmoil in Woolf's novels. Significantly, the desire 'To tear at a dark-faced garden' speaks of a bitter rejection of the bourgeois nurturing of the 'black flowers' of wartime. The subject's isolation is emphasised by placing him 'On the edge of a bricked and streeted sea'. By 1972 'the whole / Boiling will be bricked in' ('Going, Going', CP, 190) but the process starts in the 1940s as the natural world, which provides solace in many of *The North Ship* poems, is put out of reach by wartime's divisive geography. Whether *The North Ship*'s oblique manner is part of a quietistic wartime mood when critical debate was cautious, or whether Larkin's change of voice was due to his exclusion from combat, it is clear that these early poems criticised military activity and its diminishment of man's natural empathy.

The poems written immediately after *The North Ship*, between mid-1945 and 1946, were destined for the projected volume, *In the Grip of Light*, which was rejected by a succession of publishers in 1948. For Regan, this volume anticipates the realist method of Larkin's later style and he interprets these poems against the backdrop of a precise historical context: 'The coming of peace with the end of World War II gave rise to the popular notion of "a new dawn" . . . that was long and protracted, beset with anxieties and insecurities' (BTH, 2000, 121–2). Focusing on the uncertain post-war mood, Regan sees the title as 'ironical . . . rather than one of unqualified joy and optimism' (BTH, 2000, 123) and this encourages reading the volume as distrustful of the 'enlightened' attitudes that dominated public opinion in 1946.

The need to discard conventional modes of perception is evident in 'Dying Day', which was later published as 'Going' in the *Collected Poems* (3). Both titles are appropriate to lines which allude to the demise of fixed categories:

> Where has the tree gone, that locked
> Earth to the sky? What is under my hands,
> That I cannot feel?

The poem appears to be an ontological riddle, though it articulates how traditional certainties are prone to disruption at a time of cultural regeneration. The end-of-line position of 'locked' highlights the certainty of established perceptions, though the subject's inability to 'feel' signals an emotional need which contemporary circumstances inhibit. 'Going' anticipates 'Ignorance' of 'what is true or right or real' in 1955 (CP, 107), but more contemporaneously, traditional structures of understanding are questioned in 'And the wave sings because it is moving' (CP, 6). Here, Larkin spurns lifestyles 'so devised to make ourselves unhappy' in favour of a free existence in which the 'search for meaning' is accompanied by 'the cries of birds across the waters'. As in *The North Ship*, the social comment in this poem is mediated through characteristically Woolfian imagery (the model is *The Waves*) similar to that used by Auden and MacNeice in *Letters from Iceland*. The earlier books' deployment of gulls, seas and breezes to counter brash modernity is echoed in the way Larkin's poem promotes 'the shout of the heart continually at work / To break with beating all our false devices.' A nightmarish vision of an enforced, tread-mill-like existence also exists in 'Träumerei' (CP, 12), in which the speaker is 'part / Of a silent crowd walking under a wall'. References to those 'Leaving a football match . . . or a pit' signal a continuing preoccupation with working-class life. The movement from individual to group protag-onist stresses the shared solidarity of those oppressed by the iniquities of an exploitative system:

> We are now shut in
> Like pigs down a concrete passage. When I lift
> My head, I see the walls have killed the sun,
> And light is cold.

The triumph of the cold light of a utilitarian work ethic over a dead sun suggests the same concern as 'Toads' for those enduring cowed degra-dation for the sake of 'paying a few bills' (CP, 89). As well as looking forward to that poem's 'sickening poison' (CP, 89) these lines recall the bitter railings in Larkin's letters: 'We are all rats in a big machine that feeds us' (u/p letter, 7.xii.42). The slow, protracted discovery of the char-acters that spell 'D . . . E . . . A . . . T . . . [H]' mirrors the way in which those trapped by impoverished lives remain ignorant of their plight. The final 'T' is a 'decapitated cross' that foreshadows 'Church Going' (CP, 97) by registering how the demise of traditional worship has exacerbated social alienation in the post-war era.

Common to nearly all of the poems in *In the Grip of Light* is the theme of entrapment and the quest for new directions and meanings. The volume reflects the different modes of perception that the post-war world spawned, though there is also a personal dimension to the interest in alter-native identities and roles. Larkin was unsure of a total commitment to marriage in 1946, and this was also the year in which his interests were torn between poetry and prose. Moreover, Larkin was obsessed with the perspective of a socially isolated female who is jostled by a hostile patri-archal culture. These elements are of crucial significance to 'Wedding-Wind' (CP, 11) which unites a sceptical attitude to marriage, discomfort with the subjugation of women and a blending of narrative and lyric strategies.

The poem's narrative concerns a new bride whose joyous wedding night is disrupted by frightened horses in a nearby stable. Her husband goes to settle the animals that have been alarmed by the storm, and seeing her distorted image in a candlestick, the woman is left to contemplate questions of selfhood and identity, which seem to be mysteriously linked to the wind and the horses. The next day, whilst her husband attends the floods, she reflects further on the disparity between the drudgery of her daily chores and the sublime happiness of the night before. What is constant to both is the playing wind which seems simultaneously to soothe and unsettle. The poem's ending is ambiguous; the woman is at once content yet also entrapped by her married state.

The energetic wind provides an index to the woman's heightened emotions: repetition of the possessive pronoun – 'my wedding-day' and 'my wedding-night' – suggests the girl's pride in her special occasion, though the storm threatens disruption as much as it portends sexual consummation:

> a stable door was banging, again and again,
> That he must go and shut it, leaving me
> Stupid in candlelight, hearing rain,
> Seeing my face in the twisted candlestick,
> Yet seeing nothing.

Significantly, the girl remains passive throughout. The active agents are the 'stable door' and the 'he' (presumably the girl's husband) in the second line; the girl is left behind, as the end-of-line positioning of 'leaving me' indicates. Alone, she feels 'Stupid in candlelight' as if conscious of her diminished identity when abandoned by her male lover. Borrowing a phrase from 'Maiden Name' (CP, 101) she has been literally '*confused / By law with someone else*' (my emphasis). The 'twisted' image of herself that she glimpses in the candlestick reveals how her public identity is compromised without a man to define her role as wife and lover. A similar concern is expressed in a Sylvia Plath poem in which a conscious mirror perceives a woman searching for her true self:

> Now I am a lake. A woman bends over me,
> Searching my reaches for what she really is.
> Then she turns to those liars, the candles or the moon.
> ('Mirror', *Selected Poems*, 1985, 42)

As in Larkin's poem, Plath's reference to candlelight (particularly when used in conjunction with 'the moon') signifies how the male gaze categorises women as romantic figures. In 'Wedding-Wind' the girl's shock of 'seeing nothing' implies the crisis of the self she experiences in her husband's absence. At the end of the first stanza the girl empathises with the troubled horses that symbolise instinctive natural forces: their discomfort during the storm foreshadows later hints that the girl is 'restless' with her dreary, passive role. The horses' troubled state parallels the girl's growing reservations about her married life; though the implied good sex of the opening lines augured well, the wife's frustrations become apparent as the poem develops.

The monotonous chores of daily life quickly occlude the wedding night bliss:

> He has gone to look at the floods, and I
> Carry a chipped pail to the chicken-run,
> Set it down, and stare.

The 'chipped pail' signifies the girl's flawed life and the 'chicken-run' prompts a comparison between the hens' processed lives – they are kept only for their regenerative function – and the young wife's existence. After putting down the pail, the girl's 'stare' witnesses her reappraisal of conventional married life, investing the phrase 'Can it be borne' with great poignancy. But the poem is sensitive to the husband's plight as well as the wife's. Though the active form of 'He has gone . . . ' gives him an autonomy that the girl lacks, his inspection of 'the floods' signals that he is pressurised by wider forces. Tolley reveals that an early version of the line read: 'He has gone to look at the fences' (1997, 12), which conveys a stronger sense of a husband surrounded by marital responsibilities.

If the wind blew a note of joy into the couple's life in the first line, their subdued mood in the second verse paragraph is encouraged by a threatening, angry wind:

> All is the wind
> Hunting through clouds and forests, thrashing
> My apron and the hanging cloths on the line.

The predatory and aggressive wind threatens to disrupt the girl's domestic activity; rather than sanctioning marriage, nature opposes the restrictions it imposes. Seeing marriage from the male perspective, the speaker of 'Dockery and Son' (CP, 152–3) similarly questions the 'Innate assumptions' of conventional lifestyles, thinking that 'To have . . . no wife, / . . . seemed quite natural'.

At the end of the poem the loose narrative recedes into a dense poetic mode. Roberts notes how Larkin's poems 'engage with narrative but ultimately refuse it, closing the sociality of narrative with the isolated speaker in the Bakhtinian "poetic" mode' (Roberts, 1999, 15). Here, the 'poetic' voice attempts to balance the 'perpetual morning' of the girl's oppressed life with the 'new delighted lakes' of passion which characterise the relationship, but also speculates as to whether the 'lakes' of the marriage will 'dry up'. The final lines are ambivalent; the phrase 'kneeling as cattle' conveys a sense of being joyfully receptive to the world, but also hints that marriage can subjugate and oppress. The focus is not just on the girl's condition, but on 'Our' condition, suggesting that the man is as much a victim as the girl in being constrained, or as a later poem indelicately puts it, 'fucked up', by marriage (CP, 180). The final phrase is ironical – the conventional depiction of marriage as a generous tonic offers, in reality, subservience and monotony. Like the mothers in 'Afternoons' (CP, 121), both partners are pushed 'To the side of their own lives' by the pressures of orthodox roles. Moreover, the first wedding described in 'The Whitsun Weddings' – 'Where sky and Lincolnshire and water meet' – is a natural union unlike the artificial human marriages in which participants 'All posed irresolutely' (CP, 114).

If 'Wedding-Wind' examines how women are constrained by a traditional institution, 'One man walking a deserted platform' (CP, 293) considers how men tolerate the conventional nine-to-five routine. The image of 'One man restlessly waiting a train' evokes the frustrated commuter who resents 'To be each dawn perpetually journeying' at a time 'when lovers re-embrace'. Despite his soulless existence, the man's heart longs to be 'riding / The winds as gulls do'. The poem's title for *In the Grip of Light* was 'Getaway', representing the desire to escape a diminished life. Only the subject's 'ambition' and the need to provide for 'a wife or child' ensures his conformity. In 1946 Larkin's ambition of dovetailing a writing career with his library job would have preoccupied him for much of the time. Motion suggests that 'Deep Analysis' (CP, 4) is a vicarious exploration of the feelings of exclusion and helplessness that Larkin's girl-friend, Ruth Bowman, would have experienced (Motion, 1993, 142). The tender and beseeching voice of a female speaker tries to soothe an anxious partner:

> Why would you never relax, except for sleep,
>   Face turned at the wall,
> Denying the downlands, wheat, and the white sheep?

Like 'Wedding-Wind', the voice is that of a questioning woman. Carey argues that Larkin's adoption of the female perspective allows him to confront the negative aspects of his masculinity that were 'locked into . . . fear and inhibition' (BTH, 2000, 54). For Carey, the source for the poem may have been Layard's Oxford seminars, about which Larkin wrote to Sutton that women are 'the priestesses of the unconscious' who 'help men to regain all the vision they have lost' (BTH, 2000, 55). Significantly, Larkin shared Layard's creed with his sister, telling her in 1941: 'The way of salvation lies not away from the instincts but into them' (u/p letter, 15.v.41). Another poem which seems to celebrate the instinctive aspects of conventional 'femininity' is 'Portrait' (CP, 309). The poem focuses on the vulnerability of a caring female whose 'hands intend no harm' yet who is threatened by 'everything that strives / To bring her cold and darkness'. Larkin adopted the title 'The quiet one' for *In the Grip of Light*; the old title addresses, more suggestively, the girl's passivity and the stoicism with which she endures 'Winds [which] are her enemies'. Summerfield has shown how the demobilisation of women returned them to the traditional domestic sphere after a period of temporary responsibility and social status. Suggesting that 'Her hands are not strong enough / Her hands will fall to her sides', the poem sympathises with how women, suddenly curtailed by the government's re-emphasis on traditional family values after the war, were powerless to fight the winds of change: 'And no wind will trouble to break her grief'.

The poem has a further significance in its obvious reference to a particular genre of painting or drawing. István Rácz shows how 'The Card-Players' (CP, 177) was inspired by Cézanne's painting (Szaffkó and Bényei, 1999, 292) and 'Portrait' might also have been influenced by the visual arts. Larkin was probably familiar with Sutton's portraits, in which his friend and fellow-artist presents distorted faces and bodies with a distraught and anxious quality (see Plates 1 and 2). Sometimes, the women are angrily crying out, whilst at other times there is a passive note conveying resignation in the face of reduced circumstances. Occasionally, the image suggests a rare moment of exaltation and release, though, more commonly, surroundings conspire to constrict and constrain. Sutton never dated his work, though the family believe that the oil paintings pre-date the charcoal sketches. In the light of Larkin's choice of title and his close artistic collaboration with Sutton it seems entirely possible that Larkin would have seen at least one of these portraits, which raise the same questions about the closed lives of women as those expressed in his poetry and prose. A painting in Maeve Brennan's private collection is more attributable to a specific period because of its realist style. Plate 3 depicts a girl in the military-style clothes typical of women workers during the war. The girl's hairstyle suggests the fashion of the mid-1940s with its severe side-parting and the hair swept upwards to show off the face. The liberal, alternative blueprints for sexual politics that Sutton advocated to Larkin – his displeasure at 'Crumpet talk' and 'the pose of being manly' (u/p letters, 14.ix.41; 30.x.41) – prompt us to see in this picture a celebration of independent young womanhood as depicted in wartime (and post-war) recruiting posters for the W. R. A. C. and W. A. A. F. (see

Appendix, pp. 187–8). However, there are significant differences between the poster girls' confident bearing and the attitude of Sutton's model. In the painting the subject's wistful gaze signals anxiety as if the door (clearly visible behind the subject) has closed on the world of new opportunities afforded by war. 'Portrait' is acutely sensitive to what Summerfield terms the 'regendering' of the labour market in the post-war period:

> At the end of the war the idea of women's marginality to the work-force was loudly proclaimed. It was evoked in Parliament and the press as central to post-war reconstruction, and hence as the route to social stability and harmony. (Summerfield, 1998, 207)

Larkin's lines 'But wax and wick grow short: / These she so dearly guards / Despite her care die out' alludes to the snuffing-out of wider opportunity as the bio-sexual functions of marriage and motherhood were redefined as 'natural' for young women in 1946.

Larkin's discomfort with traditional gender roles can also be detected in the unpublished poems of the period. Workbook 1 contains a working draft of the poem 'That girl is lame':

> That girl is lame: look at my rough
> Hands. Can there be skill enough
> On earth to ease the bone back to its place?
> Is human patience wise enough to take
> Wandering pain? And were I allowed to find
> Grief's mainspring, could as sick a mind
> Give comfort?
> (u/p poem, 13.xi.46)

The poem articulates sympathy for the marginalised status of a disabled girl: her physical illness is a metaphor for the way that women are weakened by a bullying male culture. Significantly, the speaker is conscious of his 'rough / Hands' and perceives them as a hindrance to the girl's recovery. Having 'as sick a mind' as the girl's suggests not just empathy with her but also awareness of his own ailment – a 'masculine' mindset – which makes him powerless to assist. This is another of those occasions when, as Carey suggests, Larkin rebels against his convention-ally masculine self (BTH, 2000, 54). Whereas the girl is physically disabled, the speaker is crippled by the values of a patriarchal culture; though he observes her pain, as a man he is unable to 'Give comfort'. A later speaker is in a similar predicament when his gendered perspective forbids him to 'Console' a rape victim in 'Deceptions' (CP, 32).

One of the least noted of the poems selected for *In the Grip of Light* is 'Past days of gales' (CP, 310). Written in late 1945, only months before the publication of *Jill*, its plea that 'we still could turn, / Speak to each other in a different way' shows the same desire for 'connection' between the sexes that the novel addresses. By the autumn of 1946, Larkin channelled his frustration with the dead-end values of his sex and culture into a different medium. Despite his legendary rejection of modernist writers, he told the Paris Review that he 'admire[d] *Murder in the Cathedral* as much as anything Eliot ever wrote' (Larkin, 1983, 66) and Larkin's own experimental verse drama, *Night in the Plague* (1946) is loosely modelled on Yeats's play, *The Countess Cathleen* (1911). Larkin's play remains unpublished, though it is preserved in one of the notebooks in the British Library. As in Yeats's play, the interest of *Night in the Plague* gathers around the struggle between two universal ways of life – the humanist and the materialistic – for control over the characters' general philosophies. *The Countess Cathleen* uses as its material the convergence of pagan and Christian traditions and some critics detect a political dimension in Yeats's characters, the Countess and the Demons. David Clark finds a 'parallel between British imperialists and the demons' (Clark, 1965, 131) though Yeats insisted that 'The play is not historic, but symbolic, and has . . . little to do with any definite place and time' (1899). The rhythms and cadences of *Night in the Plague* are reminiscent of the earlier play and Larkin's action is removed from 'any definite place and time'. Just as *The Countess Cathleen*'s symbolic pattern prompts political interpretations, so the structural framework of *Night in the Plague* is alert to the limitations of social and cultural codes. Larkin utilises the constructed images of an unspecified earlier period in order to criticise the failings of his own.

Night in the Plague is a short one-act play in which the action is confined to a house in a town stricken by the plague. A wealthy merchant, more concerned with loss of business than the suffering of his neighbours, is preparing to leave for the country. Before escaping with his daughter he has taken the necessary measures to safeguard his possessions. Knowing that they have extra room in their coach, Anne, the merchant's daughter, requests that they also take James, her lover, away from the doomed town. The father rejects this out of hand, claiming that James is a foppish, idle man who is too weak to support himself, let alone a future wife. Anne persists until her father agrees on the condition that James sets out his request in a letter. Anne is delighted, but when she tells James, he immediately spurns the offer, saying that he has no use for charity and that he would be ridiculed as a coward if he were to accept. Anne chides him for his arrogance, saying that he is risking death with such foolish pride. At the end of the play the father contracts the plague, and forgetting his hostility to James, advises him to flee with Anne whilst there is

James Ballard Sutton, untitled
portraits of girls, oil on canvas,
private collection of Daphne
Ingram, London. Photographed
by S. Cooper, January 2001.

James Ballard Sutton, untitled portraits of girls, wash on paper, private collection of Daphne Ingram, London. Photographed by S. Cooper, January 2001.

2

James Ballard Sutton, untitled portrait of a girl, oil on canvas panel, private collection of Maeve Brennan. Photographed by S. Cooper, October 2000.

(a) James Ballard Sutton, untitled building scene, oil on canvas, private collection of Daphne Ingram, London. Photograph reproduced by Maeve Brennan, May 2000.

(b) James Ballard Sutton, untitled girl on bed, charcoal on paper, private collection of Daphne Ingram, London. Photographed by S. Cooper, January 2001.

still time. Instead of leaving, however, Anne and James accompany the character Death into the old man's sick room. The curtain falls.

Representing the worst elements of an acquisitive regime, the father is anxious that 'All valuable things like plate and candlesticks' are 'put in the bank's keeping'. He shows no pity for those who are infected:

> All Bedlam's loose. There's one goes wailing about
> It says – 'Lord, pity us! Lord have mercy upon us!'
> I whacked him with my stick to clear the road.
> Is supper ready?

The father's cruel tones echo the description of the Merchants in *The Countess Cathleen*. According to Aleel, 'One drew his knife, / And said that he would kill the man or woman / That stopped his way; and when I would have stopped him / He made this stroke at me' (*The Countess Cathleen*, 28). The Merchants' ruthless pursuit of wealth symbolises Ireland's increasing materialism and the demise of older customs at the beginning of the twentieth century. In *Night in the Plague*, the father's casual references to supper, whilst persecuting the weak, raises disturbing questions about fascist psychology at a time when the Nazi atrocities were being publicised. The stern request for food that he issues to his daughter identifies him as an unswerving patriarch who is as unfeeling to his own as he is to strangers. Whilst his neighbours lie dying, he comforts himself that 'money does not catch the sickness' and vows that he 'shall not go to bed, / But sit accounting'. Mindful of her father's vice-like grip of authority, his daughter reflects that he 'must be obeyed' and her love for James meets with fierce disapproval:

> *Anne*: He loves me.
> *Father*: Not enough
> To sicken himself with work for you, as I did
> For your mother. That's the test.

As with the *In the Grip of Light* poems, the unremitting codes of a bourgeois work ethic dominate the father's life, blinding him to the joys of loving relationships. Attempting to persuade Anne that leaving James is the best course, he reminds her that 'Many are staying: / Some have to, for their business requests it'. These lines anticipate the crippled characters of *The Less Deceived* who endure obligation's 'sickening poison – / Just for paying a few bills' (CP, 89), though the play's aesthetic objective subverts the need to conform more forcefully than 'Toads'.

If the father is hopelessly bound to a 'masculine' ethic of independence – albeit one which, itself, is dependent on materialistic acquisition – then so is his would-be son-in-law. James's fear of being regarded as 'the young man scared of the plague / Who couldn't be parted from Anne' suggests how he, too, is at the mercy of conventional opinion, which sees financial self-sufficiency as the essential attribute of masculinity. Anne inhabits the play's moral high ground, though her song reveals how her compassionate creed is swamped by hostile forces:

> Love through solitary days
> Falls like corn beneath the rain
> I am forgetting all your ways—
> When will you come again?
> When will you come again?

In a heartfelt speech to James, she rejects the rational world of commerce in favour of a shared communality:

> Do men think of nothing but money. [sic] Here I have told
> My father to give you room in the coach – not as he would,
> By drawing up a deed with witnesses—
> But as one man helping another from danger . . .

Anne tells James that he is 'blind' to what is important and asks him: 'What's all / The imagined insult in the world / If death is missed?' Her attempt to enlighten him recalls the trauma of embracing unorthodox perceptions in 'I see a girl' and 'The North Ship'. As in those poems the play challenges the traditional model of independent masculinity, preferring instead a 'feminine' ideal of mutual assistance. The play's final twist is heralded by the appearance of a fourth character, Death:

> *Anne*: There's no one in the house.
> [*Death* appears behind *Father*. The clock stops ticking.]
> *Death*: I am in the house.
> [A moment of realisation. *Father*, under the look of *Death*, goes
>   slowly and unsteadily back into his bedroom. *James* and *Anne* at
>   the foot of the stairs.]
> Do not hurry away.
> I offer you safe conduct for tonight,
> Come up these stairs, and see how a man dies.
> [*James* and *Anne* begin to climb the stairs. The curtain is lowered to
>   denote the passing of a few hours.]

Whichever creed is adopted, whether it is the code of independence or of communality, death subsumes our efforts into its grander design. As well as peddling the theme of humanity's 'timeless human condition', the play addresses contemporary events. At an early stage, the father reflects on the changes that the plague will bring:

A battle or two on foreign ground is nothing,
It clears the streets of quarrelsome boys and beggars:
Trade can be kept up. This is a different case.
No ships come up the river, the customs are idle.

The father believes that war will cleanse society of marginal groups, allowing commercial interests to flourish. Such views run dangerously close to the right-wing militaristic policies which oversaw the gassing of 'subversives' and gypsies in the death camps of Dachau and Auschwitz. The play is alert to how wartime's intolerance and inhumanity spills over into civilian life: pleased that 'Trade can be kept up' during conflict, the tyrannical merchant feeds off war like Mother Courage: 'Oh well, war's off to a good start. Easily take four, five years before all countries are in. A bit of foresight, don't do nothing silly, and business'll flourish' (Brecht, 1940, 22). If the father shares Courage's exploitation of the business opportunities that battle affords, Anne is more than the placatory female; she represents an alternative mode of conduct to the uncompromising male arrogance that starts world wars. Critics insist on seeing Larkin as a pedlar of unsavoury right-wing thought, yet they have singularly failed to take account of his 1940s writings, which reject the 'value' of the entrepreneurial spirit and instead support claims for a less patriarchal, more female-influenced society.

After his father's death in 1948, Larkin wrote a poem suggesting he had internalised the unorthodox constructions of masculinity ascribed to various speakers throughout the 1940s. 'An April Sunday brings the snow' (CP, 21) is a twelve-line elegy that laments the passing of Sydney Larkin in terms which celebrate the male's potential for intuition, a quality that is yearned for repeatedly in *The North Ship*. Inspired by the falling snow, the speaker tidies his father's jam stock and poignantly reflects on how the preserve symbolises a final reminder of his father's life. The poem throws into disarray conventional notions about what constitutes masculinity by cautioning how initial apperances can mislead:

An April Sunday brings the snow
Making the blossom on the plum trees green,
Not white.

Like the opening of *The Waste Land* this reverses traditional expectations: just as Eliot turns a view of spring as propitious and hopeful on its head ('April is the cruellest month . . .'), so Larkin creates a different way of seeing. The 'green' plum blossom illuminates how meanings and categories, far from being fixed, are flexible and dependent on their context;

similarly, the line break between 'green' and 'Not white' formally mirrors our surprise at seeing familiar things in a renewed light. As elsewhere, it is snow that effects the transformation of perspective, so that the contours of usual understanding are obscured. Conscious that the alternative landscape of perception will only last an 'hour or two', the speaker sets about 'moving between / Cupboard and cupboard, shifting the store / Of jam you made of fruit from these same trees'. Significantly, both the speaker and the father pursue activities that are conventionally designated 'feminine'. Whereas the speaker shuttles from 'Cupboard to cupboard', the father's hobby of jam-making and the sheer abundance of his produce – he has 'More than enough' – signals an affinity not only with what is derogatorily termed 'woman's work' but also with Nature's bounty and fruitfulness. Throughout, the tone of the poem is tender and loving, and the last stanza is particularly moving in its tribute to the speaker's late father:

> Behind the glass, under the cellophane,
> Remains your final summer – sweet
> And meaningless, and not to come again.

Just as the jam is preserved in its jars, so the dead father is now 'Behind the glass', which divides death from life. The 'cellophane' seals invoke the packaging of the flowers left respectfully at the graveside and the jam becomes a symbol for the distilled harvest of the father's life. As the 'hour or two' of altered perception draws to an end, a hard-headed viewpoint is imposed. Like the jam, the father's 'final summer' is 'sweet / And meaningless, and not to come again' but during the brief moment of a fresh perspective, the jam and the dead man's life were intrinsically and symbolically linked, the one informing and arousing memories of the other.

Though it was written for a father by a son, this poem is devoid of conventional masculine sentiment – what Sutton termed 'the pose of being manly' (u/p letter, 30.x.41). Instead of a gruff, documentary-style memorial, the speaker is uninhibited in adopting a visionary, lyrical idiom in which the father is remembered, above all else, for jam-making – a pursuit which involves the caring attributes of nurturing and providing and eschews the traditional male configuration of courage, logic and manliness.

Larkin's writing in the 1940s unsettles traditional assumptions about sexual politics and gender roles. Criticism of *The North Ship*, historically seen as a derivative of Yeats, ignores more significant influences that clarify the volume's seemingly overwrought imagery. But Larkin's correspondence, and his affinity with Auden and MacNeice, situate the volume as a non-partisan exploration of wartime culture. Though employing a more indirect mode of discourse than *In the Grip of Light*, *The North Ship* also overturns sexual and social orthodoxies, and prefigures the bolder use of a narrative framework in *The Less Deceived*.

4

Sexuality, Utopias and the Later Poems

Parodying Larkin's judgement on Auden's early and late styles, Stan Smith speculates on the seemingly irreconcilable divisions between Larkin's poems written before 1950 and those written after this date:

> I have been trying to imagine a discussion of Larkin between one person who had read nothing of his after 1950 and another who had read nothing before . . . a mystifying gap would open between them, as one spoke of a tremendously exciting social poet full of energetic unliterary knock-about and unique lucidity of phrase, and the other of an engaging, bookish talent, too verbose to be memorable and too intellectual to be moving. (Smith, 2000, 255)

Conducting 'a statistical breakdown of how [Larkin's] vocabulary differs between the two periods' (Smith, 2000, 260), Smith locates a linguistic watershed in the poet's career. This form of inquiry typifies critics' eagerness to explain Larkin's change of idiom in the middle of the twentieth century.

For Smith, the most likely turning point is *XX Poems* (1951), though the inclusion of 'Going' and 'Wedding-Wind', which have all the hallmarks of the later idiom and were included in *The Less Deceived* (1955), disrupts any clear separation between the two phases: these two poems were written five years previously and were even selected for Larkin's earlier *In the Grip of Light* (1947). Moreover, this volume's direct and socially aware idiom is similar to the metonymic style of the mature work.

The poet's explanation for his change of direction is equally problematic. Larkin suggests that 'Waiting for breakfast' (1947) marks the recovery from the 'Celtic fever' of Yeats and hints that the poem's bolder, empiricist grasp of experience was the result of an impassioned early morning reading of Hardy (Larkin, 1983, 29–30). The poem's recording of tangible experience and its first-person narrative clarity anticipate many of the later poems, though the sudden conversion from Yeats to Hardy is too simplistic to be tenable. For Motion, Larkin's most effective poems achieve their effects through a dialectic between the lyrical and the prosaic (Motion, 1982, 37) and Everett detects a parodic use of symbolism in the later poems 'Sympathy in White Major' and 'High Windows' ([CP, 168, 165], Everett, 1986, 234, 239). In addition, Larkin's account makes no mention of either Auden or MacNeice, who provided vital inspiration throughout the early period and whose influence endured well into the later stages of Larkin's career.

Whatever the timing of Larkin's stylistic transition, and however it is identified, the desire to trace the differences between the early and late periods distracts from the strong thematic continuities which pervade all of Larkin's writing. The major poems' questioning of conventional attitudes is best understood by a broad historicist approach that explains the emergence of forthright diction as symptomatic of the popular reassessment of established ideals in the post-war era. Whereas the mellifluous tones of *The North Ship* were an apt vehicle for a cautious wartime critique, a more lucid and colloquial style was more in keeping with the new freedoms of peacetime. Accordingly, Regan sees *XX Poems* as part of 'the period of post-war settlement in that they constitute a reappraisal and reconstruction of what had previously been regarded as "traditional" values and ideals, including attitudes to work, religion and marriage' (Regan, 1992, 78). Such concerns were cryptically debated in *The North Ship*, though by 1955 *The Less Deceived* confronted such topics by adapting Ayer's shrewd philosophical method in *Language, Truth and Logic* (1936). Ayer's insistence that insights and propositions should be founded on 'sense-experiences' (1936, 21), as opposed to elusive metaphysics underpins the logical processing in the major poems. Larkin intended the volume to convey 'a sad eyed (and clear-eyed) realism' (Hartley, 1988, 299) which is appropriate as it implies 'a measure of disenchantment and lost idealism but also a corresponding . . . determination to approach life in a rational and logical way' (Regan, 1992, 79).

Another crucial factor to influence Larkin's poetic voice was his enduring commitment to writing novels. Larkin wanted to be a novelist rather than a poet and he confided in the *Paris Review* that he 'didn't choose poetry: poetry chose [him]' (Larkin, 1983, 62). When he failed to complete *A New World Symphony* in 1953, his abundant narrative skills found their way into his poetry. Commentators have discussed the poetry's debt to the fiction from several angles. David Lodge identifies a *metonymic* tendency in the mature verse and ascribes this to Larkin's natural instinct for novelistic technique. Whereas the traditional poetic mode is inherently *metaphoric*, the suffusion of metonymic detail creates powerful 'indices of a certain recognisable way of life' (Regan, 1997, 77). This accords with Regan's notion that Larkin's poetry unites 'a traditional poetic lyricism with a distinctively colloquial and contemporary idiom that derives from a lower-middle and working-class speech community' (Regan, 1992, 78). Prototypes for Larkin's metonymic catalogues first appeared in prose form, though for Lodge, one of Larkin's chief attributes is his ability to conclude a poem with an abrupt disturbance of the metonymic surface 'allowing . . . metaphorical language to flow into the poem, with the effect of a river bursting through a dam' (Regan, 1997, 79). Swarbrick argues that Larkin's poems foreground the metonymic aspect and the 'personae or "masks" by which Larkin ventriloquises attitudes evolve from his command of idiom'. There is a sense in which the major poems can be seen as '"performative" in being constructed with an explicit consciousness of the impression they are creating'. This 'multi-vocal polyphony' (Regan, 1997, 215–16) in the poems is a phenomenon more usually associated with the novelist than with the poet. Swarbrick traces the collision of characters and voices to Larkin's fiction in the early 1940s, though Larkin was still consolidating these narrative techniques in his unfinished novels in the early 1950s.

Penelope Pelizzon asks, 'why [did] Larkin [write] poems rather than plays: if indeed he did exploit carnivalesque heteroglossia, why didn't he take advantage of the opportunity for multiple voices he could have maximized on stage?' (BTH, 2000, 215). Larkin's unpublished oeuvre does contain experiments in this genre though it was the possibilities of uniting narrative and performative techniques within the disciplined form of a lyric poem that really attracted Larkin. Tellingly, he once explained the arrangement of poems in *The Less Deceived* in theatrical terms: 'I treat them like a music-hall bill: you know, contrast, difference in length, the comic, the Irish tenor, bring on the girls. I think 'Lines on a Young Lady's Photograph Album' is a good opener, for instance; easy to understand' (Thwaite, 2001, 55). Similarly, he praised Randall Jarrell (who also makes poetic use of colloquialism) for his sense of performance: 'He is not afraid to dramatize an emotion . . . so that some of his poems need almost to be acted rather than read' (Thwaite, 2001, 66). Notwithstanding significant exceptions, Larkin's first major volume combines theatrical and novelistic ploys with a colloquial idiom in order to probe settled attitudes in the 1950s.

Deceptions of Convention

In the first 'performance' in *The Less Deceived* a lecherous voyeur gloats over the charms of a young woman, though the structural logic of 'Lines on a Young Lady's Photograph Album' (CP, 71) admonishes rather than sanctions the speaker's behaviour. The opening phrase, 'At last', suggests his impatience with the girl for withholding the album, though the fact that it is finally 'yielded up' and now lies 'open' suggests that the speaker's interest in the 'Matt and glossy' images is purely sexual. The girl's 'nutritious' images feed the speaker's lustful appetite, but such 'confectionery' reduces the girl's charms to a trifling sweetmeat. The implication is that the agent is merely 'distracted' from the more serious concerns of manly activity. In the final line the verb 'choke' is ambiguous: on one level it conveys the speaker's lustful desire, though on another it suggests how the speaker balks at his own rapaciousness. The poem questions the chauvinistic attitudes that its speaker parades. Like 'I see a girl', in which the speaker was 'choke[d]' with desire (CP, 278), this poem also bends back on itself to interrogate the speaker's sexist stance.

Stanza two opens with the stereotypical images of male sexual desire captured by the agent's 'swivel eye' as it 'hungers from pose to pose'. In each snapshot the girl is presented as both innocent and sexually suggestive. The sporting of 'pigtails', schoolgirl fashion, or the 'furred' robes of graduation feed a certain kind of male interest, as does the captive imagery implicit in 'Beneath a trellis'. Nevertheless, the poem does not endorse such stereotypes of male fantasy as readily as the speaker. The detail of the 'reluctant cat' draws attention to the image's artificial construction and the 'sweet girl-graduate' is not as compliant with the male gaze as she first appears. The phrase is lifted from Tennyson's 'The Princess', where it is applied patronisingly to the feminist character, Lilia. Chafing at Sir Walter's comment that strong and successful women are scarce in contemporary society, Lilia chides the arch-patriarch: '"There are thousands now / Such women, but *convention beats them down*"' (my emphasis, 'The Princess', *Alfred Tennyson*, 120). These lines occur in the previous stanza to the 'sweet girl graduate' phrase, so it is unlikely, given their frank sentiments of revolt against orthodox sexual politics, that Larkin would have missed their import. The original context of the quotation is crucial because it is spoken by an arrogant character who views women with contempt. By alluding to Tennyson's lines, Larkin draws attention to his speaker's unreasonable sexist attitude. Unsurprisingly, the speaker finds 'disturbing' the confusion of conventional gender roles suggested by the girl's 'trilby hat' – a transgression of orthodox behaviour that 'strike[s] at

[the] control' that patriarchal society takes for granted. The poem's parodying of misogyny is firmly located in time and place: the stanza's closing line ('Not quite your class, I'd say, dear') imitates the critical tones of the conservative, middle-class male who was averse to the emerging libertarian attitudes to courtship in the 1950s.

The division between the established and the progressive is brought into focus by the title of the poem. Whereas the opening 'Lines' are reminiscent of polite, eighteenth-century poetic convention, the photograph album is a new and 'empirically true' twentieth-century phenomenon that some would consider brash. In *The Intellectuals and the Masses*, Carey identifies a traditional elitist distaste for photography: 'For many intellectuals, the camera epitomized mass man's lack of imagination' and is a pastime 'favoured by clerks, suburban dwellers and similar philistine types' (Carey, 1992, 31–2). Apostrophising photography in a poetic form, Larkin embraces the ethos of The Movement – a loose collection of 1950s writers who embraced 'non-conformist, cool, scientific and analytical' principles (Hartley, 1954, 260) and argued that mass culture can also be art. Larkin exploits the precision of the photograph to rewrite traditional idealisations as false: in stanza five the leering brute's voice is replaced by a considered tone which recognises in the photographs, not the air-brushed curves of the centrefold, but 'a real girl in a real place'. Now, it is the image's 'imperfections' that are appreciated as the new voice discerns 'the cat as disinclined, and . . . / A chin as doubled when it is'.

But to return to how the girl eludes the speaker's control: her experiments with identity are implied by the 'trilby hat', and her succession of 'disquieting chaps' affronts the bourgeois' sense of 'proper' conduct. In addition, a more innocent era of uncomplicated courtship rituals is conveyed by the nostalgia of 'misty parks and motors', now 'over' and 'out of date'. The poem's consistent objective is to show that the speaker's dated sexual politics are just another facet of a world-view that is resentful of social evolution. The contemporaneous 'Hall's-Distemper boards' (decorating materials manufactured in Hull since 1903, see Appendix, p. 189) are viewed as 'blemishes' in an idealised, romantic past which the speaker constructs, a past which now 'lacerate[s] / Simply by being over'. What disconcerts the speaker and his ilk most is the 'exclusion' from a known arena of settled class, gender and identity assumptions. For Regan, the girl is 'not just an object of male desire but an emblem of an irrecoverable national past' (Regan, 1992, 98) in which roles and codes were reassuringly fixed (or 'calm and dry') as opposed to the unstable 'future' of changing social expectation.

The penultimate stanza emphasises the poem's intention to distance itself from the speaker's reactionary views. Resentful of the 'gap' between past and present, the speaker peruses the remainder of the album: 'So I am left / To mourn (without a chance of consequence) / You, balanced on a bike against a fence'. The 'gap' is cultural; the social conventions evoked by the album have changed, though the gap can also be considered emotional, as the speaker no longer feels the pressure of the relationship and so is 'free to cry'. There is also another sense in which the speaker feels detached, or unable to effect a 'consequence', over that which 'strike[s] at [his] control': as the girl presses against clearly defined barriers she challenges the construct of femininity that the speaker avidly consumed in stanza one. Larkin's bike girl may represent the Victorian 'New Woman', whom Sally Mitchell describes as 'a healthy young person in dark skirt and white shirt standing beside the bicycle that gave her freedom to travel independently' (Mitchell, 1995, 110). The 'theft' of a photograph of the girl 'bathing' suggests the speaker's attempt to regain what he perceives as the 'heaven' of former times when women were defined by the controlling male gaze.

For Diccon Rogers, the poem castigates 'the pre-programmed sexual robot [who] is a caricature of the . . . "male gaze", the gaze that objectifies and lingers erotically on the female body' (Rogers, 2002, 2). Taking the phrase 'sweet girl-graduate', Rogers suggests that L. T. Meade's novel, *A Sweet Girl Graduate* (1894) might have been as influential as Tennyson's 'The Princess' in providing the poem's parodic kernel. Meade's novel tracks the Oxbridge education of Priscilla Peel and is credited by Mitchell as being one of the pioneering texts 'for the first generation [of women] in [the] new world' of the 1890s, a time when the cultural phenomenon of the 'New Girl' was at its height (Mitchell, 1995, 22). *A Sweet Girl Graduate* complies with the criteria for the girls' school-story genre as discussed in 'What Are We Writing For?' and it also shows significant areas of overlap with *Trouble at Willow Gables*, which, like 'Lines . . .', gulls chauvinistic attitudes and applauds independent womanhood. Meade describes her heroines in tones that recall the sensual indulgence of Brunette Coleman's writing: 'Priscilla turned, and met the full gaze of lovely eyes, brown like a nut, soft and deep as the thick pile of velvet, and yet with a latent flash and glow in them which gave them a red, half-wild gleam now and then' (*A Sweet Girl Graduate*, 21). There are also similarities in the two plots: a 'bad' girl steals five pounds at Priscilla's college (St Benet's) just as she does at Willow Gables. In Meade's novel the theft is used as 'a vehicle for . . . moral expatiation' (Rogers, 2002, 3) and Larkin similarly utilises Marie Moore's supposedly 'criminal' act. Moreover, a scene in *A Sweet Girl Graduate* involves a theatrical production of 'The Princess' and Tennyson's poem provides the epigraph for Meade's novel which is, tellingly, 'Girls' / Knowledge is now no more a fountain sealed' (*A Sweet Girl Graduate*).

These details bind together 'Lines . . . ', *A Sweet Girl Graduate* and *Trouble at Willow Gables* in their attempted subversion of traditional sexual politics and their championing the autonomy of women. Rogers also suggests that *Maud* (*c.*1880s) is a source for Larkin's poem: not the poem by Tennyson, but the collected journals of Isabella Maud Rittenhouse, which were published by Macmillan in 1939, when Larkin was becoming interested in women's literature. *Maud* records the adventurous life of an independent-minded young girl and on two occasions the phrase 'sweet girl graduate' is invoked in order to be denigrated. Distancing themselves from clichéd models of femininity, Rittenhouse's heroines exclaim, '*We're* not going to have our essays tied with ribbons' and they resent how 'newspapers talk about the sweet girl graduate and her beribboned words of wisdom' (*Maud*, 103). Rogers argues persuasively from this that, even in the 1880s, the phrase was 'dated, stereotypical, patronising, amusing, and shallow' and that 'Larkin knowingly employed it as such' in 'Lines on a Young Lady's Photograph Album' (Rogers, 2002, 8). Another scene in the journals describes Maud's efforts to outwit a photographer in a manner reminiscent of Larkin's poem:

> In the middle I saw a photographer turn his camera at me from the hall back of the parapet circle. I thought him extremely impudent, so I nodded my obstinate little head, changed the position of my hands and paper frequently and thwarted him (Captain Shields afterwards told me they wanted to get a view of me reading but couldn't). (Strout, 1939, 104)

Rogers detects in these lines the same 'thwarted' controlling impulse of the male gaze that figures in Larkin's poem: 'Just as Larkin's swivel-eyed narrator, the photographer and his audience are hungry but helpless' (Rogers, 2002, 8). Rogers' findings help to redefine Larkin's sexual politics that are concerned not with misogyny, but with an enduring preoccupation with emboldened models of femininity.

Like 'Lines on a Young Lady's Photograph Album', 'Deceptions' (CP, 32) replaces the intense symbolism of *The North Ship* with an empiricist rendering of experience which owes more to Hardy than to Yeats. This is the popular view, though the thematic continuities between 'Deceptions' and Larkin's earlier texts are considerable. 'Deceptions' empathises strongly with a marginalised and exploited female. In Christopher Hitchens's words, the poem expresses 'Larkin's feeling for the woes of womanhood and the hidden injuries of class' (Hitchens, 2000, 205), and

Larkin seeks to understand the girl's predicament in terms of the social injustice that affected Augusta Bax and Katherine Lind. Moreover, though Hardy's influence allowed Larkin to deal with 'the life of men' as opposed to 'a concept of poetry that lay outside [his] own life' (Larkin, 1983, 175), the construction of this poem was inspired by a more recent poet: John Betjeman.

Larkin's admiration for John Betjeman has confounded his critics, who claim that the former poet laureate's nostalgic ramblings bear little relation to Larkin's more subtle reactions to post-war society. Nevertheless, Larkin's high regard for Betjeman is copiously recorded in the poets' unpublished correspondence. Writing to Betjeman in 1956, Larkin answers a query on 'Going' and tells his friend, 'I have a great love of your . . . poems. They give me more pleasure than any being written at present' (u/p letter, 26.iii.56). In 1960 Larkin was 'looking forward to [Betjeman's] next book with an eagerness that quite transcends "temporary notoriety"' (u/p letter, 22.viii.60), and a year later he was still pining 'for more of the poetry that only you can write' (u/p letter, 24.iv.61). Attempting to persuade Betjeman to visit Hull as writer in residence, Larkin foresees 'the chance of talking' with the future laureate as 'infinitely valuable to a student', adding, 'For me personally it would be tremendously exciting' (u/p letter, 6.vi.67). In 1971, he was 'delighted and honoured' to write the introduction to Sir John's *Collected Poems* and felt equal to the 'task of championing your poetry to American readers' (u/p letter, 26.v.71). What, for Larkin, made Betjeman 'the best Laureate since Tennyson' was the way he showed 'millions of people how to see buildings and landscapes, and listen to poems, through the only medium that reaches them' (u/p letter, 22.vi.77). Betjeman's connection with common humanity Larkin termed 'a tremendous achievement, and the nation as a whole is deeply in your debt' (u/p letter, 22.vi.77). Larkin's admiration for the ability to connect, however, formed only part of his respect for his friend. In numerous reviews of Betjeman's work, Larkin repeatedly celebrates its social awareness. Scotching the idea that Betjeman shudders 'at locutions such as "toilet"' (Larkin, 1983, 214), Larkin discerns in his friend 'a robust and responsive writer' (Thwaite, 2001, 195) whose writing goes 'quite beyond most avowed social realists' (Larkin, 1983, 214). In 'An Incident in the Early Life of Ebenezer Jones, Poet, 1828' (*John Betjeman*, CP, 49) Betjeman establishes this 'social realism' by prefacing his poem with a factual prose account of the injustices wrought by authority. The extract from Jones's 'Studies of Sensation and Event', which Betjeman cites, gives a first-hand account of how a schoolmaster-minister 'detested . . . for his tyranny' abuses a dog in front of his pupils in nineteenth-century London. The extract locates the ensuing verse in specific historical conditions that inform our reception of the poem's attitudes and events.

Like Betjeman, Larkin cites as his preface to 'Deceptions' a heart-rending prose account of social iniquity. What is most poignant about the quotation from Mayhew's *London Labour and the London Poor* (1862) is the fact that the linguistic structure creates the impression that it is the victim who speaks. John Goode notes how 'the process of sympathetic re-creation is conditioned by the temporal distance' between the original event and its literary mediation (Hartley, 1988, 127). Goode suggests that the girl 'herself creates a perspective through which she sees the events of the past' and Mayhew also 'imposes a perspective with the comment [mentioned elsewhere in *London Labour and the London Poor*] that . . . *"this woman's tale is a condensation of the philosophy of sinning"'* (Hartley, 1988, 128). When Larkin quotes from Mayhew, his work prompts a very different response to the girl's situation. The repetition of the personal pronoun – '*I* was drugged', '*I* did not regain my conscious-ness', '*I* had been ruined' and '*I* was inconsolable' (my emphasis) – aligns the reader with the girl's perception (as reconstructed by the narrator) so that we experience her exploitation. Her opening phrase, '"Of course . . . "' situates us midway through a conversation with the girl, in which she desperately beseeches us to believe her version of events. This brings us directly into the theatre of the girl's tragic world, which, as the girl's vocabulary indicates, is distinctly Victorian: 'ruined' suggests the nine-teenth-century custom of expressing sexual matters in oblique terms. Accordingly, the poem is concerned with rape, but within the context of the admonishing strictures of Victorian morality.

Just as the reader was made to identify with the girl, so the speaker of the poem shows an extreme personal involvement with her in the opening line. An empathetic bond is established, so that despite the event's being 'distant' in time, the speaker's 'tast[ing]' of 'the grief' seems as 'Bitter and sharp' as the drugged liquid 'gulp[ed]' by the girl. What began as a literal sensation for the girl becomes, for the speaker, a metaphorical one as their shared 'taste' of the experience unites them against the act's brutal reality. For Seamus Heaney, the pervasive 'main of light' in the stanza suggests clarification (see Regan, 1997, 26), though there is also a sense in which the 'enlightened' world beyond the attic threatens as much as it illumes. That it is 'unanswerable and tall and wide' implies the girl's inability to defend herself against Victorian London's overwhelming charges of impropriety. Just as the light of conventional opinion dazzled or 'gripped' characters in *In the Grip of Light*, so the girl finds the 'sun's occasional print' a blight rather than a comfort. For Goode, 'the partial light which does penetrate [the girl's gloomy situation] through men like Mayhew

... emphasises the social distinction and prevents the "*scar*" from healing' (Hartley, 1988, 130). The 'brisk brief / Worry of wheels' deftly mimics the swift movement of the carriages, though it also hints at how public opinion judges the girl's tragedy in unsympathetic terms. Even if she keeps her shame hidden, 'bridal London', with its sanctimonious intolerance for abused, unmarried women, turns 'the other way'. In every sense, the girl is alienated on account of a vicious sexual encounter for which Victorian society blames her. An attempt to 'house reclaimed prostitutes' fails in *A New World Symphony* because of society's hypocritical attitude towards irregular sexual activity: 'Society . . . liked its prostitutes where it could get at them' (BTH, 2002, 381–2). Unlike Mayhew, who sees the girl as 'a condensation of the philosophy of sinning' (Mayhew, 1862, 241), the speaker pities the girl as the lines re-create the slow, dragging hours following the rape: 'All the unhurried day / Your mind lay open like a drawer of knives'. The mid-line break, together with the enjambment, imitates the painful and protracted exposure to society's harsh judgement. As in earlier texts, this poem confronts how the dominant order is hostile towards those who transgress its codes. The final simile of the 'mind . . . open like a drawer of knives' expresses the same defiant stance against unjust treatment as that evinced by Katherine Lind who glares at the abusive Anstey 'as if he were an insect she would relish treading on' (*A Girl in Winter*, 19).

Lodge illustrates how a metonymic mode ultimately yields to metaphor in poems such as 'The Whitsun Weddings', 'Church Going' and 'High Windows' ([see Regan, 1997, 78–81] CP, 114, 97, 165). However, the opposite occurs in 'Deceptions'. The intense metaphorical pressure of stanza one ('I can taste the grief . . . the brisk brief / Worry of wheels . . . bridal London . . . Your mind . . . open like a drawer of knives') gives way to a more straightforward, realist style in stanza two ('I would not dare / Console you if I could'). This has the effect of drawing a line under the genuinely felt, though conventional, sympathy that the first stanza sponsors. The more direct manner of the second half of the poem signals the limitations of such a conventional response to the rape, without in any way invalidating its sincerity. Now, separated both spatially and temporally by 'Slums' and 'years', the speaker widens the artistic focus to include the rapist as well as the girl. After all, 'What[ever] can be said' will be of no use to the girl, who is now long dead, despite the traditional 'poetic' bonding of the opening lines. Nevertheless, some critics have found the second stanza offensive. Graham Holderness's feminist character ('Kate') recoils at what she perceives as a 'sympathetic representation of the rapist', and Rossen, while acknowledging the 'compassion for the girl's suffering' in stanza one, condemns stanza two as 'problematic because the poet also shows . . . sympathy with the man' (Regan, 1997, 89, 152). However, a consideration of the unpublished drafts indicates an enduring respect for the girl:

> All to be said
> To suffering ghost or substance is that there
> In that long scald, pretence is frozen out.

and

> Through the long slum of years from then to now
> Suffering has preserved you in its radiant frost

and

> If at this distance, your grave pinched in and lost,
> Any part of you keeps going back to that room,
> See yourself as I see you, radiant in painful frost;
> Radiant because unable to pretend.
> (Workbook 1)

The position of these excerpts in the workbook suggests that they were prototypes for the opening of stanza two. The phrase 'at this distance' highlights how the passing of time enables new angles of vision, though the idea that dominates here is that of being 'radiant in painful frost'. Larkin is fascinated by the way that the girl's unmitigated suffering grants her a 'radiance' precisely because it renders her 'unable to pretend'. Like Katherine Lind, the 'Girl in Winter' who also felt the chill of being an outsider, the raped girl acquires a sanctified state simply by being a victim. The idea of being virtuous in her exclusion from 'respectable' consideration is summed up by the oxymoronic 'radiant frost', which recalls the icy contempt for traditional angles of vision in the Sutton letters. Most importantly, the drafts display a sustained sympathy with the girl: the phrase 'See yourself as I see you' elevates her status as a wronged innocent in the speaker's eyes. In the published poem the central concern of stanza two is that the girl's 'suffering is exact', making her 'less deceived . . . / Than he was'. By making the point that the rapist is an unwitting subject of an act of cruel deception the focus shifts from the act of rape – the brutality of which has already been exhaustively depicted in stanza one – to the way that the rapist is the victim of his own violent 'Desire' that 'Dry-Point' terms the 'time-honoured irritant' of male sexuality (CP, 36). Just as the speaker of 'I see a girl' (CP, 278) felt constrained by conventional constructs of masculinity, so the rapist is under the influence (or 'charge') of the worst kind of male impulse, which plants 'the mirage of sexual triumph in [his] brain' (Carey, 2000, 156). Whilst acknowledging that such an analysis disturbs 'readings' that sympathise solely with the girl, the speaker recognises that, given her suffering, she 'would hardly care' about her attacker's deception. Longley notes how, 'for all its sympathy with the raped girl, [the poem] does not follow the path of conventional morality' (Hartley, 1988, 223). Ingelbien, too, has pointed out how the blunt fifth line wrecks the harmony that the preceding pentameters have so carefully established, thereby mirroring, formally, the break with pat conventional attitudes (Ingelbien, 2000, 477).

Larkin's comment on the volume which he sent to his publisher read: 'the agent is always more deceived than the patient . . . On the other hand suffering – well, there is positively no deception about that. No one *imagines* their suffering' (Hartley, 1988, 299). Unlike Ophelia, who is 'the more deceived' by Hamlet's antics (III.i.120), the girl is 'less deceived', in that her sense of the rape as a brutal, exploitative act is wholly accurate. On the contrary, the rapist's delusion that his rapacious desire can be realised is, in Ayer's terms, one of 'the mistakes . . . of sense-experience . . . [in which] . . . the expectations to which our sense-experiences give rise do not always accord with what we subsequently experience' (Ayer, 1936, 21). However, the poem closes without a shred of sympathy for the attacker. His '*stumbling* up the breathless stair' (my emphasis) suggests a moral imbalance as well as a physical one and the 'burst[ing]' in the last line implies not only the man's ejaculation but also the shattering of his erroneous perception. The final phrase 'desolate attic' subtly conflates the predicaments of both parties. Just as the girl was physically trapped, the rapist is also caught in the caverns of predatory male sexuality. Goode stresses the extent to which the (male) poet is complicit with 'the disgusting violence of male desire', which makes him 'only capable of a complete identification with the blind frustrated man', in contrast to a sympathy with the girl which 'can only be partial' (Hartley, 1988, 134). For Goode, the poem expresses the limited male viewpoint and the 'moral limitations of bourgeois society which believes itself to be philanthropic' (Hartley, 1988, 134). However, in the light of reading the poem alongside the unpublished drafts – and the sympathy shown to wronged women elsewhere in Larkin's writing – the poem also expresses a greater empathy for the rape victim than Goode allows.

The overbearing pressures of a dominant order are also felt in 'At Grass' (CP, 29) which is similarly based on a vivid evocation of oppression. This time the exploited subjects are animals rather than people. Not all readings have stressed the poem's concern with oppression, focusing instead on the speaker's fondness for a 'better' past. Smith sees the poem's wistful reflections as 'the very stuff of nostalgia' (Regan, 1997, 178), and

Regan discusses how it 'reveals the way in which great achievements are "fabled" in memory' (1992, 82). Blake Morrison detects in the poem 'feelings of loss and regret' and considers how 'for a certain section of the British populace [these feelings were] unusually pronounced around 1950' (cited in BTH, 1992, 83). Accounting for the poem's 'Edwardian nostalgia', Paulin reads the poem allegorically, claiming that the 'horses are heroic ancestors – famous generals perhaps'. For Paulin, the closing lines represent Larkin's (essentially negative) 'response to modern social democracy', and the groom and his boy signal the 'last vestiges of traditional hierarchy' (Regan, 1997, 163, 164).

Other critics contend that, far from embodying nostalgia for an imperial past, the horses have escaped the limitations that fame bestows. Swarbrick describes the animals as 'icons of anonymity' (Swarbrick, 1995, 62) and for Timms this 'anonymity is . . . a model of the oblivion' longed for elsewhere in Larkin's work (Timms, 1973, 74). Edna Longley's account also endorses the idea of release from human pressures: 'The horses' years of co-option contrast with their merging back into undifferentiated nature' (BTH, 2000, 41). Booth highlights the 'metaphysical distance between the horses' world and that of humanity' (BTH, 1992, 84), a view put more forcefully by Roger Day, to whom the horses are 'victims of the human world' (Day, 1987, 10). For Petch, 'The horses have escaped the fictions imposed on them as symbols of human aspiration' (Petch, 1981, 60), whilst Everett draws on the references to commerce in the worksheets and speculates that 'money played its part in defining the worldly corruption of the animals' racing career' (BTH, 2000, 20).

Reference to the worksheets encourages a reading of the poem as a rejection of the repressive forces that are bitterly opposed in Larkin's earlier writing. As well as providing important information about the poem's thematic framework, these drafts suggest a method of composition that is decidedly prose-like. To understand the poem, however, it is necessary to return to Oxford, in the winter of 1942, when Larkin was voraciously feeding his appetite for Jungian psychoanalysis. At the end of the Michaelmas term Larkin wrote to Sutton, telling him: 'Jung is bloody interesting . . . The unconscious, instead of being a garbage heap of shame and guilt, is the fountain of life, and contains the healing powers of everyone. How to get at them I still am not sure' (u/p letter, 21.xii.42). Inspired by John Layard's seminars, Larkin and a college friend embarked on an ambitious plan of charting their subconscious lives. Larkin describes the venture in a letter to Sutton in 1943:

> Philip Brown and I started recording our dreams, and Karl [Jung] gave us a leg up. Since then I have recorded 95 odd, and am still going

strong. I feel I am gradually curving into a state of union – for a bit – but it's been a long job because I am a hard case in many ways. In fact I still have a long way to go. But if once my unconscious shows the green light, I shall feel (I hope) happy and contented, because a man lives by his unconscious as you remarked, and I feel the pattern will emerge in my own actions. (Thwaite, 1992, 53)

What Larkin refers to as 'a state of union' is, for Jung, the ultimate goal of the 'individuation process' whereby the 'Self' strives to overcome the deceptions of the cultural milieu (Stevens, 2001, 81). Larkin recommended Layard's classes on 'natural instincts' (u/p letter, 15.v.41) to his sister, and his insistence here that 'a man lives by his unconscious' reveals a similar allegiance to Jungian doctrine: 'most of our difficulties come from losing contact with our instincts, with the age-old unforgotten wisdom stored up in us. And where do we make contact with this old man in us? In our dreams' (*Psychological Reflections*, 76). Dream 43 in Larkin's 'Record of Dreams' is particularly relevant to 'At Grass':

Standing on a raised plain, or little hill, I could see a racecourse in a semioval in front of me.

The horses started at A and ran to B. There were none of the usual racetrack things – white rails, etc. – and the horses did not seem to have jockeys though I suppose they must have had. The scenery seemed wild and the course a natural gulley. The horses raced, and a black and a chestnut forged ahead, till the race was between them alone. Up to C they kept level, but after that the black gained, and the chestnut swerved away up the hillside as shown. The rider (Roger Sharrock in his green overcoat) was thrown and seriously injured. (u/p 'Record of Dreams', 22.xi.42)

Larkin declared that the poem was inspired by 'a film . . . about Brown Jack . . . a famous flat-racer and jumper' that he saw in 1950 (Thwaite, 2001, 58), though the dream-record suggests that his reservations about the harnessing of dumb animals for entertainment had their origins long before this date. Significantly, the 'racetrack' reproduced in Larkin's subconscious has 'none of the usual racetrack things – white rails, etc.' and freed from the oppressive paraphernalia of their human masters the animals enjoy a 'wild . . . course' in a 'natural gulley'. The elemental and unspoilt location signals enjoyment rather than enforcement so that when the race becomes stressful 'the chestnut swerved away'. The detail of the rider being 'seriously injured' indicates man's penalty for, as Longley puts it, 'the horses' years' of co-option' (BTH, 2000, 41) in a spectacle whose purpose they cannot comprehend. Considering their closeness in subject matter and the strong thematic similarities between dream and poem, any

November 22nd.

43. Standing on a raised plain, or little hill, I could see a racecourse in a semioval in front of me.

The horses started at A and ran to B. There were none of the usual racetrack things— white rails,etc.- and the horses did not seem to have jockeys though I suppose they must have had. The scenery seemed wild and the course a natural gulley. The horses raced, and a black and a chestnut forged ahead, till-the race was between them alone. Upto C they kept level, but after that the black gained, and the chestnut swerved away up the hillside asshown. The rider (Roger Sharrock in his green overcoat) was thrown and seriously injured.

Unpublished 'Record of Dreams' (22.xi.42)

discussion of 'At Grass' must take into account the psychological profile that Larkin meticulously recorded in the early 1940s.

The sense in which the animals are at one with their habitat is encouraged in the first line; that 'The eye can hardly pick them out' suggests an affinity with their surroundings which humanity can barely fathom. Almost invisible to the human speaker, the inadequacy of the human perspective in comprehending their true state is highlighted. The alliterative 'cold *sh*ade they *sh*elter in' alerts us to the apparent paradox of seeking sanctuary in a 'cold' place. The horses shelter here precisely because it is removed from the public glare that intimidated the girl in 'Deceptions'. The only element which 'distresses' the horses' world is the 'wind', a natural force, and there is an additional aural suggestion in the word 'distresses'. The wind ruffles their manes and tails but it also *de-stresses* them of the pressures of the racing world, so graphically depicted later in the poem. The arbitrariness of events is also striking: the horses' bodies are caressed casually by the breeze and 'Then one crops grass, and moves about'. There is no sense of coercion or order or purpose; the animals are simply being animals, acting on a primal instinct that is only vaguely understood by man. Similarly, 'crops' as opposed to 'eats' suggests a harvesting; the grass is depicted as the horses' natural and proper fare as opposed to anything bequeathed by man. The phrase recalls a description of Toby the school horse in *Trouble at Willow Gables*, who is observed to be 'peacefully *cropping* the outfield' (my emphasis, BTH, 2002, 103). Within the novella's aesthetic structure the phrasing signals the animal's unity with nature as against the man-made restrictions of school life. Larkin's use of the same verb seven years later suggests that Toby was an early prototype for the horses in 'At Grass'. Like his counterparts in the poem, Toby's natural composure invites a reassessment of the efficacy of human contrivances. The stanza's penultimate line reiterates the failure of limited human perspectives: seeing the horse as 'seeming to look on', the human spectator imposes purpose and strategy on what is simply instinctual behaviour.

The horses are also symbolic of a wider shackling of natural freedom facilitated by establishment rituals. Triumphal, the animals have regained their dignity by blending in, 'stand[ing] anonymous again', as opposed to standing out from their natural surroundings. Considering Larkin's own shyness at being paraded centre-stage, and his criticism of establishment practice in the early work, this poem is not 'the very stuff of nostalgia' that Smith suggests (Regan, 1997, 178).

Stanza two contrasts past and present. The opening signifies a turning away from the naturalness of Stanza one and there is an overwhelming sense of how the animals have been hijacked as human property and exploited for whimsical entertainment. Early drafts, written in what is more obviously a prose style, emphasise the way that humanity has used the horses for its own designs: 'they were themselves sewn in / To men's concerns' and 'They lived in terms of men, hedged in / By bet and bid' (u/p draft, Workbook 1). The straightforward narrative of these lines suggests how the poem has its roots in the clarity of prose but also how the horses have become reluctantly embroiled in human affairs. In the published poem, the arbitrariness of stanza one is replaced in stanza two with the precision of 'fifteen years' and 'Two dozen distances', suggesting the human impulse to measure and control. The latter phrase implies the course's crude simplicity, sufficient to 'fable' the horses in men's eyes. 'Fable' also points to the way that the horses have become excessively mythologised in the human world. Once again, the drafts convey, in clear, narrative terms, how the animals 'were / More famous than most men' (u/p draft, Workbook 1). Larkin's novel-writing apprenticeship is equally discernible in the final version: the metonymic catalogue of 'Cups and Stakes and Handicaps' provides the cultural signifiers of a man-made, competitive regime through which the horses' 'names were artificed'. By rights horses shouldn't have names – they are artificially imposed on them in the same way that conventional labels are imposed on oppressed subjects throughout Larkin's work. The animals have been used simply as a means of perpetuating a highly profitable human activity. As an early draft phrase makes clear, 'money rode them' (Tolley, 1997, 26) for all they were worth. An ardent supporter of animal rights, Larkin chafed at such manipulative treatment of innocent beasts.

The anti-establishment stance continues into stanza three. As well as suggesting the jockeys' colourful attire, 'Silks at the start' draws attention to the monied ambience of such sporting occasions. If the 'shade', 'wind' and 'grass' of stanza one projected the tranquil, natural aura that surrounded the animals, here the way that 'Numbers and parasols' intrude 'against the sky' highlights the way that a man-made artefact shuts out the sun, ultimate symbol of life. Arriving in 'Squadrons of . . . cars' the spectators launch an assault on the animals' natural habitat; the unsullied grass of the opening is transformed into 'littered grass' – the human world's spoiling of nature. The stanza closes with an evocation of the brash and 'unhushed' atmosphere of a race meeting, which even when over 'subside[s]' into 'stop-press columns'. Newspaper reports gratuitously reduce the animals to mere statistics, which are pedalled 'on the street' in another exploitative and profitable venture. The worksheets endorse the idea that the animals are the unwitting instruments in a human campaign of corruption and greed. An early draft of stanza three records the horses' 'Every canter, swerve or sweat / [as] Money-measured' (u/p draft, Workbook 1) and the speaker muses on the disparity between the animals' natural grace and the vice-ridden world that has claimed them:

> every race
> They ran brought small disturbances -
> One pawns his coat, one cannot pay:
> Strange such seeds to trace
> Back to such splendid energies.
> (u/p draft, Workbook 1)

In the penultimate stanza, the speaker's rhetorical question ('Do memories plague their ears like flies?') is knowingly guilty of transposing human attributes onto dumb animals, though their apparent response of 'shak[ing] their heads' is a corrective to human presumption which fallaciously interprets instinctive behaviour. In the remainder of the stanza the speaker muses on the passing of an era:

> Summer by summer all stole away,
> The starting-gates, the crowds and cries—
> All but the unmolesting meadows.

Reading this, the first impression is that the excitement of former times is wistfully longed for, though the poem's effort is to distance itself from the speaker's conventional sentimentality. What has been 'stole[n] away' from the animals is not the pressure of 'starting-gates' and 'crowds and cries', but the precious time they could have spent in the 'unmolesting meadows'. Whilst the stanza's final line ('Almanacked, their names live') appears to revere the horses' fame, it also alludes to the animals' inclusion in a human catalogue of 'great' achievement.

The poem's conclusion seems to celebrate the horses' release from a life of oppression. The run-on line 'they / Have slipped their names' imitates the manner in which the horses shed an imposed identity the way they 'slip' their 'bridles'. The speaker now perceives the horses as unnamed; they inhabit, once again, the contented, 'anonymous' state of stanza one. In light of the 'untalkative' absolutes of *High Windows* ('Here', CP, 137), Rácz sees the horses as inhabiting 'a non-verbal world', representative of 'a non-human idyll' (Rácz, 2000, 233). They are now 'at ease' – though the continued use of the military imagery hints that their service is not entirely over. The speaker's claim – that the horses 'gallop for what *must be* joy' (my emphasis) – suggests the fallacy of attributing human traits to animals, but it also implies that in former times they ran not for 'joy' but for the money their owners might win. What the speaker applauds is the way that the horses are no longer defined by the spectator's 'fieldglass', or monitored by the 'curious stop-watch'.

Paulin interprets the horses as symbols for imperial grandees who were superannuated from their duties with only memories of a glorious past to sustain them (Regan, 1997, 163). A counter-interpretation, however, contends that the horses are not symbols of authority but, rather, suppliants themselves in a human regime which has 'lost contact with [its] instincts' (Jung, *Psychological Reflections*, 76). The poem is pessimistic about the quality of the horses' retirement in the closing lines. It may be 'Only the groom, and the groom's boy' who visit the animals, but they still bring 'bridles'. To imagine that the horses have escaped from human oppression is to be deceived by a conventional romantic sentimentality. Even though they have escaped the constrictions of the racing world, they are still harnessed by the 'groom's boy'. Larkin's remarks on the equestrian crime writer, Dick Francis, support a reading of the poem as an indictment of oppression. Complaining about the shortcomings of 'the mystery parts' of Francis's work, Larkin concedes that these 'arise naturally from the greed, corruption and violence that lie behind the champagne, big cars and titled Stewards'. The essay, which is significantly entitled 'Four Legs Good', praises Francis's mystery writing for its 'concern [with] horse pulling and betting frauds, and . . . wads of used notes in anonymous envelopes' (Thwaite, 2001, 293). Despite being written thirty years after 'At Grass', this passage endorses the same revulsion at 'greed, corruption' and exploitation expressed by the poem in 1950. As the sketch in Larkin's dream-record shows, the best antidote for human limitation is a determined 'swerv[ing] away' towards the 'wild' and 'natural' realm of the instincts as prescribed in Layard's seminars on Jungian psychology.

A similar turning away from organised traditions exists in 'Church Going' (CP, 97), though the speaker's initial indifference to religion is ultimately tempered with a rediscovery of the value of faith. Like 'At Grass' and 'Deceptions', the poem features a specific narrative construct. Apprehensive lest he should disturb serious proceedings, the awkward speaker interrupts his bike ride to reflect irreverently on the religious trappings inside a parish church. He has made similar trips in the past and his dismissive tone develops into a serious consideration of existential concerns. Prompted partly by his own musings, but also by the church's unique atmosphere, the speaker concludes that despite its apparent irrelevance, the building mysteriously symbolises the human need to ratify the constructed 'compulsions' that sustain us.

The debt to narrative technique in 'Church Going' is apparent from the workbook drafts. Tolley describes Larkin's compositional method as a 'desultory groping' (Tolley, 1997, 81) though this ignores the influence of a narrative framework which informs many of the early versions. What the workbooks show is not trial and error but the methodical poeticising of a narrative structure:

> Once I am sure there's nothing 'going on'
> I steal inside, letting the door thud shut.
> ~~And stand in~~ Another church: not a distinguished one.
> (u/p draft, Workbook 3)

Larkin rejected the scored-out phrase, though reading it with the undeleted lines highlights the vivid narrative element beneath the verse. Taking a further example:

> Yet I did stop: time and again I do:
> I find myself ~~standing~~ in some cold place like this,
> ~~And~~ Wondering what to look for . . .
> (u/p draft, Workbook 3)

Reading these lines *with* the omitted words one is conscious of the sequential clarity of prose brought into focus by the absence of poetic inversion in the opening phrase. Part of the appeal of the finalised poem is its seemingly casual yet carefully contrived narrative fabric, which developed from Larkin's skills in prose fiction.

As well as its roots in narrative technique, 'Church Going' bears the imprint of a performative and theatrical heritage. Not all critics are familiar with Larkin's experiments in verse drama or his stylised debates (see Pelizzon in BTH, 2000, 215), though his early training in these genres informs the later poetry, and the dialectical element is nowhere more apparent than in 'Church Going'. In 1967 Larkin concurred with Ian Hamilton that the poem represents 'a debate' (Thwaite, 2001, 22), and since then many critics have commented on its question-and-answer strategy. The subject of the poem is one that Larkin addressed as early as 1943 in 'A Stone Church Damaged by a Bomb' (CP, 269). Here, the workings of religion are treated solemnly, though in the unpublished discussion 'At the age of twenty-six' (1948), Larkin hints at the more sceptical treatment that was to follow:

> I am one of the first generation never to believe that Christ was divine, or that each man has an immortal part, at any stage in their first twenty-five years. When we are grown to the age when we have control of things, there will be queues for the cinema on Sunday mornings. (u/p discussion, 'At the age of twenty-six', 1948)

The passage's sentiment predicts the wider indifference to churchgoing which prevailed in the following decade. Larkin suggests that transcendental questions are becoming a matter for individual reflection rather than Church governance and, entering the church that inspired the poem, he 'felt the decline of Christianity in our century as tangibly as gooseflesh' (Thwaite, 2001, 83). For Roger Day, 'Church Going' captures the 'contemporary public attitude' (Day, 1987, 46) and Corcoran reads the poem as a statement of 'English post-Christian consciousness' (Corcoran, 1993, 90). Accounting for 'the shift in the post-war years towards a more secular society' (1992, 88), Regan notes 'that the "transcendent" significance previously embodied in the Church was transferred to an ideal of "the Self"', and this need for a personal appraisal of existential problems is 'fundamental to the idea of being "less deceived"' (Regan, 1992, 88). Regan's overview of the period's zeitgeist chimes neatly with Larkin's personal rejection of traditional worship:

> I have been brought up to regard the gospel story as untrue, as silly, and, perhaps subtlest, as something which only a conventional and not-over-intelligent man would credit . . . (u/p discussion, 'At the age of twenty-six', 1948)

In the opening stanzas the speaker's disrespectful tones condemn the 'silly' appurtenances of religion revered by 'conventional . . . man'. For the speaker this is merely 'Another church'; the colloquial, irreverent observation of mundane detail – 'matting, seats, and stone, / And little books' – deprives the building of any transcendent significance that it might possess. The part-time nature of contemporary church activity is suggested by the flowers being 'cut / For Sunday' and their being 'brownish now' invites reflection on the wider sense of spiritual decay and the decline in congregation figures during the 1950s. The colloquial reference to 'brass and stuff / Up at the holy end' continues the revolt against orthodox ritual and the speaker's slang trivialises a 'serious' subject – philistine flippancy deliberately crafted to antagonise the religious believer. By the end of the stanza the speaker fuses irreverent idiom with religious terminology – 'Brewed God knows how long' (the ironic and unwitting reference to 'God' suggesting the speaker has internalised conventional religious deference more than he realises). Suitably 'Hatless' once inside the church, his removal of 'cycle-clips in awkward reverence' anticipates an affinity with transcendental knowledge that the poem's conclusion conveys. Reiterating the impatience with orthodox religion elsewhere – the 'huge, decapitated cross' in 'Träumerei' (CP, 12), the 'seedy Gothic place full of decayed clergymen' in *Jill* (134) or the 'vast moth-eaten musical brocade' in 'Aubade' (CP, 208) – the speaker suggests a latent 'hunger in himself to be more serious'.

In the second stanza the speaker inquires whether the church has been 'Cleaned, or restored?', a question relating not only to the physical structure but also to the burgeoning reconstruction of 'faith' within the speaker. His 'Move forward', running his 'hand around the font', provides a subconscious baptism into an unorthodox faith. 'Mounting the lectern', the speaker samples the believer's perspective, going through the motions of preaching in a theatrical manner. A tentative respect for a broadly 'religious' outlook is also inherent in his observation of the church's state of repair: 'From where I stand, the roof looks almost new'. As one of the first generation of unbelievers, Larkin brings a different perspective, afforded by religion's attraction, into the secular atmosphere of the 1950s. The 'large-scale verses' and biblical English ('"Here endeth"') appeal to the speaker against his will making him speak 'more loudly than [he'd] meant'. Studying the poem's 'play of etymological and current meanings', Katie Wales detects in the phrase, '"Here endeth"', an 'ironic ambiguity' which 'raises the possibility of the demise of the church as a whole, not only the end of the Lesson' (Verdonk, 1993, 94, 93). Contrary to the speaker's conviction that 'there's nothing going on' inside the church, there is an abundance of enquiry occurring in his subconscious. The poem's oscillation between acceptance and denial confirms Larkin's abiding interest in the endless revolving of antithetical positions. Unlike the Larkin juvenilia that promoted a subversive anti-establishment ethos, the mature work often resists interpretative closure. If the 'Hectoring . . . verses' recall how strict codes blinded and bullied characters in *A Girl in Winter* and *In the Grip of Light*, in '*letting* the door thud shut' (my emphasis) the speaker of 'Church Going' partly welcomes the pressure to conform. But as the poem was inspired by a visit to 'a ruined church in Northern Ireland' (Thwaite, 2001, 56) the donation of an 'Irish sixpence' implies a cynical

---

[1] The reference to the 'Irish sixpence' has caused considerable speculation. It is likely that Larkin was referring to the Eire sixpence which was in circulation between 1928 and 1969 in The Republic of Ireland. The coin was slightly larger than its GB counterpart and bore the Irish harp and bloodhound on its sides. As no Northern Irish sixpence – as distinct from the standard British 'tanner' – was ever minted, Larkin can't have been thinking of any regional variant of the mainland sixpence. The speaker's gesture of donating the Irish sixpence is, therefore, a cynical one. Larkin's comment suggests that the poem is based on a trip to a church in Northern Ireland but the donation of the Eire sixpence would not have been legal tender anywhere in the United Kingdom.

dismissal of formal religion[1]. For Morrison, the poem's opposing tugs of 'undemonstrative agnosticism on the one hand, and a susceptibility to the continuities of Christianity on the other' (Morrison, 1980, 228) are due to the Movement's mixed identity. While many of the group repudiated traditional belief, 'Christianity was [still] intimately associated with . . . literature [as studied in 1940s Oxford]' and the 'Church for the Movement was yet another example of an English continuity now threatened with extinction' (Morrison, 1980, 228).

In stanza three the speaker suggests that sustained effort (his church visits occur 'often') extends his understanding though, as in Edward Thomas's poems, the speaker's geographical journey overlays a spiritual one fraught with setbacks. If the confiding tone of 'Yet stop I did' suggests the speaker's tenacity in his quest, he ends 'at a loss' and 'Wondering what to look for'. Such wondering extends to practical as well as existential matters:

> When churches fall completely out of use
> What we shall turn them into, if we shall keep
> A few cathedrals chronically on show,
> Their parchment, plate and pyx in locked cases,
> And let the rest rent-free to rain and sheep.

The semantic thread running through these lines and binding them together is that of utility and commercial exchange, a shift away from a casual, personal interest, to an organised commercialism that insists on practical value and resourceful application. Nevertheless, it is still possible to discern the allure of 'spirituality' which vies with the speaker's materialist outlook. Longley suggests a similarity between Thomas's natural, 'quasi-religious, quasi-mythological . . . faith' in 'The Mountain Chapel' and Larkin's implication in 'Church Going' 'that all religious formulations, "belief" and "disbelief" are much of a muchness,' noting that Larkin can identify even his own scepticism with the "compulsions" that have brought people to "this accoutred frowsty barn"' (Longley, 1974, 78). Larkin's forecast that 'rain and sheep' shall one day tenant the church echoes what Longley describes as Thomas's faith that 'natural forces . . . will succeed man and his monuments' (Longley, 1974, 78). This yearning for 'natural' faith reverberates throughout Larkin's writing. As the poem develops, the stark opposition between orthodox religion and irreverent secularism gives way to a transcendental awareness that defies definition.

Unable to penetrate the church's attractions by focusing on its material aspects, the speaker considers the way that superstitious ritual is nourished by a 'blent air' of mystery in stanza four. What strikes the speaker is the clandestine way that 'dubious women . . . / . . . make their children touch a particular stone' and the 'Power of some sort' that survives 'In games [and] in riddles' long after formal religious practice has ended. Such 'random' activities, however, are as transient as the organised ones:

> superstition, like belief, must die,
> And what remains when disbelief has gone?
> Grass, weedy pavement, brambles, buttress, sky

Implicit here is the notion that natural flux will unpick the fabric of human understanding, regardless of whether it embraces or rejects conventional belief. The speaker ponders who comes closest to recognising the 'purpose more obscure' that the church fulfilled. Is it 'one of the crew / That tap and jot', 'Some ruin-bibber, randy for antique' or the 'Christmas-addict'? The question is couched in the vernacular, signaling his iconoclastic credentials as he deflates the pretentiousness of self-conscious antiquarians and religious devotees. As in Larkin's early work the poem gains its éclat by admonishing conventional sources of wisdom. It is the bicyclist rather than the specialist who is an authority on how the church's 'special shell' provides a focus for existential musings: 'what . . . is found / Only in separation – marriage, and birth, / And death, and thoughts of these'. As the speaker passes 'Through suburb scrub' to reach the church it becomes clear that despite its unprepossessing appearance, the urban landscape is still able to provide a path to spiritual awareness. Unlike John Betjeman, who denigrated the mediocrity of modern citizens (the 'tinned beans / [and] Tinned minds' of 'Slough' [*John Betjeman*, CP, 20]), Larkin suggests their potential for sustaining consolations.

Wales refers to 'the dramatic interplay of the dual-voiced, split personalities' in the poem and to 'the suggestiveness of the language . . . which forces the reader to reassess the obvious interpretation of words [which] works almost unconsciously to reinforce the unsettling of fixed positions and stock attitudes'. She identifies a dialectic created by the juxtaposition of two different lexical sets, one consisting of words relating to concrete physical features, the other to more theological concerns such as 'belief' and 'superstition'. 'Through the interweavings of the lexis, the physical and non-physical modes of existence are confirmed in their own "dialectic"' (Verdonk, 1993, 92, 93, 95). Lodge similarly identifies a contrast between 'trustworthy ordinariness' and the 'current of metaphorical language' (Regan, 1997, 79). But the poem's closing insights, although presented in a highly poetic style, are simply a re-articulation of what the 'ordinary' man has already worked out. The poem's effort correlates with the way in which earlier socially inferior protagonists, John

Kemp and Katherine Lind, achieve understanding at the end of the novels. Abandoning speculation as to what the 'frowsty barn is worth', the conventionally 'poetic' speaker voices, in the final stanza, not a discovery of traditional belief, but an awareness of how the church 'recognised, and robed as destinies' the 'compulsions' which invite existential enquiry. Larkin's remark that 'Church Going' is 'entirely secular' (Thwaite, 2001, 83) supports what the title, when read in conjunction with the poem, implies: that despite falling congregation figures 'someone will forever be surprising / A hunger in himself to be more serious'. At the same time, the final lines chastise the way that the assertions of orthodox faith – how the speaker 'once *heard* [the church] was *proper* to grow wise in' (my emphasis) – rigidly maintained religious conformity. Though the poetic syntax makes it unclear, the line 'If only that so many dead lie round' weakly justifies faith on the grounds that death focuses the mind on questions of destiny. The narrative clarity of a draft version ('if only for the reason / that dead people lie around' [u/p draft, Workbook 4]) illustrates Larkin's ironical intentions much more clearly: its being a site for death is not a sufficient reason for embracing the Church.

Written in 1954, 'Church Going' confronts the problems faced by the individual in restructuring existential belief in an increasingly non-religious society. Indeed, it is noted that, 'At the beginning of the fifties under 10 per cent of the population were regular churchgoers' (Marwick, 1982, 97). In observing that 'religions [are] shaped in terms of what people want' (Thwaite, 2001, 56), Larkin acknowledges how alternative forms of 'religious' discourse were more in keeping with 'what people want[ed]'in the 1950s. Yet if the poem reflects a cultural and historical turning point, it also mirrors its author's psychological profile. Carey discerns in the fourth stanza a voice (which he terms 'female') that 'ponders more seriously humanity's need for religious mystery – to which women, rather than men, will respond' (BTH, 2000, 59). Carey traces the origins of this intuitive 'female' voice to the Jungian doctrine that Larkin encountered in Layard's seminars. Like Larkin, Jung shied away from formal religion, commenting on one occasion that his clergyman father 'was entrapped by the Church and its theological teaching' (*Memories, Dreams, Reflections*, 64–5). The speaker of 'Church Going' evades such entrapment though he is under no illusion that the British post-war demise of religion curtailed the search for answers to the profoundest of questions.

In contrast to 'Church Going', other poems possess a bold debating method, suggesting clear links with Larkin's early experiments in dramatic writing. As well as the *Round the Point* debates and the verse drama *Night in the Plague*, satirical dialogues occur regularly in the letters to Sutton. Larkin distracts his friend from army routines by expressing the mental agonies of what to write about in a micro-drama involving facets of his own personality:

> <u>Better Self</u>. Stop talking about yourself, you fool! Do you think that poor bloke wants to read all your piddly little self-praises and conscious smirks?
> <u>Self</u>. The force of your argument, my dear sir, does not escape me, but as I am going to pay 1½d to send a letter to him <u>which he asked for</u>, I'm going to indulge my whims and fancies to their fullest extent. (u/p letter, 6.ix.39)

The 'Better Self' wants to protect Sutton and is blunt and aggressive; the other 'Self' provides a reasoned case in the genteel tones of middle-class English. As in later poems the 'Better self' cheerfully ignores polite decorum whilst the conventional self is constrained by customary courtesies. In the same letter Larkin congratulates himself on 'mastering the art of literary counterpoint' and in another he informs Sutton that he is 'still to find a counterpart . . . in whom I can exist wholley [sic]' (u/p letter, 39). Elsewhere, Larkin drafts a heated exchange between '<u>Mind</u>' and '<u>Bowels</u>' in which the latter scabrously rebukes the former for being an inferior writer to D. H. Lawrence (u/p letter, 7.v.41). This dual identity is depicted graphically in a sketch showing a two-headed Larkin viewing paintings on opposite sides of a gallery:

Included in unpublished letter (20.xii.49)

Larkin was obsessed with the coexistence in the psyche of oppositional selves that continually vie for control. Invariably, one 'rebel' self chides the other for holding certain attitudes, though occasionally the rebel admits that his case is futile. Complaining about the work ethic that turns humans into 'rats in a big machine', Larkin concedes that his 'arguments would be more impressive if [he] had any alternative' (u/p letter, 7.xii.42). What to put in the place of orthodox behaviour is treated aesthetically in 'Toads' and 'Poetry of Deparures' (CP, 89, 85), though Sutton's letters suggest that the latter poem was inspired by a lifestyle recommended by the painter in 1950:

> a change might do you much good. For instance, physical work, perhaps farming, would surely tend to put to sleep your self-conscious mind? Or you could see the world as a tramp – there are casual wards for tramps where they give you a huge sandwich at night and a huge sandwich in the morning, make you have a bath, and ask no questions . . . I'd be most willing to join you in either of these ventures. (cited in Lerner, 1997, 16)

'Toads' opens with a monosyllabic tirade that is delivered by the speaker's rebellious self and addressed to the part of him that accepts the 'toad *work*' of a steady job. The rebel strives to rouse the conformer's ire through a combination of indignant questioning ('Can't I use my wit as a pitchfork / And drive the brute off?') and exasperated exclamation ('Just for paying a few bills!'). Thematically, the poem is reminiscent of 'One man walking a deserted platform' (CP, 293), though, stylistically, it owes more to Geraint and Miller's embittered dialogues in *Round the Point*, or the micro-dramas in the Sutton letters. There is a note of desperation in the poem as the speaker's subversive impulse tempts his orthodox counterpart with the means of overcoming the 'sickening poison' of routine. 'Toads' effectively captures the rhetorical strategies of colloquial speech. The repetition of 'Lots of folk', followed by an example of unorthodox behaviour – living on 'their wits' or 'up lanes' – and finally sanctioned by bullish assertion – 'They don't end as paupers' and 'They seem to like it'– creates the impression of provocative public house banter. The use of italicised typography ('*work*' and '*starves*') foregrounds the intonation of actual speech and creates an illusion of immediacy. Once the case for non-conformity has been made – 'No one actually *starves*' by opting for a life of cadging – the orthodox self responds:

> Ah, were I courageous enough
> To shout *Stuff your pension!*
> But I know, all too well, that's the stuff
> That dreams are made on . . .

Just as the rebellious voice expressed itself in colloquial speech, so the orthodox self employs the conversational connectives of 'Ah' and 'But' to imitate the fractures of oral discourse. If the italicised forms vitalised the admonishing gestures of rebellion at the start, here they signal that outright revolt is as unworkable as the clichéd terms in which it is expressed. Just as the rebellious self employs registers as socially diverse as 'nippers' and 'unspeakable wives', so the orthodox self's pun on 'stuff' embraces both vernacular expression and erudite Shakesperian allusion; the poem's dilemma is felt by a broad range of communities and classes. Considering the 'multilingual' dimension in 'Mr Bleaney' (CP, 102), Jonathan Raban notes how 'each idiom corresponds exactly to a social tone, even if the idioms are defined in rather literary terms: the declassed 'narrator', the proletarian 'character', and the essentially aristocratic voice of "poetry"' (Raban, 1971, 32). The reading of 'Toads' offered here is similar to that of 'Mr Bleaney': in both cases, 'one can't miss the richness with which [the poem] invests its linguistic community in the search for a voice . . . that will cut across the barriers of class and rhetoric and speak direct' (Raban, 1971, 33). 'Toads' concludes with a compacted final stanza that imbues it with a mystical insight that is disarmingly unclear but whose implication is that the paths of revolt and orthodoxy are interdependent and mutually complementary.

As the speaker in 'Toads' has 'both' an everyday and a fantasy life, there is a definite sense in which 'one bodies the other' (CP, 90). The poem is crafted from the clichés of popular fiction ('The fame and the girl and the money' [CP, 90]); in a review of Ian Fleming's 007 books, Larkin reveals the thinking behind this oppositional dialectic: 'the Bond novels were an adroit blend of realism and extravagance, and both were necessary: the one helped us swallow the other' (Larkin, 1983, 266). Whereas in Larkin's early writing the individual was constantly dashed by the pressures of dominant culture, in 'Toads' the individual's capacity to rebel against custom (the 'Why should I[s]' and 'Can't I[s]') is neutralised by his orthodox side, so that equilibrium is achieved at the end.

'Poetry of Departures' (CP, 85) also employs a counterpointing of styles and registers that is characteristic of the early prose. The poem is subtler than 'Toads' in its unsettling of the established antithesis between two seemingly different lifestyles. Its objective is to show that the life of the free-booting rebel is the same as the conformist's – both pursue constructions of the ideal existence. At the start the speaker is detached from what is, apparently, a general agreement on the desirability of upending life's conventions. The contrast between the colloquial expression ('*He chucked up everything*') and the speaker's measured reflection signals a difference in perception based on class rather than the intrinsic merits of non-conformity. As the speaker ponders the problem in his educated tones, it is clear that all social types, even those with 'The good books, the good bed' and the 'life, in perfect order' want to cut loose from the familiarity of 'specially-chosen junk'. The use of three different pronouns in stanza two ('they . . . I . . . We') confirms the widespread appeal of escape and the speaker's description of his possessions as 'junk' signals how all classes, regardless of their social standing, disparage the mundane in the quest for adventure.

In stanza three the speaker is attracted to the stock gestures of the adventure novel which leave him 'flushed and stirred'. What keeps him 'Sober and industrious' is the knowledge that the heroism of fiction is available to him as a fantasy ideal: 'I can, if he did'. The speaker recognises the stereotypes of runaway, rake and fighter as constructions, which are as separate from his real life as the italicisation is from the rest of the typography. In the final stanza the speaker imagines himself in a variety of heroic poses. Couched in a pastiche of adventure fiction such gestures are comic, though the speaker's serious concern is to show that even if such attitudes were struck, they would merely constitute 'a deliberate step backwards / To create' what he already has: 'Books; china; a life.' Describing the rebellious life in the same terms as the orthodox one, the poem enacts its coup. Just as the speaker's conventional routines were 'in *perfect* order' so the act of revolt is 'Reprehensibly *perfect*' (my emphasis): both are flawed in their offer of a contrived, ideal life. As Barthes reflects in *Mythologies*: 'Any kind of freedom always in the end re-integrates a known type of coherence' (Barthes, 1973, 82).

For Rossen, the speaker's 'dissatisfaction is cast in terms of a stark set of choices' (Rossen, 1989, 134) but the poem works to dispel the illusion that choice exists. Osborne deploys Kierkegaard's *Either/Or* (1843) to demonstrate the poem's exposure of the 'crass . . . reductive opposing of "authentic" and "inauthentic"'. The Existentialist needs 'a dominant value-system to define himself against . . . quite as much as the conforming majority needs its rebels'. Rather than being distinct entities, 'authentic and inauthentic . . . are [simply] relational terms that need each other in order to signify' (BTH, 2000, 160, 161). Reasserting the validity of the poem's dialectic, Regan historicises 'Toads' and 'Poetry of Departures', seeing them as part of 'the sustained debate about freedom after 1945'. The mood of the poems is 'quietistic' in that they 'weigh a desire for escape and release with a dutiful commitment to the status quo' (Regan, 1992, 91). Robert Crawford uses both poems to support the complex synergy of duty and craft and imposes a biographical reading upon the poems, claiming that the 'Gauguinesque clearing off . . . seems to have been a kind of balancing mechanism, a dream of wildness that kept [Larkin] at his [library] desk' and suggesting that the poem is 'psychologically acute' (Crawford, 2001, 268, 267).

To identify, in 'Toads' and 'Poetry of Departures', the same psychological influence which pervaded 'At Grass' and 'Church Going', it is necessary to remember what Jung required of his patient:

> He is taught to see his symptoms as arising from an unbalanced mode of existence, which is itself a result of thwarted archetypal intent. Treatment consists of helping him to recognize and find ways of correcting his archetypal frustration, abandoning his one-sidedness, and bringing about a new equilibrium between the opposing forces in his personality as a whole. (Stevens, 2001, 128)

It is easy to detect, in the yearned for release of 'Poetry of Departures', not just a construct of elusive ideals, but a narrow prescription for 'one-sided' masculine behaviour. In stanza three the speaker's fantasy life is informed by the conventional male archetypes of seducing women and punching villains. These ideals remain 'thwarted' for many of Larkin's male speakers, who feel unjustly coerced into aspiring to such stereotypes. In the final stanza, the speaker momentarily pictures himself in poses that recall the traditional romantic leads of Hollywood films. In 'Toads', too, the speaker is pulled to 'The fame and the girl and the money', though his remark that he will not get these 'All at one sitting' signals their untenable nature (CP, 90). Just as Larkin's 1940s writing questioned conventional notions of masculinity and proposed alternatives to traditional gender models, the speaker of 'Poetry of Departures' 'opt[s] out of the coercive force of contemporary sexual ideology' (Clark cited in Regan, 1997, 127). In turning down his part of being 'Stubbly with goodness' the speaker is rejecting the image of an unshaven man as symbolising a form of 'goodness' in post-war popular culture (i.e., the unshaven Allied soldier returning victorious from the battlefield). The subversive force of 'Toads' and 'Poetry of Departures' is indebted to Jungian doctrine. If 'At Grass' and 'Church Going' advocate 'contact with our instincts' (*Psychological Reflections*, 76), 'Toads' and 'Poetry of Departures' peel back 'the false wrappings of the persona' which impose identities that are culturally prescribed (*Collected Works VII*, para. 269).

The departure from fixed identities pervades *The Less Deceived*. What offends the poems' speakers, throughout the volume, is blind obedience to society's prescribed guidelines. 'Places, Loved Ones' (CP, 99) begins in a defiant mood as the belligerent speaker rejects the expectation to settle down with 'that special one'. He resents how an orthodox, domestic existence provides 'no choice' in the planning of alternative goals and lifestyles. What troubles him most is the pressure of being 'Bound . . . to act / As if what [he] settled for / Mashed [him]'. Objection to the idea that bachelordom is a kind of second-best which must be stoically tholed rather than enjoyed is returned to in 'Reasons for Attendance' (CP, 80). The speaker asks 'what / Is sex?', announcing the start of a diagnostic process, that seeks to deconstruct the ideals of sexuality and cohabitation that are supposed to constitute universal mature human cravings. The poem calls for a value system that is individual and unique; the repeated use of the personal pronoun and the insistence 'I too am individual' emphasises the need for a private 'working through' of convictions and preferences. Whilst, for some, 'the lion's share / Of happiness is found by couples', for the speaker, who prefers the solitary life of art, such a conception is 'sheer // Inaccuracy'. The poem's exhaustive logic and its vigorous testing of conventional platitudes relates it to the logical positivism of A. J. Ayer, though the final line throws human judgement into question. The poem recalls the misjudgements of human knowledge in *A Girl in Winter* but it also looks forward to the limits of reason in *The Whitsun Weddings* and *High Windows*.

'Born Yesterday' and 'Spring' (CP, 84, 39) refute the idea that only certain people qualify for life's pleasures. The first poem commemorates the birth of Kingsley Amis's daughter, though it avoids wishing her 'the usual stuff / About being beautiful' which conforms, too neatly, with stereotypical assumptions about qualities we 'ought' to have, qualities that Larkin later, ironically, describes as 'Essential' (CP, 144). By contrast, the equation of what is 'ordinary' and 'dull' with what is desirable (an 'enthralled / Catching of happiness') turns traditional categorisation on its head, recognising the need to be 'flexible' in assessing what constitutes the 'ideal' personality. The poem's reversal of conventional signification recalls Butterfield's re-evaluation of his academic 'failure' as 'contentment' in a value system which is detached from customary thinking (BTH, 2002, 440). Similarly, 'Spring' counters the view that only couples with children (the 'Green-shadowed people') can appreciate the season's charms. In a moment of insight recalling the sudden illuminations in the 1940s poems ('flashing like a dangled looking-glass, / Sun lights the balls that bounce, the dogs that bark'), the speaker glimpses the wonders of 'earth's most multiple, excited daughter'. Tellingly, the speaker is brought close to nature despite his seemingly unfit childless status as 'An indigestible sterility'. Whilst conventional romantic sentiment suggests that families and 'Their children' are best placed to commune with spring's fertile promise, the detail of the 'untaught flower' signals how nature is unschooled in such presumptuous human conceptions.

There are links between 'Absences' (CP, 49) and *The North Ship*: in the title poem of the latter volume a seafaring metaphor explores alternative values, though in 'Absences' 'there are no ships' and the surrounding seascape is curiously 'shoreless'. This suggests a joyous separation from the constrictions of human identity (a space 'cleared of me'), though the absence of ships also signals the difficulty of reaching distant shores of understanding – shores that remain 'out of reach' in *The Whitsun Weddings*. Similarly, 'Wires' (CP, 48) pushes against the boundaries of orthodox structures: straining 'against the wires', the steers fail to realise that there are 'limits to their widest senses' of freedom. Unlike the cattle, the characters of *The Whitsun Weddings* discover that restrictions exist 'Beyond the wires' and that freedom is a chimera – another fenced existence. *The Whitsun Weddings* is concerned not only with physical release, but also with the more difficult task of escaping the ideological imprisonment inside our heads.

Weddings and Divisions

The 1960s saw an unprecedented increase in mass consumerism. Advertisers eagerly promoted goods and opportunities to a population keen to escape wartime constraints. For some, however, the decade's aspirational culture was a false grail of unattainable happiness. In its aesthetic representation of how political and economic forces mould our beliefs, *The Whitsun Weddings* is as much a product of the decade as the 'mixers, toasters, washers, [and] driers' that are catalogued in 'Here' (CP, 136). The volume contemplates the invidious process that converts goods and lifestyles into craven 'desires', though its scope extends beyond the specific conditions of the 1960s, confronting the insistent way that dominant models of social and sexual politics infect the collective consciousness; the poems also challenge the way that language inadequately expresses the longed for antidotes to commercial excess.

'Sunny Prestatyn' (CP, 149) is a penetrating indictment of commercial irresponsibility and crude masculine sexuality. John Bayley claims that, 'The degradation of daily circumstance does not alter [the girl's] transcendent nature' (Bayley, 1984, 63) whilst Booth sees the poem as 'a lament for the vulnerable transience of the beauty and happiness' that the girl represents (BTH, 1992, 122). For Swarbrick, the 'poem measures dream-image against bleak reality' (Swarbrick, 1995, 117) and Clark claims that a potentially appropriate reaction for the male reader is to be 'appalled by [the] depiction of his own "tuberous" sexuality' (Regan, 1997, 123). Whalen detects the 'false promise' of desire (BTH, 2000, 115) and Pelizzon discerns in the poem 'an attack on an ordered society . . .

which functions by purveying unobtainable images' (BTH, 2000, 219). The poem's disdain for crass advertising ploys and its critique of certain aspects of male sexuality ally it to similar sentiments in the early work and the private papers.

The poem considers a poster for a seaside resort whose central 'hook' is a scantily-clad girl. The vandalised image questions the moral standing of advertisements that peddle misleading constructs of happiness to those gullible enough to be enticed. As well as raising issues about the commercial exploitation of idealised images of women, the poem considers the advert's irrelevance for those excluded from the affluent 1960s. Lisa Jardine objects to the 'steady stream of casual obscenity' and the 'derogatory remarks about women' (Regan, 1997, 5) in Larkin's letters; here, though, this material is woven into the poem's structural aesthetic as a means of criticising the attitudes Jardine finds offensive. 'Sunny Prestatyn' employs such 'casual obscenity' as an efficient way of deflating the construct of the romantic and idealised world promoted by the advertising campaigns of the 1960s. Larkin was delighted by Maeve Brennan's appalled reaction after she had read the poem: '"That's exactly the reaction I want to provoke, shock, outrage at the defacement of the poster and what the girl stood for"' (cited in Brennan, 2002, 60). Though Larkin's use of pornography caused a furore, he in fact adapts such material, as well as his scatological invective, to question the sexual consumerism of the period.

The girl of the poster tempts us with the fine weather of what is claimed to be an idyllic resort: '*Come To Sunny Prestatyn* / Laughed the girl on the poster'. The clean-cut image of the happy holiday girl is wholesome and appealing, though there is a gap between the girl's sentiments and the main voice in the poem. The girl is the product of an advertising industry that cajoles the consumer into the belief in a fantasy land of blue skies and unspoilt beaches. Inevitably, the poster's cheap promise of perfection has an alienating effect for some viewers. Larkin's dual-voiced writing is apparent: the girl's proclamation of an unspoilt haven is countered by the earthy rebuff of the wall-writer's defacement. Rather than responding to the cheery innocence of the message, Titch Thomas perceives the girl as a sex object whilst the reader is titillated by a series of erotic potentialities. The poster depicts a utopia that is forever out of reach, pandering to the worst aspects of male sexual desire which, as in 'Deceptions' and 'Two Portraits of Sex' (CP, 32, 36), frustrates rather than gratifies. The language is simultaneously innocent and overtly sexual, suggesting that modern selling techniques rely on provoking the base sexual attitudes that Titch Thomas graphically illustrates. The crude gestures are an apt expression of the bitterness felt by those excluded from the economic feast of the

1960s, but they also convey the grotesque realities of the male who is made to '*Come To Sunny Prestatyn*' in a sexual rather than a geographical sense.

Images conspire to form an erotic fantasy of a girl who is available for loveless sex. 'Kneeling up', 'tautened white satin' and a 'hunk of coast' which is significantly placed 'Behind her' convey how the poster sexually objectifies the girl in an explicit marketing ploy. 'Hunk' is colloquially suggestive of a sexually attractive male, and the drafts depict the girl 'Beckoning with thighs half open': sex is the main commodity being advertised here (u/p drafts, Workbook 6). Titch Thomas's diminutive stature suggests that he is as undependable as Prestatyn's weather, though social pressure controls his posturing as much as the girl's. The poem identifies one archetypal aspect of consumerism – the exchange of money in an act of prostitution. The selling of Prestatyn is as ignoble and exploitative as the observer's lusting over the girl. Holidays provide temporary solace for those leading mundane lives; free time and leisure are commodities to be paid for and like Titch Thomas, consumers cannot resist the charms on offer.

In the second stanza the picture of the girl 'slapped up one day in March' suggests abuse on several levels. By trading on the girl's sexuality the poster is abusive of her appearance but the way that the poster is 'slapped up' against the wall suggests a physical assault on the girl herself. Whilst her sexually vulnerable pose resembles the pornographic images collected by Larkin (see Motion, 1993, 234), its poetic function is to equate advertising methods with the rape that the exhibition of her semi-naked body incites. Far from speculating on an innocent away day in Wales, the male spectator desecrates the poster: 'Huge tits and a fissured crotch / Were scored well in'. Anglo-Saxon diction denotes the darker side of male desire but Titch Thomas's violent act demystifies the process that sets impossible ideals for both sexes:

> Someone had used a knife
> Or something to stab right through
> The moustached lips of her smile.

Penetration of the girl's lips destroys the smile which so tempted the speaker in the first few lines. The knife and the graffiti disfigure the girl's face, robbing her of the power of physical attraction that she had over men. It is not the girl who is raped, but her socially constructed representation that symbolises how, in the terms of an earlier poem, 'Reprehensibly perfect' images are paraded for consumption ('Poetry of Departures', CP, 86).

Like 'Deceptions' (CP, 32), the poem is balanced in its sympathy for the man and the girl. Of the poster girl: 'She was too good for this life'.

The girl shouldn't have to suffer Thomas's gross sexual attention though, equally, she shouldn't be manipulated by 'the dubious glamours of advertising' (Regan, 1992, 101). The last three lines allude to the self-gratifiying nature of consumerist society:

> Very soon, a great transverse tear
> Left only a hand and some blue.
> Now *Fight Cancer* is there.

Given Larkin's references to the subject in his letters, 'a hand and some blue' is a double reference to the private male perusal of pornographic material ('blue' being slang for pornography). Society's obsession with transient gratification in the 1960s (the 'Cheap suits, red kitchen-ware' and 'sharp shoes' ['Here', CP, 136]) was also a form of masturbation which provided release from an onerously materialistic world. The poem concludes with the substitution of one poster for another – the new slogan, '*Fight Cancer*', serving as a powerful displacement of fantasy and a chilling reminder of mortality.

The poster that inspired the poem is one of a series of advertisements for holiday destinations that are discussed in *Today* in 1963, one year after the poem was written (see Appendix, p. 190). The article addresses the 'gross deception' that the constructed nature of the poster perpetrates on the (male) observer and it provides a historical record of the attitudes with which the reader is assumed to be complicit. '"If that's what they have on the beaches of Kent" . . . you say as you fight your way to the ticket-office with your umbrella, raincoat and wellingtons under your arm, "then the sooner I get down to Ramsgate . . . the better!"' (*Today*, 17.viii.63). 'Sunny Prestatyn' questions sexist attitudes like these by recreating the posters' provocative appeal in order to explore the motivations for, and the reception of, demeaning sexual stereotypes for men and women.

The similar use of posters in earlier works implies Larkin's disenchantment with advertising began before the 1960s. Returning to Huddlesford after the air raids, John Kemp sees 'great gouts of clay [which] had been flung against posters' and ponders the shattered dreams of a population (*Jill*, 215). In *A New World Symphony*, Butterfield muses on the false promise of material gains when he sees 'a little boy . . . defacing a house-agent's advertisement' (BTH, 2002, 432). The boy is a prototype for '*Titch Thomas*' suggesting that Larkin's discomfort with consumerism existed prior to the social climate of the 1960s. *Jill* and *A Girl in Winter* repeatedly question commercial practices, and the subversive element in the letters and in the poetry and verse drama of the 1940s suggest a sustained disillusionment with man's acquisitiveness throughout Larkin's work.

In Larkin's dream-record the subconscious mind yearns to 'swerv[e]' away from human oppressions, and 'Here' imagines the most extreme form of detachment (CP, 136). Like 'Toads' and 'Poetry of Departures', the poem is also about release, but whereas the earlier poems employed a debate between different selves, 'Here' contains no self at all. For Swarbrick, 'the reader experiences the [poem's] journey without . . . a mediating voice' (Swarbrick, 1995, 104) and Smith refers to its 'pseudo-specificities' (Regan, 1997, 182), both in terms of its speaking voice and in its call for something elusive, or 'out of reach'. Syntactically, 'Here' is unusual in that the first three stanzas and part of the fourth consist of a single sentence in which the only apparent 'subject' is the participle, 'Swerving', signalling 'a violent wrench away from some other straight or direct course' (Rossen, 1989, 54). The poem rejects human values and endeavours together with the constraining boundaries that corporeal identity imposes. This correlates with the yearning for space 'cleared of me' in 'Absences' (CP, 49), but it can also be traced to passages in the fiction where a non-human mode is longed for. In the opening chapter of *A Girl in Winter* the absence of a subject and numerous passive constructions signal the enveloping of human activity by elemental forces and in *Trouble at Willow Gables* a series of past participles suggests actions which are mysteriously disembodied and ethereal:

> Time passed . . . Water began to boil, fires were lit, bacon cut up, sausages sprinkled with flour, shoes of all shapes and sizes were cleaned and polished, floors and steps scrubbed, and the brass plate on the front door, as well as innumerable doorknobs, were brightly rubbed. (BTH, 2002, 91)

Later, 'Tea steamed and was sipped: bacon cut and eaten, the rinds curling on the edges of innumerable plates: toast was buttered and bit' (BTH, 2002, 92). Indifference to human concerns also exists in *A New World Symphony*:

> Among the rafters dust blew along dark quills of wind, and piled up: a piece of newspaper left behind by the workmen turned yellow, was sanded over. Here and there a window began an individual rattle, a door an individual squeak. (BTH, 2002, 413)

The technique recalls 'Time Passes' in *To the Lighthouse*, where an uninhabited house grants natural phenomena free rein. The similar lack of a subject in 'Here' intensifies the separateness, not just from topographical features, but also from the 'unfenced existence' at the end.

Imitating a railway carriage's changing angle of vision, the opening lines suggest a deliberate avoidance exacerbated by the threefold repetition of 'Swerving'. Left behind are the 'rich industrial' areas that cast their 'shadows' over a landscape scourged by post-war expansion. An early draft implies that commercial excess has caused the blight: 'Swerving east, away from money's shadows / And more important traffic, to fields' (u/p draft, Workbook 6). The published lines instead emphasise the 'all night' activity of the 'traffic', recalling the 'Traffic . . . / Always on the move' in MacNeice's 'Letter to Graham and Anne Shepard' (LFI, 1937, 30). However, the draft focuses on the undervalued route 'to fields', suggesting how the 'rich' industrial centres compare unfavourably with the wealth of 'piled gold clouds' that anticipate the natural coin of 'Solar' (CP, 159). But the nature descriptions fall short of Wordsworthian grandeur: 'thin and thistled' does not invite communion with the Earth Mother and the most ardent Romantic would struggle to wrest transforming visions from unpropitious 'mud'. The direction of travel is not towards a pastoral idyll, but hurtles towards a bleak environment where 'Workmen at dawn' shelter at 'a harsh-named halt'. This is the only indication that the poem tracks a train journey but the clumsy application of language suggests the difficulties of veering away from human meddling. The stanza ends, however, on a note of subdued appreciation: the MacNeicean catalogue 'Of skies and scarecrows, haystacks, hares and pheasants' captures not only the region's rural textures but also its panoramic vastness that beckons at the end.

The second stanza portrays the delicate cohesiveness of a diversified social history in which different cultures and lifestyles are bound together: 'spires' jostle with 'cranes', signifying the haphazard human constructions of different periods and the 'barge-crowded' water dilutes what another poem describes as a quasi-religious 'devout drench' ('Water', CP, 93). The eclectic confusion of buildings and events is mirrored by the human groupings. Socially diverse 'consulates' and 'grim head-scarfed wives' also vie for space in a 'cluster', subsuming class divisions in humanity's chaotic tumble and the 'Cheap suits' and 'red kitchen-ware' are the 'metonymic' emblems of a mediocre post-war consumerism that has compromised human identity. Like the girls in 'The Large Cool Store' (CP, 135), fashion has deprived consumers of their individuality, making them as cheap and

---

[2] The early draft chimes with Larkin's anti-slavery remarks in *All What Jazz*: 'The American Negro is trying to take a step forward that can be compared only with the ending of slavery in the nineteenth century. And despite the dogs, the hosepipes and the burnings, advances have already been made towards giving the Negro his civil rights under the Constitution that would have been inconceivable when Louis Armstrong was a young man' (1985, 87).

tacky as the 'cut-price' goods they purchase. However, the reference to 'the slave museum', an allusion to Hull's Wilberforce House (a draft describes its ugly contents as 'Sickening with whips' [u/p fragment, Workbook 6]) provides a depiction of humanity's darkest injustice[2]. In the published lines, 'Fast-shadowed wheat-fields' become the 'raw estates' at the town's 'mortgaged half-built edges'; financial obligations oppress synthetic existences. For Whalen, this shows 'an alertness to the . . . capitalist forces which beat . . . down' the 'small beauty of the human being', a theme he identifies throughout the later poems (Whalen, 1997, 149).

The final stanza seeks seclusion from human gatherings in isolated 'villages, where removed lives / Loneliness clarifies' calling to mind the 'Villages [that] were cut off' at the start of *A Girl in Winter* (11), yet which were stirred by a force beyond human understanding. The ending's transcendent element, which has variously been termed 'epiphanic', a 'metaphoric current' and a 'symbolist' mode (Regan, 1997, 27, 79, 51), pines for an absence of human structures where natural processes flourish unaided: 'leaves unnoticed thicken', 'Hidden weeds flower' and 'neglected waters quicken'. The 'Luminously-peopled air' contrasts with the town's drab population, suggesting how animated insects surpass humanity's 'rich [industry]' but capturing, too, the desire to populate the airy oblivion in the closing lines.

The 'shapes' on the beach are the last indistinct vestiges of human forms before the contemplation of the ultimate escape from earthly constraints: 'Here is unfenced existence: / Facing the sun, untalkative, out of reach'. Appealing to the sun recalls the wonder at the 'fire-spilling star' in 'The North Ship' or the 'petalled head of flames' in 'Solar' (CP, 302, 159) but the bonds of language prevent a total release in their prescription of limited human knowledge. Just as the girl's natural intuition is occluded by the 'written skies' in 'Like the train's beat' (CP, 288), the 'untalkative' experience of airy spaciousness is thwarted by verbal articulation, which puts it 'out of reach' to human consciousness. Commenting on the 'limits to perception' that the poem sets, Regan terms 'Here' a *post-romantic* poem . . . [that] seriously questions the autonomy of the imagination and the transforming powers of "vision" on which Romantic poetic theory is posited' (Regan, 1992, 106).

'MCMXIV' (CP, 127) also comments on humanity's separation from natural processes. Here 'the countryside [is] not caring' about a significant moment in twentieth-century history. The poem focuses on the change in attitudes and lifestyles brought about by the First World War and, in Larkin's words, laments 'the irreplaceable world that came to an end' (Thwaite, 2001, 85). Various critical approaches have therefore tended to concentrate on the nostalgia evoked in the first two stanzas. For

Ricks, the poem is 'ominously idyllic' (Ricks, 1974, 9), whilst for Roger Day the poem is an 'idealised view of the pre-war era' (Day, 1987, 63). Clark adopts a different approach, seeing the 'accumulation of cultural signifiers' as a fictitious idyll that never existed (BTH, 2000, 176). Swarbrick similarly distrusts the poem's patriotic tones, suggesting that it trades in 'cultural myths [which are] as potent as those purveyed in the advertising images of other poems' (Swarbrick, 1995, 118). For Osborne, 'Larkin's most patriotic poem, "MCMXIV", with its refrain of "Never such innocence again" . . . is rendered somewhat less patriotic by its origins in part four of that anti-nationalistic poem *Hugh Selwyn Mauberley* by . . . [Ezra] Pound' (BTH, 2000, 147–8). Reference to Larkin's unpublished dream-record and other fragments suggest that, rather than expressing nostalgia for a golden era of patriotism and duty, the poem indicts the sacrifice of innocent men for dubious ideals.

An unpublished poem of 1950 shows that Larkin was capable of portraying contempt for those responsible for the events of 1914–18:

> Last of all, when a great war has ended
> (Humped iron sheds ruined, shut roads overgrown)
> Governments sell equipment they intended
> To fit out men they can now leave alone.
> (u/p draft, Workbook 1)

The war's destructive effect upon society's superstructure is obvious; the decision to sell military equipment argues that innocent civilians are cynically manipulated by their elected representatives. The fragment reflects on how the drudgeries of labour are a poor reward for active military service:

> So men in battledress lay bricks on mortar . . .
> Dust settles on them, dirt and chips of stone
> Rain smudges in: all crease in lines of effort.
> Anonymous discoloured shapes, they own
> No special dignity. Yet old and weathered . . .
> (u/p draft, Workbook 1)

Exploitation on the battlefield is replaced by exploitation in the workplace, a theme also addressed in *No For An Answer*. Like Porky, the ex-servicemen in the poem become 'discoloured shapes' who are accorded 'No special dignity'; instead, they adopt the debilitating routines of conventional masculine behaviour that leaves them 'old and weathered'.

Larkin commended Owen's poetry, hoping that 'the carnage, the waste, [and] the exploitation' that Owen describes 'should all be brought home to innocent non-combatants' (Larkin, 1983, 160). Larkin wrote this in 1963, though its anti-war sentiment is consistent with that expressed in the unpublished poem in 1950. There is a consistency, too, in his attitude towards the two World Wars. The Sutton correspondence suggests that Larkin was as resolutely opposed to the Second World War as he was to the First, wishing Sutton 'all luck in any kind of anti-army activity' (u/p letter, 29.vi.42). Larkin's 'Record of Dreams' also contains passages recording his discomfort with the hostile attitudes towards the enemy that dominant wartime culture endorsed. In Dream 36 Larkin is a captive in a prisoner-of-war camp in Germany: 'Each night a little ceremony was held with a lit candle to "inspire" us in hope of ultimate British victory. We had to do it in turn – it was not my turn then, but it would be' (u/p 'Record of Dreams', 18.xi.42). The depressed tone of the final phrase suggests Larkin's revulsion at wartime heroics and elsewhere in the dream he tries to connect with his captors: 'I felt I could learn German myself if I had a chance to talk to Germans' (u/p 'Record of Dreams', 18.xi.42). A month later, the roles are reversed and in Dream 85 Larkin is in a position of authority: 'I was an officer, in officer's uniform, standing outside a café where there was a dinner of Pacifists going on inside. I felt I should break it up, it being wartime etc.' (u/p 'Record of Dreams', 27.xii.42). Larkin is uncomfortable with the obligations of a dutiful and patriotic soldier, and considering his rejection of wartime attitudes elsewhere, it is hard to believe that a poem whose title refers to 1914 presents an 'idealised view of the pre-war era' (Day, 1987, 63). 'MCMXIV' is not a lament for an 'irreplaceable world' (Thwaite, 2001, 85), but an expression of sorrow at how that world's reverence for traditional constructs of national identity promoted a casual compliance with death and destruction.

Couching the title in 'roman numerals, as you might see it on a monument' (Thwaite, 2001, 85) calls to mind a sense of loss and rememberance, but the Roman style also cautions that imperial prowess is as susceptible to destruction as the naïve innocence of the queuing men. 'Those long uneven lines' at the start evoke the eagerness with which men waited 'patiently' to join up. Their 'Grinning' expressions and perception of war as 'An August Bank Holiday lark' reveals their attitude of gauche expectation, as if the excitements of a football or cricket match beckoned. The language recreates the distinct feel of life in the 1910s – the 'crowns of hats', 'moustached archaic faces' and the wonderfully innocent 'lark'– but these are the knowing and poetically constructed signifiers of a 1960s nostalgic ideal. Beneath the surface the poem expresses anxiety for men behaving '*as if*' (my emphasis) they awaited pleasure, when in reality their destiny was trench warfare. The men are deceived into readily accepting their fate through a complete integration into institutions to which they feel inextricably linked. The use of participles ('Standing', 'Grinning') heightens the sense of an established continuity of acquiescence with society's demands, their 'archaic faces' signalling the difference in outlook between now and then, but also implying that they represent others before them who contentedly accepted the dominant construction of historical processes.

The poem is ambivalent towards tradition, at once nostalgic and yet profoundly aware of the limitations of the securities of the past. The opening 'And' of stanza two promotes a wistful lyricism and the subsequent tumble of period detail gives the 'effect of impressions gathered at second hand from a sepia photograph' (Regan, 1992, 121). Overwhelmingly, the stanza's cultural signification of 'farthings and sovereigns' marks the gulf between past and present: 'And the shut shops, the bleached / Established names on the sunblinds'. This indicates the pre-war reverence for appropriate behaviour, though the 'bleached' blinds are a fading of conformist values. The 'Established names' on the sunblinds obscure what is natural by erecting their own version of 'how life should be' (CP, 144). Similarly, the 'dark-clothed children at play', whose conservative dress and suitable behaviour contrast with gaudier modern attire, are 'Called after' monarchs, echoing their parents' respect for traditional hierarchies but also their lack of imagination in deferring to what is known and trusted. Adverts for 'cocoa and twist' evoke period consumer taste, yet also provide comfort against wider wartime uncertainties.

The third stanza highlights nature's indifference to social structures, evoking a parallel elemental domain where human codes carry little weight. The 'countryside not caring' and the 'place-names all hazed over' underline the folly of ambitious human design: the undergrowth obscures human indicators and recalls the blurred boundaries in *A Girl in Winter*, ominously shadowing the 'Domesday lines / Under wheat's restless silence'. Symbolising the enduring power of nature, the wheat that has grown since the Domesday survey eclipses human endeavour as effortlessly as it outlives those killed in France, and the stanza's evocation of natural tranquillity puts allegiance to idealised national characteristics firmly in context. The stanza's closing lines convey a notional reverence for the past whilst noting its class differences: 'differently-dressed' servants inhabit 'tiny rooms in huge houses'. The 'dust behind limousines' depict the period's neglect of the national estate, masked by a façade of wealth and respectability.

Though the poem lacks the force of Yeats's conclusion to 'Easter 1916' ('All changed, changed utterly', *Selected Poems*, 119), the last stanza conveys a similar sensitivity to the change in human consciousness brought about by a significant historical event. The repetition of 'Never' in the first two lines emphasises the watershed in values that the war represents. The lines recall 'The Malverns' in which Auden comments, of England: 'now it has no innocence at all' (*The English Auden*, 142). Composed in 1933, Auden's poem addresses the political uncertainties of the 1930s and regrets that a certain construction of Englishness is under threat. Larkin's lines are reminiscent of Auden's, though the echo is ironical, as in 'MCMXIV' the men's 'innocence' signifies their naïve compliance with wartime jingoism. The concluding stanza reflects on the colossal shift in attitudes to duty and to nation that occurs 'Without a word'. Nature's insistent forward push in the previous stanza suggests the inevitability of change which makes human pronouncement irrelevant. Like the 'untalkative' aspect of 'Here', or the wordless insights of 'High Windows', the altered perceptions of 'MCMXIV' are beyond controlling human forces.

If this poem presents a nostalgic snapshot of an innocent age, it is, as Clark contends, to 'comment . . . on the process of mythicization that the poem itself performs' (BTH, 2000, 176). 'MCMXIV' uses the emotive vocabulary of a historical period to evoke feelings of mournful longing, though the language reconstructs a set of social values that inspired the tending of gardens prior to fighting wars. Rather than a nostalgic vision, the poem's aesthetic structure delivers a serious comment on flawed ideals.

Not all critics hear the poem's chastising tones. Neil Corcoran finds it 'impossible to gauge what kind of irony, if any, may attach to the notion of "innocence"' (Corcoran, 1993, 92) though he assumes that the poem's objective invites concurrence with the social iniquity it cites. Such a view is the consequence of insisting on Larkin's reactionary impulse: 'It is obviously possible for a poem written in 1960 to favour a traditional English class hierarchy; but it is hardly to be believed that such a thing might constitute an element of "innocence"' (Corcoran, 1993, 92). Corcoran reads the poem as a straightforward evocation of certain ideals, which ignores its performative element, in which the speaker's contrived acquiescence deconstructs the social order it claims to uphold. 'MCMXIV' makes the same charges of cultural indoctrination as 'Conscript' nineteen years earlier and it anticipates the contempt for 'Wreath-rubbish in Whitehall' that makes the speaker 'throw up' in 'Naturally the Foundation will Bear Your Expenses (1961, CP, 134). Rather than expressing different social outlooks, 'Conscript' and 'MCMXIV' are fabrics of the same subversive mind. Both of them illustrate how the 'powers which rule . . . lives have now become thoroughly internalised' such that conscripted civilians 'identify that power with their own inward being, so that to rebel . . . would be a form of self-transgression' (Eagleton cited in Regan, 1998, 244).

Larkin's most accomplished poem, 'The Whitsun Weddings' (CP, 114) illustrates the poet's stylistic and thematic culmination. Employing the metonymies of the novel, there are striking similarities between 'The Whitsun Weddings' and Larkin's fiction. As with 'Church Going', the drafts show how the finished poem emerged from a narrative framework:

> Something must have stopped me getting away
>   That Whitsuntide
> For it was after lunch on Saturday
> When . . .
> (u/p draft, Workbook 4)

The poem focuses on rites of passage; the Jungian dimension, which had its origins in Larkin's student days and exists elsewhere in the ouevre, is also present here. 'The Whitsun Weddings' tackles, in a coherent and vivid way, the diminished notions of femininity inspired by contemporary attitudes to marriage and consumerism in the 1960s.

The speaker's colloquial tones ('I was late getting away' and 'Not till about / One-twenty') define him as a representative of post-war society, but also register how his existence is regulated by the clock. Whatever responsibilities he leaves behind almost prevent the speaker's escape and, unlike John Kemp, whose window was misted over (*Jill*, 21), the traveller has 'All windows down', suggesting the potential to embrace new perspectives. The first 'wedding' the traveller sees has no human participants but focuses, instead, on 'Where sky and Lincolnshire and water meet', a vision that is often denied to the speaker by the futile 'sense / Of being in a hurry'. These lines recall MacNeice's resentment at being 'Always on the move' in *Letters from Iceland* (30). The latter text influenced 'The North Ship' and it also infiltrates the artistic impulse of 'The Whitsun Weddings'. The poem has continuities with *In the Grip of Light*, too: the phrase 'blinding windscreens' implies a unique illumination of the familiar, but also suggests how technological contrivances have an occluding effect on humanity's capacity for natural communion. The journey's movement 'Behind the backs of houses' and across 'a street / Of blinding windscreens' prompts a view of urban landscapes from an unusual or changed perspective. As with Katherine Lind's journey to London, during which she 'Only infrequently . . . [saw] things that reminded her of landscape paintings', the speaker dwells on what is shabby and uninspiring. However, just as Katherine saw the random detail as 'enshrined beneath the sky' (*A Girl in Winter*, 80), the speaker's fleeting glimpses 'uniquely' transform scenes and events.

Contemplating the 'new and nondescript' landscape on a 'sunlit Saturday' the speaker notices how the tide of modern production processes has wrecked 'dismantled cars', leaving behind a nauseous wake of 'industrial froth': the 'short-shadowed cattle' are not only victims of the sun's angle, but natural symbols that have been rudely eclipsed by mechanistic endeavour. One of the poem's great merits, however, is the way it balances despair and negativity with the potential worth of what is mundane and mediocre: 'A hothouse flashed uniquely' in the sun aptly intimates how regenerative stirrings can be nursed to health despite the inauspicious setting of a drab post-war landscape.

By the end of the third stanza, the speaker's contempt for his surroundings extends to those who live there. The 'porters larking with the mails' are ignored by the traveller, who 'went on reading' instead, suggesting his class-conscious belief that intellectual activity outweighs an interest in common humanity. Similarly, the reference to 'girls / In parodies of fashion' is imbued with the speaker's élitist, sneering tones. Smith detects here the patronising attitude towards a society 'where mass tastes and values prevail, and the charming yokels of an earlier pastoral have turned into menacingly actual travelling companions, claiming equal rights' (Smith, 1982, 176). As Swarbrick cautions, though, 'this kind of criticism unquestioningly accepts the voice speaking these lines as one it is intended we approve' (Swarbrick, 1995, 106). The speaker chides himself for his rash condescension: 'Struck, I leant / More promptly out next time, more curiously, / And saw it all again in different terms'. Speakers throughout the volume try to 'see the same subject "in different terms", to modulate, change perspectives' (O'Neill cited in Hartley, 1988, 196), and this realigning of viewpoints is most apparent in the title poem. At first, the speaker's revised impression of the wedding parties seems just as contemptuous as his earlier estimation, particularly his references to 'nylon gloves and jewellery-substitutes', implying it is not only their clothes, but the brides themselves who are second-rate. What the speaker is really alert to is how 'the descriptions of women's fashions . . . present them as the means by which contemporary society constructs femininity' (Osborne cited in BTH, 2000, 152). Seen in these terms, the poem is sympathetic to the brides' predicament. They are 'Waving goodbye / To' a pre-marital existence, when conventional codes of dress and conduct were less stringently applied. As they embark on married life they are labelled, or 'Marked off . . . unreally', much like the 'synthetic' products in 'The Large Cool Store' (CP, 135). For David Trotter, the poem involves a rite of passage for the brides 'which celebrate[s] the connection between individual experience and shared meaning' (Trotter, 1984, 180–2), but hearing 'An uncle shouting smut' is demeaning rather than celebratory. If the poem traces a Jungian 'individuation' ritual, this is achieved not by offensive initiation rites but in spite of their degrading influence.

The next stanza registers the journey's momentary cohesiveness as the travellers become 'loaded with the sum of all they saw'. However, there are doubts as to how 'Free' the brides are. Stanza six evokes the women's intuitive understanding of events:

> The women shared
> The secret like a *happy funeral*;
> While girls, gripping their handbags tighter, stared
> At a *religious wounding*. (my emphasis)

Longley claims that '"The Whitsun Weddings" has . . . more to do with gender than with class . . . For the women in the poem, marriage is tribal initiation as violation' (BTH, 2000, 42). Just like the speaker's earlier perception of the brides, the oxymorons here suggest not only marriage's joyous sanctity but also its deadening and destructive effects. The heady conflation of disparate scenes – 'Now fields were building-plots' – that the journey facilitates is diminished by the way that the weddings have somehow injured the girls, or snuffed out part of their identity. In 'gripping their handbags tighter' they struggle with questions of self-definition and the association of marriage with death persists into the penultimate stanza. Just as in 'Toads', italicised typography mimics direct speech; the phrase '*I nearly died*' refers to the bride's colloquial response to wedding-day nerves, further suggesting, with a touch of black humour, the demise of the single life and all its possibilities. The symbolic import in the lines, 'walls of blackened moss / Came close, and it was nearly done, this frail / Travelling coincidence' suggest that the ending is not as full of 'hopefulness' as Larkin claimed (Haffenden, 1981, 124–5). Death threatens to derail whatever unique coalescence has occurred. The poem's famous closing imagery achieves this precarious balance between hope and despair.

Rushing southwards and conscious of the unifying experiences both within and without the train, the speaker has a sudden vision of the metropolis: 'I thought of London spread out in the sun, / Its postal districts packed like squares of wheat'. These lines contain, for many readers, an uplifting note: the newly-weds' homes will be places of abundant fertility where their offspring will grow with all the vigour that the wheat simile implies. The 'packed' capital suggests the plenitude of the new shoots of humanity and rather than overcrowding there is a harmonious merging of what were once disparate neighbours:

> They watched the landscape, sitting side by side
> – An Odeon went past, a cooling tower,
> And someone running up to bowl – and none
> Thought of the others they would never meet
> Or how their lives would all contain this hour.

Here is an eclectic mixture of different Englands that are accorded equal status by the traveller's edifying gaze. According to this interpretation, just as the couples, who were once separate, now exist 'side by side', so the landmarks of different national traditions – both the urban and the pastoral – become wedded in the overarching vision.

A second reading reveals that the lines sustain an interpretation that is directly contrary to the optimistic theme discussed above. Considering the phrase 'Now fields were building-plots', London's 'postal districts packed like squares of wheat' now seem to be unappealingly busy and urbanised to an inhuman degree. The wheat simile is darkly ironic, implying that London can barely sustain grass, let alone 'squares of wheat'; in the words of 'Going, Going', what is rapidly filling the spaces where wheat used to grow is 'concrete and tyres' (CP, 190). The metaphors in the final stanza are equally fraught with ambiguity. On the one hand, the concluding image contains a positive note: like 'rain', the latent fertility of the marriages refreshes the drought of disharmony that blights the nation, a theme that links the poem to *The Waste Land*. On the other hand, the strength of unity that marriage suggests is diminished by being sent 'out of sight, somewhere' in the form of an 'arrow-*shower*' which connotes dissolution rather than a replenishing deluge.

Carey suggests that the poem's oscillation between the joyful and the pessimistic does not have to be reconciled. The poem's two 'voices' – one pragmatic and conventionally 'masculine' and the other intuitive and conventionally 'feminine' – are endemic, not just to this poem, but to Larkin's work as a whole (BTH, 2000, 51–65). Such a view has its attractions, though there is another explanation for the poem's seemingly built-in contradictions. On 4 March, 1941 Larkin borrowed from the Bodleian Library W. Y. Tindall's *D. H. Lawrence and Susan His Cow*. Larkin's admiration for Lawrence is well recorded in the Sutton letters, where he declares that the novelist is so important he should be 'read out in churches' (Thwaite, 1992, 57). At various points, Larkin uses Lawrentian imagery and adapts his thematic concerns; the central section of 'The Whitsun Weddings' is indebted to chapter 5 of *The Rainbow* in its portrayal of a wedding party (see Whalen, 1986, 83). However, Larkin's reading of Tindall is important because the book cites a letter written by Lawrence to his sister in 1911, where God is described as:

> a vast shimmering impulse which waves onwards towards some end
> . . . When we die, like rain-drops falling back again into the sea, we
> fall back into the big, shimmering sea of unorganized life which we
> call God. We are lost as individuals, yet we count in the whole. It
> requires a lot of pain and courage to come to discover one's own
> creed, and quite as much to continue in lonely faith. Would you like

a book or two of philosophy? or will you merely battle out your own ideas? I would still go to chapel if it did me any good . . . It is a fine thing to establish one's own religion in one's heart, not to be dependent on tradition and second-hand ideals. (cited in Tindall, 1939, 19)

At the end the sentiments are reminiscent of the speaker's re-articulation of orthodox belief in 'Church Going', though earlier in the passage Lawrence addresses a theme similar to the closing lines of 'The Whitsun Weddings'. Does the 'arrow-shower' represent a life-enhancing force, or a dissolution of former strength that is now 'out of sight'? Lawrence's philosophy embraces both of these possibilities. In the letter's terms, the newly-weds of the poem, like the disparate scenes around them, become 'lost as individuals, yet . . . count in the whole'. A *North Ship* poem advances a similar thesis: 'Far out beyond the dead / What life they can control – / All runs back to the whole' (1944, CP, 272). Similarly, the shadow of death and despair which haunts 'The Whitsun Weddings' returns us to 'the big, shimmering sea of unorganized life' which Lawrence calls God and which Larkin construes as having the potential for meaningful coalescence. Both 'The Whitsun Weddings' and Lawrence's philosophical musings have a shared imagery – rain, a sense of falling and the fusion of separateness into wholeness – and Larkin's widespread use of water to signify mystical union is also indebted to Lawrentian philosophy.

The poems discussed cover a wide range of topics: advertising, the permissive society, the First World War and a journey through England in the 1960s. What they share is an overriding concern with the way that roles, lifestyles and identities are imposed on the individual. 'Sunny Prestatyn' and 'Essential Beauty' deconstruct how an idealisation 'Of how life should be' (CP, 144) is aggressively sold, whereas in 'MCMXIV ' and 'Here', coercion is subtly packaged under ennobling or liberating idioms. The constrictions of stereotypical gendered behaviour are repeatedly paraded, as in the 'unfocused she' of sensual billboard fantasy (CP, 144) or as the mediocre existence of the Whitsun brides. *The Whitsun Weddings* is acutely conscious of the way that women's conventional obligations '[push] them / To the side of their own lives' ('Afternoons', CP, 121), but it is also conscious of how domestic routines are equally crushing for the husband who 'has no time at all, // With the nippers to wheel round the houses / And the hall to paint in his old trousers' ('Self's the Man', CP, 117). For Clark, this poem is an 'appalling evocation of socially constructed and responsible masculinity' (Regan, 1997, 100) though the speaker's doubts about his own life (he can only 'suppose' that it's better) anticipates the mistrust of human speculation at the end of

'High Windows'. In 'Wild Oats' (CP, 143), what divides the subject from happiness is a socially constructed desire for an archetypal 'bosomy English rose' who is conventionally 'beautiful' yet totally unattainable for the awkward speaker. Realising this, he settles for 'her friend in specs' but the affair cools because he is 'too selfish, withdrawn, / And easily bored'. The poem speculates on how cultural forces package 'beautiful' women as the most appropriate objects for male sexual interest. The 'two snaps / Of bosomy rose' serve as 'Unlucky charms': their glossily 'perfect' images of idealised femininity preventing the speaker's relations with real women.

'Dockery and Son' (CP, 152) assumes a decentred perspective in portraying the begetting of sons. For the speaker 'To have no son, no wife, / No house or land . . . seemed quite natural', though he is conscious of the 'Innate assumptions' that inscribe these things as basic requirements of manly contentment. The poem's title closely resembles that of Charles Dickens's *Dombey and Son* (1848), also concerned with questions of patrilineal descent. The speaker is arrested by Dockery's conviction that 'he should be added to' and his belief that 'adding meant increase'. The choice of verb is crucial, as the notion that fathering a son *adds* to the begetter's reputation implies that the male offspring is a material asset that can be quantified and invested in a way that a daughter – under the auspices of a traditional patriarchal society – cannot. Like *Dombey and Son*, 'Dockery and Son' suggests a family business run on patriarchal lines in order to make a profit. Larkin's poem exposes the chauvinistic principles (not the 'truest, or [what we] most want') upon which family businesses are based in the same way that the structural principles of Dickens's novel indicts the shameful misogyny of its principal character: 'But what was a girl to Dombey and Son! In the capital of the House's name and dignity, such a child was merely a piece of base coin that couldn't be invested – a bad Boy – nothing more' (*Dombey and Son*, 2). *High Windows* develops *The Whitsun Weddings'* treatment of the relative merits of both natural and monetary coinage, as well as further commenting on the failings of patriarchal sexual politics. *The Less Deceived* also questioned the 'printed directions of sex', lifestyles and religion ('Wants', CP, 42) that the dominant culture stringently records. Throughout his career, Larkin destabilised the very attitudes that his detractors accuse him of purveying.

Windows of Perception

There is an unmistakable correspondence between the breakdown of [post-war] social consensus and the fractured linguistic contours of

Larkin's final poems. If *High Windows* is sometimes savage and vehement in its outlook, it is also the most socially committed and ideologically engaged collection of poems that Larkin produced. (Regan, 1992, 124)

An ideological social commitment, evident in *High Windows*, can also be found in Larkin's early poetry, particularly *In the Grip of Light*. Swarbrick also argues for Larkin's thematic continuities, seeing in *High Windows* a 'deepening anxiety about the relationship between self and community' (Swarbrick, 1995, 124) and reading it as a 'despairing conclusion to Larkin's lifelong quarrel with himself about his own identity' (Swarbrick, 1995, 124, 123). *High Windows* shows the same contempt for social and sexual conventions that pervaded the earlier writing, though some critics insist on its stylistic and thematic separation from the subversive impulse in Larkin's earlier work. For Trotter, the critical tone in *High Windows* is a new departure for Larkin: '[the volume shifts] to a far more militant and assertive stance than he had ever adopted before . . . The shaming pragmatism of the sixties drove him to speak his mind, to give his poems the authority of conscious and unequivocal dissent' (Trotter, 1984, 184–6). Trotter notes the important shaping factors of the cultural and social ambience, though he overplays the 'change' in Larkin's work; radical enquiry in verse is in fact a mainstay of the poet's oeuvre. Since the mellifluous idiom of *The North Ship* in the early 1940s Larkin's work has expressed a 'conscious and unequivocal dissent' from orthodox belief; it is this disdain for oppressive human systems which continues to dominate his poetry in the 1960s and 1970s.

Noting the links between the first and third of the major volumes, Ian Almond comments that 'in Larkin systems are resented . . . for their inhibitive . . . bullying nature . . . One thinks immediately of the "hectoring" bible in "Church Going", or the "bonds and gestures" in "High Windows", the oppressive presence of the priest' (BTH, 2000, 183). In a candid gloss, Larkin himself remarked of the title poem: 'It shows humanity as a series of oppressions, and one wants to be somewhere where there's neither oppressed nor oppressor, just freedom' (Thwaite, 2001, 59).

In 'High Windows' (CP, 165) the 'oppressions' are those of sexual desire and religious belief, both of which tyrannise human existence. The poem's narrative suggests that just as the speaker is envious of the younger generation's sexual freedom, so the older generation were similarly covetous of the speaker's non-churchgoing habit. The wordless emptiness of the final stanza implies that such human constructions of freedom are themselves restrictive and illusory. What is yearned for instead is an elemental void that is tantalisingly 'beyond' human comprehension. The luminous exaltation of stanza five longs for a desireless state, separate from the corporeal and linguistic boundaries of human existence, though the poem's compositional fabric ruthlessly undermines clichéd modes of understanding.

In the first stanza the speaker views the 1960s sexual revolution as a 'paradise' in which the 'Bonds and gestures' of the traditional marriage contract are as redundant as 'an outdated combine harvester'. In the hedonism of the 1960s, sexual behaviour has all the impersonality, as well as the mechanical efficiency, of agricultural hardware. The 'long slide' that 'everyone young' plays on signals that sex is now practised with the abandon of children in a recreational park, though its worth is questioned by the detail of 'going down' which is reminiscent of *The Waste Land*: 'Marie, hold on tight. And down we went' (*T. S. Eliot: Selected Poems*, 51). As in Eliot's poem, a physical descent is matched by a moral one so that what the speaker perceives as a sexual utopia is re-evaluated by the poem's aesthetic logic as a *dystopian* nightmare.

The speaker's convictions are also undercut in the way that his *knowledge* (line 4) is based merely on 'see[ing]' and 'guess[ing]' (ll. 1–2), suggesting the precarious nature of his understanding. Even when the focus is widened to 'Everyone' in stanza two, they only 'dreamed' of a utopian existence and in stanza three the speaker can only 'wonder' about the previous generation's attitudes towards his own behaviour. These verbs consistently imply wishful thinking rather than definitive insight, but the speaker's limitations are marked, more than anything else, by his crude language.

According to Larkin his 'bad language' was used simply 'to shock' (Thwaite, 2001, 61), though various critics have provided alternative theories as to its function. James claims that it 'is put in not to shock the reader but to define the narrator's personality' (James, 2001b, 49), and Burt interprets Larkin's 'dirty words as subcultural indicators . . . powerful ways of calling into question who the poet sounds like, who he wants to sound like, and why' (Burt, 1996, 18). The narrator's use of expletives would have shocked some readers in 1974, though they also define him as aggressive, cynical and overtly chauvinistic. Significantly, 'he's *fucking* her' while 'she's / *Taking* pills or wearing a diaphragm' (my emphasis) implying that men enjoy sex while women suffer the anxieties of contraception. This is the kind of sexism that offends Jardine but, as Burt's analysis implies, the construction of such a character and his repellent sexual politics are invoked precisely to be undermined. The chauvinistic yearning for a world where sexual activity is entirely enjoyed and directed by men is just another of the dubious 'utopias' that the poem's objective challenges.

Larkin's other perceived 'oppression', religion, should also be mentioned. The central, italicised section of the poem ventriloquises the previous generation's attitude towards the apparent 'freedom' of the first speaker's agnosticism. He is envied for having a life in which there is '*No God any more*' and for being able to voice openly '*What you think of the priest*'. Once again, though, the details of the poem conspire to nullify the idea that this is another 'paradise'. It is not described as such by the first speaker and the phrase '*That'll be the life*' recalls the expectant '*Till then*' of 'Next, Please' in its hope for an elusive ideal (CP, 52). The image of the 'long slide' is re-invoked to emphasise the reductive nature of the quest: '*He / And his lot will all go down the long slide / Like free bloody birds*'.

The aspiration towards an ideal of happiness is put into a wider context at the end of the poem. 'Rather than [the] words' which are used to articulate 'happiness' in the first four stanzas, the last lines suggest a realm 'beyond' human codification. Whereas the poem's predominant movement has been 'down', thereby stressing the futility of human reasoning, the focus at the end is upwards to the 'high windows'. As in 'Here' (CP, 136), the ultimate view is not transcendent or visionary, but instead 'shows / Nothing, and is nowhere, and is endless'. The poem suggests the *un*seeing nature of human perspectives and is reminiscent of 'Like the train's beat' (CP, 288) which ruptured conventional syntax to depict how the 'written skies' of spoken communication balked, rather than aided, meaningful connection. Similarly, the attraction of the 'blue air' of 'High Windows' resides in its being *un*inscribed with human understanding. The syntactical arrangement emphasises the snub to human insight. Throughout the poem, 'knowledge' has been gathered by an identifiable agent – '*I see*', '*I . . . / . . . guess*', '*I know*', '*Everyone . . . dreamed*', '*I wonder*' and '*Anyone . . . thought*'. In contrast to this '*the* thought' in stanza five has no accompanying subject (my emphases); it simply 'comes', as Petch says, 'to resolve the imaginative tussle of the earlier verbs . . . the absence of a pronoun here is essential to the poem's movement towards generalization' (Petch, 1981, 98). What constitutes the poem's ultimate 'oppression' is flawed human knowledge which the ending negates. Tracing the poem's debt to French symbolism, Everett re-articulates the human need to construct:

> '*L'azur*' (the blue) is Mallarmé's most consistent and philosophical symbol, delineating both the necessity and the absence of the ideal, an ideal which we imprint on the void sky by the intensity of our longing . . . (Everett, 1986, 239)

For Everett, Larkin's model for 'High Windows' was Mallarmé's 'Les Fenêtres', though there are other sources: Whalen sees in the poem 'concern for the living presence of the elements' as shown in Lawrence's 'Blueness' (Whalen, 1986, 62). For John Whitehead, the end of Larkin's poem resembles the last line of 'Old Man' by Edward Thomas (see Whitehead, 1995, 234). Speculation on the precise location of the high windows is equally varied. Booth claims that the windows of Larkin's top floor flat, in Pearson Park, provided the inspiration (see BTH, 1992, 167) whereas Roger Day argues that it was the windows of another Hull site, The Brynmor Jones Library, that kindled the poem (see Day, 1987, 81).

As well as textual and topographical influences, it is important to consider the impact on the poem of Larkin's friendship with James Sutton. Of particular relevance to 'High Windows' is an untitled, surrealist work by Sutton (Plate 4a) which, according to Daphne Ingram, greatly impressed Larkin. Maeve Brennan describes the painting as showing 'building workers trapped in a dark upper room with no doors. The only means of escape [is] through a small window high up on the wall' (Brennan, 1998, 26). Writing to Brennan, Sutton describes the sky as 'the clearest infinite blue imaginable' and though he was initially unsure as to the picture's meaning, he finally realised that the subject was 'sex (the plaster) & the freedom to indulge, or not, in sex without fear' (cited in Brennan, 1998, 26). Sutton believed that in 'High Windows' Larkin '[took the idea] a stage further to accommodate the Sixties sexual revolution' (letter to Maeve Brennan, 8.ix.88).

Sutton's interpretations correlate with the critics' view of the poem, but above all else, the painting suggests the oppressive nature of labour and its power to define people's existence. The cowed posture of the worker in the foreground shows that he is utterly overwhelmed by the flowing plaster that dominates the canvas. The plaster symbolises how labour encroaches on the worker's sense of self. Just as the main figure is subsumed by the symbolic plaster (his feet are already invisible), so the minor characters act out a tableau of 'oppression' in the background. The 'foreman' character on the far right threatens a third figure with a spade whilst at the same time urging him to work harder. The hapless third figure is literally forced into his work as his head is pushed into his plasterer's hawk that screens out his face and so erases his identity. Sutton emphasises the way that work delineates our existence by framing the scene within the wooden supports of an access platform so that the workers are oppressed, not merely by their labour, but also by the invidious industrial relations that erode any sense of fellow-feeling. The concerns of Sutton's painting are replicated in Larkin's poetry, prose and drama. In *A Girl in Winter* Katherine is exploited by the tyrant-manager, Anstey; in *Night in the Plague* the Father puts business interests before compassion and in 'Träumerei', 'One man walking a deserted platform' and 'Toads', workers are beaten down by gruelling routines. Given Larkin's artistic affinities with Sutton, it seems extremely likely that he appropriated the painting's striking blue windows to suggest freedom from oppression in all its forms. As in the poems, however, ultimate freedoms are 'out of reach' ('Here', CP, 137) and the figures who bask in the intense light at the back of the picture yearn for a brightness beyond the 'sun-comprehending glass' yet remain in the room, hopelessly bound by their human existence.

Larkin's appreciation of Sutton's work can also be used to counter his alleged racist[3] and sexist tendencies. The main figure in the picture is a black male whose clothes and demeanour clearly signal his humbled, lower-class status though the picture's objective is to sympathise with his plight. The shaft of light emanating from the windows illuminates his face and makes clear his potential for higher understanding. Similarly, one of Sutton's charcoal sketches (Plate 4b) depicts a young girl wistfully gazing out of an attic window implying her desire for a wider experience than her conventional feminine identity permits. The bleakness of the room and the bars of the bed-frame exacerbate her confinement. The speaker of 'Ugly Sister' (1943–4, CP, 292) is also confined, though her bed is a refuge from the iniquities of adolescent love. She finds solace in music and nature but remains cut off from the external world. 'Wedding-Wind', 'Like the train's beat', 'Portrait', 'The Whitsun Weddings', 'Deceptions', *A New*

---

[3] Roberts has contextualised some of Larkin's alleged racist remarks. In a letter to Sutton, Larkin refers to Louis Armstrong as 'you niggah' and 'youleader-man', encouraging him to 'jam dat ole horn' (4.viii.39). For Roberts, 'there is nothing racist about Larkin's imitation of Black American idiom here, at least by the standards of 1939'. Writing to Charles Monteith in 1971 Larkin praises Armstrong as a 'Trojan horse of Negro values'. Moreover, in *All What Jazz* Larkin looks forward to a time when 'the Negro is as well housed, educated and medically cared for as the white man'. At the end of his life Larkin was concerned that the book 'now reads very anti-black, insofar as most of the people I bollock are black', but added in mitigation, 'most of the people I praise are black too' (cited in Roberts, 1999, 8–9).

Larkin's empathy with the predicament of the black male is also evident in his dream-record: 'I am a negro . . . I go to an American racecourse where I go in the negroes' entrance & use the negroes' very rickety lavatory. I then meet Hilly, and we walk arm in arm . . . it's terrible to think I cd. be killed (ie lynched) for walking with her . . . She agrees, and says something about Russia – a similar atrocity (u/p 'Record of Dreams', 28.xii.42).

World Symphony and *A Girl in Winter* all share Larkin and Sutton's compassion for women who are socially marginalised.

Like 'High Windows', 'This Be The Verse' (CP, 180) uses demotic language to launch a Freudian assault on our parents. If the former poem decried the idea that sexual freedom constitutes happiness, the latter work denounces 'hav[ing] any kids yourself' and the invidious hereditary traits that this engenders. The fine pun of the opening phrase suggests the mechanical nature of the sex act, in which children are, quite literally, 'fucked' into existence; but it conveys, too, how being conceived is equated with ruination. In colloquial terms we are all 'fucked up' when we inherit the previous generation's 'faults'. The inevitability of this process is implied by the jaunty iambic rhythm that bullies the reader into accepting the poem's claim. This coercion is best seen in the first line, where the cosy and familiar 'mum and dad' is on the receiving end of a coarse expletive. The application of vulgar terminology to what is conventionally thought of as safe and reliable disrupts settled assumptions about family relationships. Depicting parents as the enemy is exacerbated by the prolific use of the anonymous word 'they'. It appears no fewer than six times in five lines and it has an estranging effect, dehumanising the familiarity of the family.

In the second stanza, every generation, it is argued, has been corrupted by the 'old-style' values of the parents, though it also hints at the much more sinister damage that domestic relations can inflict. By isolating the first line from its surrounding context ('they were fucked up in their . . . ') Clark teases out the suggestion that domestic violation sometimes extends to areas beyond the mental sphere (Regan, 1997, 99). As well as the potential molestation that conventional familial relations can mask, the second half of the stanza highlights what is, at the best of times, the deceitful nature of parenting. Behind the child-deceiving 'soppy-stern' persona are the adult realities of married life – passion and conflict – which the phrase 'at one another's throats' so effectively conveys. The implication is that family life is founded on duplicitous principles.

Considering these charges against marriage and parenthood it is hardly surprising that readers are advised to 'Get out as early as [they] can' in the final stanza. The phrase renounces all sexual as well as institutional entanglements, urging a withdrawal not only from marriage but also from the woman herself. Some might interpret this as misogynistic, though the blame for the failings of procreation is apportioned exclusively to males ('Man hands on misery to man') implying that it is the specific responsibility of siring that is at fault. Moreover, the cynical, aggressive idiom of the first two stanzas modulates into a bardic voice at the end which chastises not 'the saloon bar crony' but informs, instead, a sophisticated audience that is more likely to ponder the poem's only simile. But what is the 'misery' that 'deepens like a coastal shelf'? Does the line refer merely to the hereditary ills that increase as each subsequent generation is born? Or does it suggest, as Carey argues, the 'unpopulated geographical space . . . that other Larkin poems [such as 'Here' and 'High Windows'] open out into' (BTH, 2000, 52)? As in those poems, the meaning of 'This Be The Verse' resides in its apparently unresolvable contradictions. Human beings are clearly locked into the regenerative chaos that the poem depicts, though a plane of human absence is still wistfully yearned for. As in so many of Larkin's poems, human understanding is the major oppressor and this is impossible to escape.

In particular, it is language that imprisons the speakers of the poems. Gary Day notes that 'Larkin's problem is how to construct . . . [a] sense of self using a language which has already constructed a self for him' (Day and Docherty, 1997, 41), and other critics have argued that swearing provides an exit from the restrictive signification of ordinary language. For Rossen, Larkin's four-letter words constitute a kind of 'non-language' which suit his purposes by providing an alternative 'code of language which at the same time tears a hole in [conventional] language' (Rossen, 1989, 130). Burt interprets Larkin's foul lexicon as a revolt against a wide range of orthodox structures: 'It . . . foreshadows and reflects the same self-isolating, sadly certain rejection of ordinary language and society . . . in a negationist gesture out of and away from everything' (Burt, 1996, 19).

Whilst complete abdication from the human condition is the ideal escape, the characters of *High Windows* settle for a release from human institutions. The closing counsel of 'This Be The Verse' couldn't be simpler: 'don't have any kids yourself'. 'How Distant' (CP, 162) shows how those trapped in conventional 'masculine' roles – 'Cattlemen, or carpenters' – are 'keen / Simply to get away / From married villages', locations where traditional conduct is prescribed at home and at work. Grumbles about society's constrictive mores are familiar characteristics of Larkin's work, though the alternatives are not always coherent. Larkin either denounces convention or seeks to escape it; or better still, escape altogether the bodily form which 'Surrounds us with its own decisions' ('Ignorance', CP, 107). The move towards more organic principles of social organisation informs part of Larkin's cure for the commercialisation that infects both relationships and nations alike. In order to identify the other part, however, it is necessary to reflect on how other intellectuals' have conceived of their perfect world.

A theme shared by several of the extracts in *The Faber Book of Utopias* (Carey, 1999) is the radical reshaping of conventional sexual politics.

James Lawrence describes his vision of a matriarchal world in which the hypocrisies and stigmas of the nineteenth century have been swept away. Carey summarises:

> All property . . . belongs to [women] and passes to their daughters at death. They enjoy absolute freedom in love. A man may propose sex to any woman and be sure of 'a gracious compliance or a polite refusal'. Social gatherings usually end in love-making, partners in the last waltz generally spending the night together. All mothers are single mothers, and the care and management of children is their concern . . . Motherhood is publicly honoured – soldiers, for example, salute pregnant women. The name of the father is, however, unknown . . . [These women] have emancipated themselves from the false modesty that (as Lawrence saw it) helped to keep [them] subjugated in Europe and Islam . . . They appear naked before men without a second thought. (Carey, 1999, 181)

Charles Fourier, another nineteenth-century utopia-seeker, is equally impatient of traditional taboos and calls for an 'unashamed' sexual freedom:

> The qualification for admission to [Fourier's] 'amorous nobility' will be a generous sexual nature, capable of carrying on several affairs at once (this will be tested under examination conditions). Polygamy and adultery will be praiseworthy in Harmony, and they will be open and unashamed – there will be no secrecy – whereas monogamy will be despised as the narrowest sort of love. (Carey, 1999, 212)

In Fourier's 'Harmony' both sexes are able to surrender themselves to the 'unfettered impulses of simple nature' (Carey, 1999, 214), though Charlotte Perkins Gilman confronts the way that sexual personality is, itself, socially constructed:

> [Herland is home to] a race of calm, dignified, athletic, rational women, who seem beautiful yet strangely sexless, lacking the charms and the fragility that the young men have been culturally conditioned to associate with femininity. (Carey, 1999, 382)

Gilman's 'Herland' is a 'sisterhood, without social classes or competitiveness' (Carey, 1999, 382) and is similar to 'Walden Two', the utopia conceived of by B. F. Skinner in 1948:

> Communal living replaces private houses, releasing women from domestic labour. Husbands and wives have separate rooms, which makes them happier and better adjusted. Children are reared communally ('Home is not the place to raise children'), and regard all adults

as their parents . . . In Walden Two . . . Competetiveness has vanished, along with heroes, hero-worship, the cult of leadership and the idea of personal triumph. (Carey, 1999, 426)

The Faber Book includes a social audit of women's opinions gathered in 1995. In responding to the question 'What do you want?' interviewees spoke candidly about their prerequisites for a better world. A London woman asked for 'The freedom to enjoy pornography without being labelled by feminists as anti-feminist' and a Coventry participant asked simply 'To be free of what society expects . . . to be married for only six months of the year and be by myself for the other six!!' (Carey, 1999, 500–1). These views echo those expressed by another Coventry writer: Larkin admitted to 'want[ing] sex very much indeed. But I take leave to refuse it on the terms offered in the particular culture pattern we have the misfortune to inhabit' (BTH, 2002, 486). This extract chimes perfectly with the sentiments expressed in the Faber anthology. Tellingly, Philip Larkin presents a code of sexual honesty that could have issued from the pen of either Fourier or Gilman:

> I think the most sensible arrangement would be sort of sex clubs, rather like tennis clubs, where men and girls could meet each other with as little misunderstanding as to why they were there as if they had met at a tennis club. Contraceptives would be on sale and beds available. Of course, anything permanent would have to be carried on outside. (BTH, 2002, 487)

The scheme could be misconstrued as corrupt or degenerate, so the writer takes care to stress how it will liberate respectable citizens of both sexes. It will achieve this by eradicating the guilt of those who practise non-marital sex in the conventional 'culture pattern':

> It seems to me that as soon as you admit a desire for extra-marital intercourse everyone instantly assumes that you're a tough fit for nothing but drink and money, or an oily-haired swine with a dressing-gown and a portfolio of etchings, and that in either case you have instant and cut-price access to the *demi-monde*. Well, that's just not the case, do you hear me? I'm not less sensitive than these married bastards, I'm more sensitive, otherwise I should be married myself. I'm not going to deceive girls and then pretend it was their own look-out . . . I want to screw decent ordinary girls of my own sort without being made to feel a criminal about it. In our particular culture-pattern that's impossible. (BTH, 2002, 492)

Larkin's wishes appeared in the debate *Round Another Point* (1951), which remained unpublished and neglected until 2002. The piece is clearly humorous, but it is also important to the literary appraisal of Larkin's work because it depicts a reasoned scenario that is neither exploitative nor sexist. Here, Larkin is neither pervert nor bigot. On the contrary, Larkin is at pains to point out that there will be 'little misunderstanding as to why they [are] there' (BTH, 2002, 487) and he resolutely states that he's 'not going to deceive girls' (BTH, 2002, 492). The relationships are to be conducted only with self-respecting partners who freely consent, namely, 'decent ordinary girls of my own sort' (BTH, 2002, 492). Most importantly, Larkin wants to practise his unorthodox lifestyle 'without being made to feel a criminal' by 'our particular culture-pattern' (BTH, 2002, 492). Critics insist upon reading the poems against the sexist outbursts of the letters, though the ideas expressed here suggest that the letters themselves utilise such utterances parodically, and that Larkin regarded them as fit for parody given the systematic way that he undermines them in his poetry and prose. The debate depicts in a coherent and rational way Larkin's objections to the hypocrisies of conventional sexual politics that hamper the lives of both sexes in equal measure. In her memoirs, Maeve Brennan cites a letter in which Larkin detaches himself from the conventional sexual politics that he decries in the debate:

> I don't connect [your letters] with *flirtation or my taking advantage of you . . . or any other cliché of human relations*: they were just one person showing kindness to and concern for another. And this is a jolly rare thing in my experience. (my emphasis, 18.iv.61, cited in Brennan, 2002, 42)

'Annus Mirabilis' revisits the ideas contained in the debate (CP, 167). Despite the fact that sexual freedom has, in 1963, arrived 'just too late' for the speaker, the poem achieves a positive note by identifying the chief characteristics of a revised model for sexual politics. Like the debate, the poem scorns the customary rituals of courtship and marriage ('A sort of bargaining, / A wrangle for a ring'), preferring instead the freer attitudes to sex about which, in the 1960s at least, 'Everyone felt the same, / And every life became / A brilliant breaking of the bank'. The metaphor that runs through these lines and ties them together is that of bartering or commercial exchange. Whereas in former times a sexual partnership would be secured by 'bargaining', in 1963 what is celebrated is the 'breaking of the bank' signalling how questions of sexual and personal attachment have been liberated from the world of financial obligation. The phrase also recalls the popular gambling expression suggesting how the establishment (or 'bank') has been toppled by the new code of ethics that 'Everyone' wants. An early draft of stanza three began: 'Then all at once the quarrel sank / Both sexes felt the same' (u/p draft, Workbook 7). The reference to 'Both sexes' emphasises the point made in the debate that the alternative lifestyle will not be exclusively male in its conception but will be endorsed (as an even earlier draft of the line expresses it) by 'men and women alike' (u/p draft, Workbook 7). Twenty seven years previously 'Out in the lane I pause' (1940, CP, 253) similarly hoped for sexual democracy: 'Girls and their soldiers from the town / Who in the shape of future years / Have equal shares'.

Such a democratic ideal contrasts with the way that commerce tyrannises human relations throughout the volume. In 'Posterity' (CP, 170) the speaker uses 'the money sign' to symbolise the oppression of family commitments and in 'The Building' (CP, 191) it is noted 'how much money goes' on the futile fight with death. However, there is one poem which reveals that like that other human measure, language, money is ultimately of little value. Like 'Toads' and 'Poetry of Departures', 'Money' (CP, 198) uses a debating format to achieve its effects. Unlike the earlier poems though, the speaker is already detached from the frenzied world of getting and spending:

> Quarterly, is it, money reproaches me:
>   'Why do you let me lie here wastefully?
> I am all you never had of goods and sex.
>   You could get them still by writing a few cheques.'

Money 'reproaches' the speaker because he spurns the consumerist ethic that equates 'goods and sex' as undifferentiated marketable items. Money's wheedling tones represent a psychological profile that measures everything in terms of cash value. Everett notes that 'by rhyming "sex" and "cheques" [Larkin enjoys] a hard laugh . . . at the Consumer Society in the head' (BTH, 2000, 15). The money-character recalls the other misguided souls in Larkin's writing who are similarly entranced by the false grail of commercial gain. Wagstaff senior and Anne's father pursue its charms at the cost of losing their children's affection only to see the error of their ways too late, though in the poem's closing lines the speaker has the perspicuity to see beyond money's tarnished surface to the corrupt reality it promotes:

> I listen to money singing. It's like looking down
>   From long french windows at a provincial town,
> The slums, the canal, the churches ornate and mad
>   In the evening sun. It is intensely sad.

The singing money-character is reminiscent of the siren's call and, as in 'High Windows', the speaker's downward view of its achievements stresses its limited accomplishments. The penultimate line implies not only that its legacy is one of social deprivation and drab industrial landscape, but that money has turned religion into a senseless decoration. What is 'intensely sad' is the way that human civilisation has waned due to its over-reliance on money as a gauge of ultimate worth. In 'Nothing To Be Said' (CP, 138) 'measuring love and money [are] / Ways of slow dying' and *The North Ship* instructs: 'Throw away . . . / That jewel in the head / That bronze in the breath' (CP, 297). Even the speaker of 'Homage to a Government' (CP, 171) regrets that 'All we can hope to leave them now is money'. Regan sees 'Money' as a 'quintessential statement of alienation' (Regan, 1992, 136) which recalls Marx's conviction that as a 'universal, self-constituted value of all things' money 'has . . . robbed the whole world, human as well as natural, of its own values' (McLellan cited in Regan, 1992, 137).

For Everett, 'Money' addresses 'the painful strangeness of living in a world without transcendentals to judge by, a world of only "money"' (BTH, 2000, 14) and earlier poems, such as 'Here' and 'High Windows', similarly reject how a soaring absolute can miraculously satisfy humanity's yearnings. Like his earlier writing, Larkin's final volume draws on a familiar set of natural motifs and communal values, which, after the revolts against social, sexual and commercial constrictions, provide at least some sanctuary against what the works repeatedly see as the pallid routines of twentieth-century existence.

In contrast to the cheap human coinage of 'Money', the purer 'Gold' in 'Solar' (CP, 159) 'exist[s] openly' and 'give[s] for ever' without the strings and preconditions of man-made devices. Like *A Girl in Winter*, 'The Explosion' (CP, 175) deploys Lawrentian natural coin imagery to express the resilience of working-class communities in times of tragedy: 'Larger than in life they managed – / Gold as on a coin, or walking / Somehow from the sun towards them'. 'Dublinesque' (CP, 178) also evokes the dignified solidarity of mourners who possess 'an air of great friendliness' despite their loss. The poem shares with *A New World Symphony* the stalwart mood of *Dubliners*, though in 'Livings II' the oceanic imagery is reminiscent of *Letters from Iceland*: 'Lit shelved liners / Grope like mad worlds westward' (CP, 188). As in *The North Ship*, to sail west is to embrace the decadent forces of capitalism: forces that 'Show Saturday' (CP, 199–201) ominously dubs as 'time's rolling smithy-smoke'. What this poem ultimately celebrates is the 'Regenerate union' of shared human endeavour which, 'like strength, [lies] below / [the] Sale-bills and swindling' of corrupt commercial enterprise.

None of these instances of political liberalism in any way eliminates or compensates for Larkin's vicious, right-wing rantings. The desultory lines of 'Homage to a Government' (CP, 171) contain the reactionary sentiments that dismayed many of his politically-correct critics in the 1990s. Sympathetic readers such as Andrew Motion and Martin Amis suggest the folly of judging the art by the life (Motion, 1993, 2) and of according undue literary weight to the irrational outbursts in the letters (Martin Amis, 2001, 164). Nevertheless, the author of crass utterances such as 'Bring back the cat' and 'Kick out the niggers' (Motion, 1993, 410) sits oddly with a conception of Larkin as a subversive radical. There are, it seems, two Larkins: one is the idealistic rebel deconstructing the dogmas of the other entrenched conformist persona, unwriting or parodying the vindictive tirades expressed in the letters. Such aspects of Larkin cannot be ignored. But these 'limitations' are mapped onto the geography of the poems, where they are ridiculed, taunted and rejected so that – aesthetically transformed – they become enlisted in Larkin's career-long campaign against clichéd narratives.

Whatever the ambiguities in Larkin's political beliefs, the wide array of writing now available, which includes prose and drama as well as dream-records and other miscellaneous texts, enables a more coherent and complete appraisal of his work. The extended Larkin canon clarifies the poetry's debt to narrative and performance, both at a stylistic and thematic level, but at the same time provides evidence to counter Greer's charge that the poems are 'racist, sexist, and rotten with class-consciousness' (Greer, 1988, 27). In 1992 Regan hoped for an interpretative reappraisal of Larkin: 'it seems likely that many readers will come to regard the poetry of Philip Larkin as an imaginative declaration of resistance and solidarity against the aggressive and demeaning self-interest that has characterised the final decades of the twentieth century' (Regan, 1992, 141–2). In light of the extended scope of insight into Larkin afforded in the decade since, it is predicted that Larkin will indeed come to be remembered as amongst Britain's poet-rebels and enfants terribles of the twentieth century.

Appendix

1 Upublished drawing from *Life With A Phairy Phantasy: A Morality in Pictures*. Drawn by Mr P. A. L. 1943. Bodleian Library.

2 University Labour Federation leaflet, *A Grave Step*, Cambridge. Enclosed in an unpublished letter from Philip Larkin to Catherine Larkin, May 24, 1941. Brynmor Jones Library.

3 W. R. A. C. recruitment coupon, *Daily Mirror*, May 30, 1953.

4 W. A. A. F. recruitment poster, *c*. 1941. Imperial War Museum.

5 Leaflet, early 1900s.

6 Article in *Today*, weekly magazine, August 17, 1963.

1 Unpublished drawing from *Life With A Phairy Phantasy: A Morality in Pictures.* Drawn by Mr P. A. L. *c.* 1940–3. Bodleian Library.

A GRAVE STEP

DLN/3/2a

which affects the future of all University students, future generations of students, the whole British people,

has been taken by the Government in its latest announcements about Entrance to the Universities and Call-Up of University students.

FOR THE UNIVERSITIES
it means that:

UNIVERSITIES will be peopled by students chosen not mainly for their academic qualifications, but for their potential ability as officers.

MILITARY EDUCATION is likely to become a more important part of University life than academic achievement.

STUDENTS will live in constant fear of being removed from the Universities and sent into the Army in the middle of their courses.

CONSCIENTIOUS OBJECTORS have no guarantee that they will be allowed a University career.

AN EMASCULATED ONE-YEAR COURSE will not fit students for any job which today requires a University training, and will be virtually useless to themselves and to the community.

Is it in the interests of
THE COMMUNITY that:

THE PEOPLE should be deprived of the teachers, social workers and civil servants which it so badly needs now and in the future?

DOCTORS AND SCIENTISTS should be turned out half-trained to positions of great responsibility?

THE MEAGRE EDUCATIONAL OPPORTUNITIES built up through a century of struggle should be curtailed still further?

ALL EDUCATION should have military ends?

2   University Labour Federation leaflet, *A Grave Step*, Cambridge. Enclosed in an unpublished letter from Philip Larkin to Catherine Larkin, May 24, 1941. Brynmor Jones Library (*continued on next page*).

All students must act together
to demand

1. Entrance to the Universities to be based on *academic,* not military, qualifications.

2. The number of students not to be reduced below its present level.

3. *No one-year courses.* All students admitted to be allowed a full course.

4. Students, while at the University, to be under academic, not military, authority.

5. Military studies not to be allowed to interfere with academic work.

This Government has shown

by its attacks on the living standards of the people, by the accentuation of existing social and economic inequalities, by its denial of adequate air-raid protection that it **ACTS IN THE INTEREST OF ONLY A SMALL SECTION OF THE POPULATION.**

by allowing the Universities to degenerate into Technical Colleges for the war machine, in contrast to the tremendous development of education in China and Spain during war, that **IT HAS NO INTEREST IN THE MAINTENANCE OF HIGHER EDUCATION.**

by its attack upon free speech and freedom of discussion, and by allowing military education to become a substitute for academic study, that **IT IS EMULATING ITS NAZI RIVALS.**

If you are prepared to prevent further steps on the road to Fascism

Be in the forefront in the fight against these measures.

Unite with the organisations of the people who are experiencing similar attacks.

Work to replace the present Government by a People's Government which will maintain education and extend democracy.

Issued by the University Labour Federation, 22 King Street, Cambridge, and printed by the Farleigh Press, Beechwood Works, Beechwood Rise, Watford, Herts.

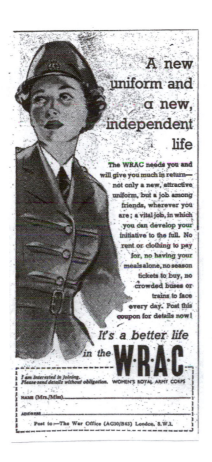

3   W. R. A. C. recruitment coupon, *Daily Mirror*,
May 30, 1953.

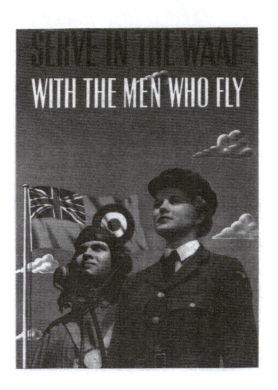

4 W. A. A. F. recruitment poster, *c.* 1941.
Imperial War Museum.

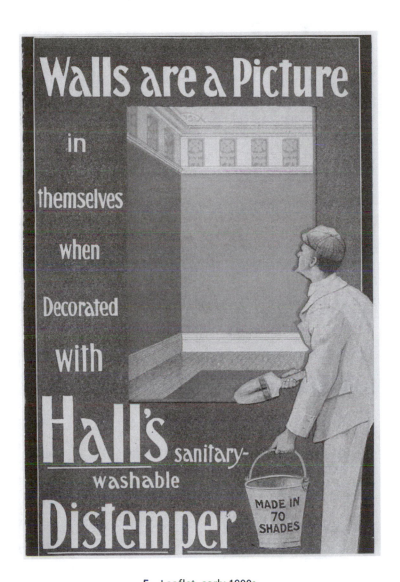

5   Leaflet, early 1900s.

Four gir
wrong tr

AND IT'S ALL THANKS TO Dr. BEECHING

IF you're planning to catch an express train to the coast soon, maybe it's because you've fallen for one of British Railways' glamorous new poster popsies.

They're all over the country, these platform pin-ups. There's almost certainly one on Platform Two of your local station, slap on the site that used to show corny-old-man - and - the - kids - building-sandcastles pictures.

If the man next to you peers anxiously through the window every time your train stops, he's not worried about passing his stop. He's just trying to get another glimpse at a full-colour popsie.

Gross deception

I have sad news for him today, however. Little does he know the gross deception to which he has fallen victim!

Little does he know how cunningly he is being used as a pawn in the battle for the cheap-day excursion!

It is all the fault of Dr. Beeching. His Southern Region have chosen a dishy beach girl to represent each of their four most popular holiday counties.

There's KENT—a sulky titian-haired beauty in a black bikini, her left knee clutched between dainty hands, a where-are-you look in her eye, and four red apples dangling tantalisingly by her right ear.

There's SUSSEX—raven-haired and green-eyed, the light reflecting gorgeously on her red lips, dressed in a striped, low-cut bathing-suit.

There's HAMPSHIRE—golden hair sweeping left shoulder, head undeniably tilted in come-hither fashion, red-and-white striped swimsuit with black pants.

And there's DORSET—auburn-haired, wide-eyed, clad in an orange bikini, a swan about to swim into the side of her head.

"If that's what they have on the beaches of Kent" (or Sussex, or Hampshire, or Dorset), you say as you fight your way to the ticket-office with your umbrella, raincoat and wellingtons under your arm, "then the sooner I get down to Ramsgate (or Worthing, or South-sea, or Swanage) the better!"

I hate to break it to any of you who have already spent fruitless weekends and a lot of money scouring the beaches for such international class beauties, but there has been a little . . . shall we say . . . misrepresentation.

Oh! the shame

For not one of the popsies being admired daily on the platforms is a native of the county she represents.

Furthermore (Oh! the shame of it!), not one has any intention of lying around this summer on the beaches of Kent (or Sussex, or Hampshire, or Dorset), or, indeed, of England.

All, alas, are professional actresses or models.

And the holidays *they* have in mind will be in Italy (or Spain, or France, or—at the very least—Jersey). Take Miss Holidays-in-Hampshire, inviting you to

Miss Holiday-in-Hampshire isn't even British. She is German. Holidays? In Italy

"Arrive Earlier by Train" at Christchurch, Portsmouth, New Milton and many other equally desirable places.

A Hampshire girl? She's not even

SLIM
THE ROMAN WAY!

OVERWEIGHT is the greatest single cause of our worst fatal disease: coronary thrombosis. It kills about ten times more middle-aged Britons today than it did only thirty years ago. What's the answer to the killer? According to Professor Yudkin, Head of the Department **by STEPH** of Nutrition at London University plenty of physical activity and a complete revolution in our diet instead of much boosted slimming cures.

"Our ancestors chose the righ

6 Article in *Today*, weekly magazine, August 17, 1963.

ls on the
ack

British. She's twenty-two year old German-born Gundel Sargent.

"I'm off to Italy this year, looking for the sun," she told me.

"Hampshire? Hampshire? Oh yes—I was in Bournemouth for a weekend once. Nice for a couple of days, but for a holiday? No."

Miss Kent is a near-miss. She

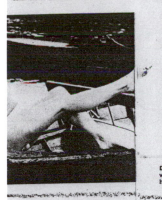

comes from neighbouring Sussex and is twenty-one year old cabaret singer Lisa Page.

"I've been too busy to take a holiday for three years," she said, "but I'm off soon to do cabaret in Israel. Kent? Well—hardly."

The girl trying to entice you into Dorset comes, in fact, from Walthamstow, Essex. She's model Barbara Smith.

When she marries next month, she and her husband will not honeymoon in Weymouth. Nor yet in Swanage. They're going to Jersey.

"We want to be sure of some sun," said Miss Smith. "Actually, my favourite holiday place is Spain, though.

"Dorset? I've been through it on my way to other places. The countryside is *pretty* . . ."

From Somerset

Girl number four, Miss Sussex, is Eve Eden. She comes from Bath, in Somerset. And she dreams of the South of France.

All this is not going to go down very well with the real beauties of Kent (or Sussex, etc., etc.). Not to mention their mums.

In Eastbourne, Mrs. Dorothy

by PATRICK GOLDRING

Power put in a strong claim for her sixteen-year-old schoolgirl daughter, Elizabeth, this year's Eastbourne carnival queen.

"I really do think they might have chosen a Sussex girl for the Sussex poster," she said.

"Now, my Elizabeth would make a very good poster girl. She's blonde, blue-eyed, and she was chosen from twenty-seven others for her attractiveness, intelligence and personality. . . ."

Such pleas fail to move the cynical hearts of British Railways, however.

At his Waterloo office, a Southern Region official told me: "We were quite cold-blooded about this."

"It didn't matter to us whether the girls on our posters had any actual connections with the counties.

"We just wanted the most attractive poster girls we could find."

He gave the posters a long, penetrating look. "And I think we've got 'em," he said with a grim smile.

That might well be. But there are going to be some right old barneys down on the beaches when the truth leaks out, I can tell you.

There are signs that it is leaking out already.

At one London suburban station last week I saw the lovely face of Hampshire's German come-hither girl, Gundel Sargent, wearing a pencilled moustache and beard.

It could be some genuine Hampshire girl getting her own back.

Dorset's girl, Barbara Smith, will soon be a bride. Her honeymoon won't be in Dorset

type of diet because they instinctively selected nutritious food," he says. "If they hadn't, the human race wouldn't have survived."

It is only in the last eight thousand years that we turned from natural foods and began to produce food, vegetables, cereals and sugar. And began to give ourselves those ever-present weight and health problems.

What's the "complete revolution" in our diet that Professor Yudkin suggests? Eat as our ancestors did—choose our foods for their nutritious contents, not for their tastiness.

With this idea in mind, some astute businessmen recently opened an ancient Roman-style restaurant in London. There customers can have the succulent meat dishes that kept our conquerors so content and healthy.

"The favourite dish here is *Pollo del Diavalo*," says chef Michele

When in London, eat as the Romans did!

Frangimore. "It's chicken, served with red wine, ham, garlic and a special gravy. It's delicious—but it's not fattening.

Another favourite is *Maialino de Latte Ripieno*—stuffed suckling pig. It's stuffed with pork, chestnuts, eggs and liver and served with cooked apples. It can fill the

hungriest man without making him put on weight—because it's all natural food."

Don't get the idea that Professor Yudkin ignores all tasty meals in his battle against coronary thrombosis. Far from it. He's a gourmet —and enjoys dishes based on meat, fish, eggs, cheese and cream.

"The only thing I'm against," he says, "is putting the joy in food before our instinctive choice."

IF we allowed instinct to take over, would we choose the right foods? Recently some six-month-old babies were left to choose their own diets from a wide range of foods—and selected everything that was nutritious. Although there was no sugar, cakes or sweets in their menu, they developed as well as babies who existed on conventional diets.

Keeping oneself in trim isn't only a problem for the figure conscious starlet—it's a life and death threat to us all.

Bibliography

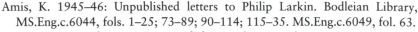

Amis, K. 1945–46: Unpublished letters to Philip Larkin. Bodleian Library, MS.Eng.c.6044, fols. 1–25; 73–89; 90–114; 115–35. MS.Eng.c.6049, fol. 63.

Amis, M. 2001: *The War Against Cliché*. London: Jonathan Cape.

Auchmuty, R. 1999: *A World of Women*. London: The Women's Press.

Auden, W. H. [1977] 1986: *The English Auden*. Edited by Edward Mendelson. London and Boston: Faber and Faber.

—— and MacNeice, L. [1937] 1985: *Letters from Iceland*. London and Boston: Faber and Faber.

Ayer, A. J. [1936] 1990: *Language, Truth and Logic*. Harmondsworth: Penguin.

Barthes, R. [1957] 1973: *Mythologies*. St. Albans: Paladin.

Bayley, J. 1974: 'Too Good for This World'. *TLS*, 21 June, 654.

—— 1984: Larkin and the Romantic Tradition. *Critical Quarterly* 26 (1–2), 61–66.

Betjeman, J. [1958] 2000: *Collected Poems*. London: John Murray.

Booth, J. 1992: *Philip Larkin: Writer*. Hemel Hempstead: Harvester Wheatsheaf.

—— (ed.) 2000: *New Larkins for Old*. Basingstoke: Macmillan.

—— (ed.) 2002: *Trouble at Willow Gables and Other Fictions*. London: Faber and Faber.

Brecht, B. [1940] 1996: *Mother Courage and her Children*. London: Methuen.

Brennan, M. 1998: James Ballard Sutton 1921–97. *About Larkin*, April, 24–27.

—— 2002: *The Philip Larkin I Knew*. Manchester and New York: Manchester University Press.

Brownjohn, A. 1975: *Philip Larkin*. Harlow: Longman.

Burt, S. 1996: High Windows and Four Letter Words. *Boston Review* 21 (5), 18–19.

Carey, J. 1992: *The Intellectuals and the Masses*. London and Boston: Faber and Faber.

—— 2000: *Pure Pleasure*. London: Faber and Faber.

—— 2002: Larkin's female alter-ego. *The Sunday Times*, 5 May, 38.

—— (ed.) 1999: *The Faber Book of Utopias*. London: Faber and Faber.

Clark, D. [1965] 1993: *W. B. Yeats and the Theatre of Desolate Reality*. Washington D.C.: The Catholic University of America Press.

Coleridge, S. T. and Wordsworth, W. [1798] 1976: *The Lyrical Ballads*. London: MacDonald and Evans.

Cooper, S. 1999: Larkin and the 1940s. *About Larkin*, October, 25–26.

Corcoran, N. 1993: *English Poetry Since 1940*. London: Longman.

Crawford, R. 2001: *The Modern Poet*. Oxford: Oxford University Press.

Day, G. and Docherty, B. (eds.) 1997: *British Poetry from the 1950s to the 1990s*. Basingstoke: Macmillan.

Day, R. 1987: *Larkin*. Milton Keynes: Open University Press.

Dickens, C. [1848] 1999: *Dombey and Son*. Oxford: Oxford University Press.

—— [1854] 1980: *Hard Times*. Harmondsworth: Penguin.

—— [1860] 1978: *Great Expectations*. Harmondsworth: Penguin.

Eliot, T. S. [1919] 1932: Hamlet and his Problems. In *Selected Essays 1917–1932*. London: Faber and Faber.

—— [1922] 1987: *Selected Poems*. London and Boston: Faber and Faber.

—— [1935] 1974: *Murder in the Cathedral*. London: Faber and Faber.

Everett, B. [1986] 1991: *Poets in Their Time*. Oxford: Oxford University Press.

Forster, E. M. [1908] 1980: *A Room with a View*. Harmondsworth: Penguin.

Gardner, P. 1968: The Wintry Drum. *Dalhousie Review*.

Greer, G. 1988: A Very British Misery. *Guardian*, 14 October, 27.

Haffenden, J. 1981: *Viewpoints: Poets in Conversation with John Haffenden*. London: Faber and Faber.

Hamilton, I. 1964: Interview with Ian Hamilton. *London Magazine* 4 (8), 72.

Hardy, T. [1974] 1977: *Poems of Thomas Hardy*. Edited by T. R. M. Creighton. London and Basingstoke: Macmillan.

Hartley, A. 1954: Poets of the Fifties. *Spectator*, 27 August, 260–1.

Hartley, G. (ed.) 1988: *Philip Larkin 1922–1985: A Tribute*. London: The Marvell Press.

Hawkes, T. [1983] 1997: *Structuralism and Semiotics*. London: Routledge.

Hitchens, C. 2000: *Unacknowledged Legislation*. London: Verso.

Ingelbien, R. 2000: Seamus Heaney and the Importance of Larkin. *Journal of Modern Literature* 23 (3/4), 471–482.

James, C. 2001a: *Even As We Speak: New Essays 1993–2001*. Basingstoke and Oxford: Picador.

—— 2001b: *Reliable Essays*. Basingstoke and Oxford: Picador.

Joyce, J. [1914] 1973: *Dubliners*. Harmondsworth: Penguin.

—— [1922] 2000: *Ulysses*. Harmondsworth: Penguin.

Jung, C. G. [1905–61] 1971: *Psychological Reflections*. London: Routledge and Kegan Paul.

—— [1953–78] 1994: *Collected Works*. London: Routledge.

—— 1963: *Memories, Dreams, Reflections*. Edited by Aniela Jaffé. London: Routledge and Kegan Paul.

Kierkegaard, S. [1843] 1992: *Either/Or*. Harmondsworth: Penguin.

Kuby, L. 1974: *An Uncommon Poet for the Common Man: A Study of Philip Larkin's Poetry*. The Hague: Mouton.

Larkin, P. [1946] 1985: *Jill*. London and Boston: Faber and Faber.

—— [1947] 1975: *A Girl in Winter*. London and Boston: Faber and Faber.

—— [1970] 1985: *All What Jazz: A Record Diary*. London and Boston: Faber and Faber

—— [1988] 1990: *Collected Poems*. Edited by Anthony Thwaite. London and Boston: The Marvell Press and Faber and Faber.

—— 1938–49: Unpublished letters to James Sutton. Brynmor Jones Library, DPL/174/2/1–141.

—— 1941: Unpublished letters to Catherine Larkin. Brynmor Jones Library, DLN/3/1–4.

—— 1942–43: Unpublished 'Record of Dreams'. Brynmor Jones Library, DPL (2)/1/2/12.

—— 1943: *Ante Meridian: The Autobiography of Brunette Coleman*. Transcribed by James Booth. Brynmor Jones Library, DPL (2)/1/13 (a).

—— 1940–3: *Life With A Phairy Phantasy: A Morality in Pictures Drawn by Mr P. A. L. 'The onlie forgetter'*, unpublished. Bodleian Library, MS.Eng.c.2358, fols. 1–19.

—— 1943: *Michaelmas Term at St. Bride's by Brunette Coleman*. Transcribed by James Booth. Brynmor Jones Library, DPL (2)/1/13.

—— 1943: *Trouble at Willow Gables by Brunette Coleman*. Transcribed by James Booth. Brynmor Jones Library, DPL (2)/1/12.

—— 1943: *What Are We Writing For?: an essay by Brunette Coleman*. Transcribed by James Booth. Brynmor Jones Library, DPL (2)/1/1/13.

—— 1945–60: Unpublished workbook No. 5. Brynmor Jones Library, DPL/1/5/1.

—— 1946: *Night in the Plague*, unpublished verse drama. British Library. Additional Manuscript, MS.52619.

—— 1946–50: Unpublished workbook No. 1. Brynmor Jones Library, DPL/1/6/66.

—— 1947: 'Augusta', novel fragments. Transcribed by James Booth. Brynmor Jones Library, DPL/4/4.

—— 1948: 'Wagstaff', novel fragments. Transcribed by James Booth. Brynmor Jones Library, DPL /4/5.

—— 1948: 'At the age of twenty-six', unpublished discussion. Brynmor Jones Library, DPL(2)/1/2/15.

—— 1950: *Round the Point*, debate. Transcribed by James Booth. Brynmor Jones Library, DPL/4/10.

—— 1951: *Round Another Point*, debate. Transcribed by James Booth. Brynmor Jones Library, DPL(2)/1/3/15.

—— 1953–54: Unpublished workbook No. 3. Brynmor Jones Library, DPL/1/3/3.

—— 1954–57: Unpublished workbook No. 4. Brynmor Jones Library, DPL/1/4.

—— 1957–82: Unpublished letters to Sir John Betjeman. Special Collections, McPherson Library, University of Victoria.

—— 1960–63: Unpublished workbook No. 6. Brynmor Jones Library, DPL/1/6.

—— 1962: Unpublished letter to Rosemary Hewitt. Brynmor Jones Library, DLN/3/5.

—— 1964–67: Unpublished workbook No. 7. Brynmor Jones Library, DPL/1/7.

—— 1977: Unpublished letters to Barbara Pym. Bodleian Library, MS. Pym.152, fols. 16–30.

—— 1983: *Required Writing*. London and Boston: Faber and Faber.

—— *c.* 1943: Unpublished undergraduate essay. Bodleian Library, MS.Eng.c.3895, fols. 28–40.

Lawrence, D. H. [1915] 1978: *The Rainbow*. Harmondsworth: Penguin.

—— [1928] 1980. *Lady Chatterly's Lover*. Harmondsworth: Penguin.

Lerner, L. 1997: *Philip Larkin*. Plymouth: Northcote House.

Lodge, D.1990: *After Bakhtin*: *Essays in Fiction and Criticism*. London: Routledge.

—— [1977] 1997: *The Modes of Modern Writing*. London: Arnold.

—— and Wood, N. (eds.) 2000: *Modern Criticism and Theory*. Harlow: Longman.

Longley, E. 1974: Larkin, Edward Thomas and the Tradition. *Phoenix* 11/12, 63.

Lopez, T. 1999: W. S. Graham and the 1940s. Larkin and the 1940s Conference, London, 17 July.

Marwick, A. [1982] 1996: *British Society Since 1945*. Harmondsworth: Penguin.

Mayhew, H. [1862] 1967: *London Labour and the London Poor*, IV, 'Those That Will Not Work'. London: Frank Cass.

Meade, L. T. 1894: *A Sweet Girl Graduate*. London: Cassell and Co.

Mitchell, S. 1995: *The New Girl; Girls' Culture in England 1880–1915*. New York: Columbia University Press.

Morrison, B. 1980: *The Movement: English Poetry and Fiction of the 1950s*. Oxford: Oxford University Press.

Motion, A. 1980: *The Poetry of Edward Thomas*. London: Routledge and Kegan Paul.

—— 1982: *Philip Larkin*. London: Methuen.

—— 1993: *Philip Larkin: A Writer's Life*. London: Faber and Faber.

—— 1993: Too Close for Comfort. *Guardian*, 31 March, 27.

Orwell, G. [1945] 1951: *Animal Farm*. Harmondsworth: Penguin.

—— 1968: *The Collected Essays, Journalism and Letters of George Orwell* vol. II, 'My Country Right or Left: 1940–1943'. Edited by Sonia Orwell and Ian Angus. London: Secker and Warburg.

Paulin, T. 1992: Letter to the *Times Literary Supplement*, 6 November, 15.

Petch, S. 1981: *The Art of Philip Larkin*. London: Sydney University Press.

Piette, A. 1995: *The Imagination of War: British Fiction and Poetry 1939–1945*. London and Basingstoke: Papermac.

—— 1999: Childhood Wiped Out: Larkin, his Father and the Bombing of Coventry. Larkin and the 1940s Conference, London, 16 July.

Plath, S. 1985: *Selected Poems*. Edited by Ted Hughes. London and Boston: Faber and Faber.

Pym, B. 1961–75: Unpublished letters to Philip Larkin. Bodleian Library, MS. Eng.lett.c.859, fols. 1–22; 23–48.

Raban, J. 1971: *The Society of the Poem*. London: Harrap.

Rácz, I. 2000: Experience, Words and Meaning in Philip Larkin's *The Less Deceived*. *Neohelicon* 27 (2), 211–235.

Regan, S. 1992: *Philip Larkin*. Critics Debate Series. Basingstoke: Macmillan.

—— (ed.) 1997: *Philip Larkin*. New Casebooks Series. Basingstoke: Macmillan.

—— (ed.) 1998: *The Eagleton Reader*. Oxford: Blackwell.

Ricks, C. 1974: *The Whitsun Weddings. Phoenix* 11/12, 6.

Rittenhouse, I. M. [*c.* 1880] 1939: *Maud.* Edited by R. L. Strout. London: Macmillan.

Roberts, N. 1999: *Narrative and Voice in Postwar Poetry.* London: Longman.

Rogers, D. 2002: Stolen from the local girls' school: The New Girl, 'Brunette Coleman' and 'Lines on a Young Lady's Photograph Album'. Larkin in Context Conference, Hull, 29 June.

Ross, A. 1967: *Poems 1942–67.* London: Eyre and Spottiswoode.

Rossen, J. 1989: *Philip Larkin: His Life's Work.* Hemel Hempstead: Harvester Wheatsheaf.

Salwak, D. (ed.) 1989: *Philip Larkin: The Man and His Work.* Basingstoke: Macmillan.

Shakespeare, W. [1595] 1969: *A Midsummer Night's Dream.* Edited by Allan Rodway. London and Glasgow: Blackie.

—— [1600] 1963: *Hamlet.* Edited by Edward Hubler. New York: Signet Classic.

Shaw, G. B. [1916] 1970: *Pygmalion.* Harmondsworth: Penguin.

Sinfield, A. 1989: *Literature, Politics and Culture in Postwar Britain.* Oxford: Blackwell.

Smith, S. 1982: *Inviolable Voice: History and Twentieth-Century Poetry.* Dublin: Gill and Macmillan.

Smith, S. 2000: Something for Nothing: Late Larkins and Early. *English* 49, 255–275.

Stevens, A. 2001: *Jung: A Very Short Introduction.* Oxford: Oxford University Press.

Summerfield, P. 1998: *Reconstructing Women's Wartime Lives.* Manchester: Manchester University Press.

Sutton, J. B. 1941–51: Unpublished letters to Philip Larkin. Brynmor Jones Library, DP/182.

Swarbrick, A. 1995: *Out of Reach: The Poetry of Philip Larkin.* Basingstoke: Macmillan.

Szaffkó, P. and Bényei, T. (eds) 1999: *Happy Returns: Essays for Professor István Pálffy.* Debrecen: KLTE Press.

Tennyson, A. [1847] 2000: *Alfred Tennyson.* Edited by Adam Roberts. Oxford: Oxford University Press.

Thomas, E. [1903] 1932: *Oxford.* London: A. and C. Black.

—— 1964: *Selected Poems of Edward Thomas.* London and Boston: Faber and Faber.

Thwaite, A. (ed.) 1982: *Larkin at Sixty.* London: Faber and Faber.

—— (ed.) 1992: *Selected Letters of Philip Larkin 1940–1985.* London and Boston: Faber and Faber.

—— (ed.) 2001: *Further Requirements.* London: Faber and Faber.

Timms, D. 1973: *Philip Larkin.* Edinburgh: Oliver and Boyd.

Tindall, W. Y. 1939: *D. H. Lawrence and Susan His Cow.* New York: Columbia University Press.

Tolley, A. T. 1991: *My Proper Ground: A Study of the Work of Philip Larkin and its Development.* Edinburgh: Edinburgh University Press.

—— 1997: *Larkin at Work*. Hull: University of Hull Press.

Trotter, D. 1984: *The Making of the Reader: Language and Subjectivity in Modern American, English and Irish Poetry*. Basingstoke: Macmillan.

Verdonk, P. (ed.) 1993: *Twentieth-Century Poetry: From Text to Context*. London and New York: Routledge.

Wain, J. [1953] 1979: *Hurry on Down*. Harmondsworth: Penguin.

Walder, D. (ed.) 1990: *Literature in the Modern World*. Oxford: Oxford University Press in association with the Open University.

Whalen, T. 1986: *Philip Larkin and English Poetry*. Basingstoke: Macmillan.

—— 1997: Conflicts with Capitalism: Philip Larkin's Politics. *The Antigonish Review* 111, 143–158.

Whitehead, J. 1995: *Hardy to Larkin: seven English poets*. Munslow: Hearthstone.

Woolf, V. [1925] 1992: *Mrs Dalloway*. Harmondsworth: Penguin.

—— [1927] 1977: *To the Lighthouse*. London: Grafton Books.

—— [1928] 1979: *Orlando*. St. Albans: Panther.

—— [1931] 1980: *The Waves*. St. Albans: Panther.

—— [1938] 1978: *Between the Acts*. St. Albans: Panther.

—— [1938] 1979: *Three Guineas*. Harmonsworth: Penguin.

—— [1944] 1978: *A Haunted House*. London: The Hogarth Press.

Wordsworth, W. and Coleridge, S. T. [1798] 1976: *Lyrical Ballads*. London: MacDonald and Evans.

Yeats, W. B. [1911] 1999: *The Countess Cathleen*. Edited by Michael J. Sidnell and Wayne K. Chapman. Ithaca and London: Cornell University Press.

—— 1899: Plans and Methods. *Beltaine* 1 (8).

—— 1991: *Selected Poetry*. Edited by Timothy Webb. Harmondsworth: Penguin.

Index

Index

Index

Index